Principles of Joy in the Holy Spirit

Finney's Lessons on Romans

Volume III

C. G. Finney

Books by L.G. Parkhurst, Jr.

Principles of Righteousness:
Finney's Lessons on Romans, Volume I
Compiled and edited from the works of Charles G. Finney
Edmond: Agion Press, 2006

Principles of Peace:
Finney's Lessons on Romans, Volume II
Compiled and edited from the works of Charles G. Finney
Edmond: Agion Press, 2010

Prayer Steps to Serenity: The Twelve Steps Journey:
New Serenity Prayer Edition
Edmond: Agion Press, 2006

Prayer Steps to Serenity:
Daily Quiet Time Edition
Edmond: Agion Press, 2005

How God Teaches Us to Pray:
Lessons from the Lives of Francis and Edith Schaeffer
Milton Keynes, England: Nelson Word Ltd. 1993

How to Pray in the Spirit
Compiled and edited from the works of John Bunyan
Grand Rapids: Kregel Publications, 1993, 1998

Principles of Prayer
Compiled and edited from the works of Charles Finney
Minneapolis: Bethany House Publishers, 1980, 2001

Finney's Systematic Theology: New Expanded Edition
Compiled and edited from the works of Charles G. Finney
Minneapolis: Bethany House Publishers, 1994

Principles of Joy in the Holy Spirit

Finney's Lessons on Romans
Volume III

Charles Grandison Finney

With Commentary from Henry Cowles
The Longer Epistles of Paul

Compiled and Newly Edited for Today by
L.G. Parkhurst, Jr.

"For the kingdom of God is not a matter of eating and drinking, but of righteousness, peace and joy in the Holy Spirit."—Romans 14:17

Agion Press
AgionPress.com

Principles of Joy in the Holy Spirit: Finney's Lessons on Romans: Volume III:
   The Biblical Companion to Finney's Systematic Theology
Copyright © 2012 Louis Gifford Parkhurst, Jr. All Rights Reserved.

Published by Agion Press, P.O. Box 1052, Edmond, OK 73083-1052

No part of this book may be reproduced or transmitted in any form or by any means, graphic, electronic, or mechanical, including photocopying, recording, taping, or by any information storage retrieval system, without the prior written permission of the copyright owners.

All Scripture quotations in this book are from the *King James Version of the Bible* or *The Holy Bible: New International Version*, copyright 1973, 1978, 1984, by the International Bible Society. Used by permission of Zondervan Bible Publishers.

Cover Photo and Cover Design
Copyright © 2012 by Kathryn Winterscheidt: Used by Permission

The Charles G. Finney Lessons on Romans
    Volume I: *Principles of Righteousness*
    Volume II: *Principles of Peace*
    Volume III: *Principles of Joy in the Holy Spirit*

Publisher's Cataloging-in-Publication Data

Finney, Charles Grandison, 1792-1875.
    Principles of Joy in the Holy Spirit:
        Finney's Lessons on Romans, Volume III /
  Charles G. Finney ; compiled and edited by Louis Gifford Parkhurst, Jr.
    260 p. : port. ; 23 cm.
    1, Bible. N.T. Romans—Sermons. 2. Sermons, American.
I. Parkhurst, Louis Gifford, 1946-   . II. Title
BS2665.52.F59   2012   227'.106
ISBN 978-0-9778053-3-4 (pbk.):   LCCN 2012908848

Principles of Righteousness
Volume I

Preface

1. The Wrath of God Against Those Who Withstand His Truth
    Romans 1:18-19—1857 11
2. God's Wrath Against Those Who Withstand His Truth
    Romans 1:18-19—1858 23
3. Holding the Truth in Unrighteousness
    Romans 1:18-19—1861 35
4. On the Atonement
    Romans 3:25-26—1856 53
5. Sanctification by Faith
    Romans 3:31—1837 67
6. The Foundation, Conditions, Relations, and Results of Faith
    Romans 4:1-5—1850 79
7. The Rationality of Faith
    Romans 4:20-21—1851 93
8. God's Love Commended to Us
    Romans 5:8—1858 105
9. The Nature of Death to Sin
    Romans 6:7—1840 105
10. Death to Sin through Christ
    Romans 6:11—1853 125
11. Sanctification under Grace
    Romans 6:14—1839 141
12. The Wages of Sin
    Romans 6:23—1854 153
Study Questions for Individuals and Groups 171
Henry Cowles Commentary on Key Verses from Romans 185
About Agion Press 207

Principles of Peace
Volume II

Preface

1. Legal Experience
    Romans 7:1, 22-23—1837 1
2. Christ the Husband of the Church
    Romans 7:4—1837 17
3. Revival of Sin and the Law
    Romans 7:9—1853 31
4. Thanks for the Gospel Victory
    Romans 7:25—1856 45
5. Justification
    Romans 8:1—1843 59
6. Total Depravity
    Romans 8:7—1836 73
7. Moral Depravity
    Romans 8:7—1862 117
8. License, Bondage and Liberty
    Romans 8:15—1854 131
9. Spirit of Prayer
    Romans 8:26-27—1835 145
10. All Things for Good to Those That Love God
    Romans 8:28—1847 167
11. All Events Ruinous to the Sinner
    Romans 8:28—1847 179
12. All Things for Good to Those That Love God
    Romans 8:28—1852 193
13. Religion of the Law and the Gospel
    Romans 9:30-33—1837 205
Study Questions for Individuals and Groups 217
Henry Cowles Commentary on Key Verses from Romans 235

Principles of Joy in the Holy Spirit
Volume III

Preface

1. Men, Ignorant of God's Righteousness, Would Establish Their Own
   Romans 10:3—1855 1
2. The Way to be Holy
   Romans 10:4—1843 15
3. On Believing with the Heart
   Romans 10:10—1856 27
4. Conformity to the World
   Romans 12:2—1837 41
5. How to Prevent Our Employments from Injuring Our Souls
   Romans 12:11—1839 63
6. Being in Debt
   Romans 13:8—1839 77
7. Nature of True Virtue
   Romans 13:8-10—1843 91
8. Love is the Whole of Religion
   Romans 13:10—1837 105
9. Love Works No Ill
   Romans 13:10—1841 121
10. Putting on Christ
    Romans 13:14—1843 143
11. The Kingdom of God in Consciousness
    Romans 14:17—1861 155
12. Total Abstinence a Christian Duty
    Romans 14:21—1850 173
13. Doubtful Actions are Sinful
    Romans 14:23—1837 201
Study Questions for Individuals and Groups 221
Henry Cowles Commentary on Key Verses from Romans 235

Charles Grandison Finney
Revivalist, Pastor, and Theologian
1792-1875

"The writer is inclined to regard Charles G. Finney as the greatest evangelist and theologian since the days of the apostles. Over eighty-five in every hundred persons professing conversion to Christ in Finney's meetings remained true to God. Finney seems to have had the power of impressing the conscience with the necessity of holy living in such a manner as to procure the most lasting results."

From *Deeper Experiences of Famous Christians* by James Gilcrist Lawson, Anderson, Indiana: The Warner Press, 1978, page 175.

Preface

After a delay much longer than I anticipated, Charles G. Finney's *Principles of Joy in the Holy Spirit* has finally been published by Agion Press. One of the reasons I intended to complete this three volume set of Finney's *Lessons on Romans* is because I believe students of the Bible, evangelists, ministers, and revivalists need a comprehensive Biblical companion to *Finney's Systematic Theology*. Finney's sermons or lessons on Romans show how he drew his theological teachings from the Bible, and how he related his theology to his preaching in a very effective manner. His sermons reached the average person in the pew; while *Finney's Systematic Theology* primarily reached college students and professors, ministers and preachers. From reading his sermons on Romans; however, you will learn that his listeners were intellectually far above the average person sitting in the church today.

In Finney's publication of his *Systematic Theology*, he never completed the first volume, which would have revealed the main points of historic, Biblical Christianity that all true Christians believed in his day. He intended to publish the first volume last, because he believed that he would only be publishing what everyone already knew and believed. Because his intention to publish the first volume last (which he did not live long enough to do) has not been widely understood (and in some cases purposely ignored), Finney's Christian and ethical ideas have been misunderstood and sometimes purposely misrepresented. For example, he has been accused of not preaching salvation by grace through faith in Jesus Christ, of legalism, of preaching a religion of works, of perfectionism, and of not giving enough honor to the work of the Holy Spirit in the conversion of sinners. I believe the first volume of his *Systematic Theology* would have refuted these criticisms. In any event, if Finney's *Lessons on*

Preface

Romans are carefully studied the reader will see many of the ways Finney's critics have been in error. I believe the three volume work of Finney's *Lessons on Romans* will partially answer many questions about Finney's true beliefs, and hopefully inform some of his critics.

Charles G. Finney's *Principles of Righteousness: Finney's Lessons on Romans,* Volume I, resumed the "Finney's Principles" series, which I began with the first book in the series, *Principles of Prayer,* published by Bethany House Publishers in 1980. *Principles of Peace*, Volume II, is followed by *Principles of Joy in the Holy Spirit*, Volume III. Unlike the first series, Finney's *Lessons on Romans* include Study Questions for each lesson that can be used by the individual student for review or in a class study on Romans. Each volume includes 12 to 13 lessons for study during 3 quarters of the year. In addition, Finney's *Lessons on Romans* includes extensive excerpts from the commentary on Romans by Henry Cowles, a contemporary and colleague of Finney's at Oberlin College; therefore, in the new *Finney's Principles Series* you have a variety of tools to use in your study of the Bible.

From time to time during the last thirty years, since the beginning of this series, some have asked me how I have used what I have learned from Finney in my preaching. The best way to learn the answer to this question is to read the many weekly Bible Lessons that I have published in *The Oklahoman* newspaper for more than twenty years. For the past few years, I have published these lessons on the *International Bible Lessons* web site at internationalbiblelessons.com. These Bible Lessons are based on the Uniform Lesson Series and are used by teachers and students in many different Christian denominations around the world. Most recently, I have been writing a weekly International Bible Lesson Commentary at biblelessonforum.com. To learn how Finney's ethical and life-transforming teachings can be applied today, see my books, *Prayer Steps to Serenity The Twelve Steps Journey: New Serenity Prayer Edition* or *Prayer Steps to Serenity: Daily Quiet Time Edition*. May God bless your continuing study of His word!

Love in the Lamb of God
L.G. Parkhurst, Jr.
June 8, 2012

1

Men, Ignorant of God's Righteousness, Would Establish Their Own

1855

For they being ignorant of God's righteousness, and going about to establish their own righteousness, have not submitted themselves unto the righteousness of God. —Romans 10:3—KJV

Since they did not know the righteousness that comes from God and sought to establish their own, they did not submit to God's righteousness. —Romans 10:3—NIV

In this one verse, the Apostle Paul condensed the religious condition of the Jews and stated three facts. First, they were ignorant of God's righteousness. Second, they sought to establish their own righteousness by their self-justifications and legalistic works. Third, they did not submit to God's righteousness through faith in Jesus Christ. Basically, they wrecked their nation through their ignorance of God's righteousness. Not knowing Jesus Christ, they were always going about trying to establish their own righteousness—and they were forever unsuccessful.

Principles of Joy in the Holy Spirit — Finney's Lessons on Romans

To an alarming extent today, what was true of the Jews in Paul's day is still true of many people inside and outside of the church and among all classes of people in Christian lands. All those who are not really Christians, who do not receive Jesus Christ as their Lord and Savior, are ignorant of God's righteousness. They try to establish their own righteousness and refuse to submit to God's righteousness.

When is someone ignorant of God's righteousness?

A person is ignorant of God's righteousness when he does not truly know God; and especially when he does not know God as He revealed himself in the spirituality of His law in the Bible. The Jews failed because they did not perceive that God's law called for the inmost and perfect heart love for God and others. Their carnal eye focused on the external, legalistic, and ceremonial aspects of the law. The extensive visible performance required in the Mosaic system gratified their ambition for distinction and display; therefore, they quite overlooked those very explicit statements (everywhere frequent throughout the scriptures) which God gave to call attention to the state of the person's heart—this being the only thing of real value in God's sight. God revealed His righteousness and perfect purity of character in His law, and we learn about His character from His holy and righteous law.

A person is ignorant of God's righteousness when he does not understand God's method of making sinners righteous. The Jews did not feel they needed a system such as the gospel. They supposed that God would accept them if they merely obeyed their ceremonial laws. In this legalistic supposition they made a grand and fatal mistake. God never gave the ceremonial laws so people could justify themselves, but for another entirely different purpose. God intended for the ceremonial laws to introduce the real gospel, to point people to Jesus Christ for justification, and to prepare the way for them to accept Christ as Lord and Savior. The ceremonial laws hinted plainly at the true way of salvation and illustrated the great principles upon which the gospel rests.

Generally, sinners have no concept of God's plan for securing in them what He commands. They look no further than the precept and the

Men, Ignorant of God's Righteousness, Would Establish Their Own

penalty of God's law, and this is nothing but legalism. They seem utterly unaware that the high aim of God is to bring them back to obedience and love through faith in Jesus Christ. Therefore, through the precept and penalty of the law, God must first bring sinners under a felt sentence of death, but their return to obeying God's law will not make them righteous before God. Understanding what the law of God requires of them and then feeling they deserve the sentence of death should prepare the way for bringing them to Christ for salvation. A person is ignorant of God's righteousness when he fails to understand the conditions on which God can treat them as righteous; that is, can justify and save them. The mistake of the Jews was not understanding the conditions upon which God could justify them, and this is the mistake of all sinners. They do not understand how God proposes to make them righteous and turn them from all their sin.

When people try to establish their own righteousness.

We should inquire, "*What is meant by establishing one's own righteousness?*" Suppose a person comes into a court of justice. He is accused, and pleads, "Not guilty." In some way he justifies his conduct. Perhaps he attempts to prove his own entire righteousness in the whole transaction and insists that in every particular he has done nothing wrong and only what is right. He would trying to establish his own righteousness.

Sinners try to establish their own righteousness when they make excuses for their sins. If a person can show he was and is right under the circumstances to do what he did and does, he establishes his righteousness. So, sinners go about to avoid conviction of sin—to bring in extenuating and justifying circumstances. When they try to justify their commission of sins, God asks them: "Will you condemn me so you can be righteous?"

Making excuses for your sins arraigns God before His own court of justice. Your excuses for sins accuse God of imperfections, of doing wrong, of committing crimes. Sinner, what do you mean? Do you think God will accept your rationalizing and say He was wrong? If not, why do you present your excuses before Him? Why bring your excuses before your Almighty Judge to insult Him to His very face by impeaching His equity and justice? Every sinner who brings forward any form of excuse for his own sins is really trying to establish his own righteousness.

People try to establish their own righteousness when *they depend on their doing* right to be accepted by God. This is a common form of legalism. How often do they tell you they intend to do right; showing plainly by their manner and by their use of this supposed intention that they think in this way they can secure favor with God? They turn off God's claims with this plea. They do not believe they are in danger of being sent to hell. This is nothing else but going about to establish their own righteousness.

The same must be said of those who depend on their own reformation to establish their own righteousness. I have often met with young people who, before coming to Oberlin College, have been much more loose in many points of moral conduct (as for instance the observance of the Sabbath). But coming here, they have attempted to reform and this has greatly relieved their consciences. Of course, now they think they are in a good way, and they think themselves almost sure of heaven; however, this reformation may be wholly due to their love of a good reputation. Mingling here with people who themselves observe the Sabbath, and who have established this general habit, they are forced to conform, and do so, without any more regard for God than they had before. Such persons I have seen pass through other stages of self-righteous endeavor. They become convicted of sin and perhaps begin to pray. Still they are uneasy; therefore, they resort to some forms of external reformation. How very common is this among the masses of awakened sinners! Many of you have had this sort of experience. It took you a long time to understand that you were all wrong and that nothing would avail for you short of a most radical change of heart wrought through faith in Jesus Christ.

In the same train of feeling, some people depend on having done nothing worthy of condemnation. Indeed! What is this but going about to establish their own righteousness? They think they have done nothing that can justify God in sending them to hell. On this point they take issue with God, assuming that they have done nothing very wrong. They must know that in God's sight sin deserves hell, or else He would not have built hell nor have made hell the penalty of sin. How, then, should they dare

Men, Ignorant of God's Righteousness, Would Establish Their Own

to dispute this point with God and accuse God on the implied charge of injustice!

The same thing is seen, under a slightly different form, when people depend on their general integrity of character. This is yet another form of legalism. They have been honest and kind, and on the whole so good that they think God cannot send them to hell. They think their goodness will strike the balance of the scales of justice in their favor. They have done a great many things that are about right. They think that on the whole they have done more good than harm; therefore, they are sure it cannot be right for God to send them to hell. Their life shows more obedience than disobedience—as they insist. Indeed, sinner! What do you know of personal holiness? What experience have you of a pure heart—of real love to God—of sincere regard for doing His will because you love God? Surely, you are only going about to establish your own righteousness.

Sinners clearly display the same legalistic spirit when they hold on to the idea that they are about as good as those who profess to be Christians. They say they know of some Christians who are not any better than they are, and with whom they think their own case might compare favorably. Such sinners are going about to establish their own righteousness.

When people depend on their religious observances they are trying to establish their own righteousness. Many have learned better than to try to rely on their honesty or morality; therefore, they resort to their religious observances. Catholics virtually count their beads and prepare their senseless, unmeaning services. Even Protestants do the same: they make a merit in their observances just as the poor man who expects to go to heaven by kneeling before the holy altar, kissing the holy wafer, and saying his *Ave Marias*. This type of Protestant prays just like the Catholic; that is, with the same purpose and the same state of heart. He reads his Bible on the same principle and in the same way goes through what he calls his "religious duties." What is this but mere legalism?

Depending on their religious observances was a mistake of the Jews. They fasted twice in the week and were greatly given to prayer and alms to the poor. In these services, their scribes, priests, and Pharisees, spent a great share of their time. Thrice a year they went up to Jerusalem to the solemn feasts. Religious duties absorbed a large share of their time and money. You would be appalled to learn how much their temple cost, and their religious worship, sacrifices and offerings. On all these they placed the utmost dependence. But when people rely on other methods of salvation than God's method, they are really going about to establish their own righteousness.

The righteousness of God of which sinners are so ignorant.

In general, God's righteousness is synonymous with His infinite moral purity; but, in such connections as this, it seems to mean more specifically His integrity as a moral governor. As Supreme Governor of the universe, God is bound to sustain the interests of His government in its relations both to the unfallen and to the fallen. Under the most solemn obligations to do His utmost to secure universal obedience as a necessary means to the highest happiness, God cannot allow His law to be broken, nor rebels to live—except on the basis or ground of some satisfaction being made that shall amply sustain the sanctity and honor of His law. Of course, this quality of His character as a moral governor determines the great features of His plan of saving sinners. His plan stands revealed in His law and gospel in the Bible. The righteousness of God renders it forever certain that no sinner can be accepted on the basis or ground of any works of his own, which is legalism. God's claims are so high and the sinner has fallen so low that God can never accept any work of his hands. Even his prayers—out of relationship with Jesus Christ—and his best works are all odious to God. He is trying to put God off with something less than a perfect heart, a perfect heart of love for God and neighbor.

By the very terms and spirit of the law of God, God's law demands perfect obedience and the exigencies or needs of God's great kingdom require no less. The law in both its precept and penalty must be honored or no sinner can be saved. I do not mean that God will insist that the utmost measure of penalty shall be visited on the sinner's own person; but it must be this or a substitute that will answer the one great end of fully sustaining the dignity, influence, and authority of His law. His throne must be infinitely removed from all supposable permitting of sin or connivance with sin. Therefore, it became necessary that our Surety or

Men, Ignorant of God's Righteousness, Would Establish Their Own

Guarantor, Jesus Christ, should honor the law as to its penalty by sacrificing himself and offering His humanity on the altar of His divinity. Also, in His own Person, Jesus Christ obeyed the law of God fully. Hence, to be saved, sinners must return to real obedience, to real love for God and others through faith in Jesus Christ, who offered himself in their behalf. God's righteousness requires that the sinner repent of his sins and trust in Jesus Christ for salvation.

How God makes the sinner personally righteous.

We can now apprehend more clearly God's method of making sinners personally righteous. God opens the way by giving His Son to honor the law, so that God can come down from heaven and enter into covenant with the sinner and draw him back to life and love. This is God's method: through faith the sinner receives Jesus Christ as the sinner's righteousness, Christ having borne for the sinner the curse of the law, Christ having obeyed the law perfectly, and then Christ having suffered the penalty of sin in the place of the sinner, which the sinner must have suffered if not for the saving work of Christ. The sinner, by faith accepting Christ, becomes, in the governmental respect, united to Christ, so that, for Christ's sake, God accepts them both. Families sometimes come into such a relation to government that the children stand in the stead of the parents and are rewarded or forgiven for their parents' sake. The relationship sustained by Christ and the believing sinner to the government of God is similar, as Paul wrote, "God presented Christ as a sacrifice of atonement, through the shedding of his blood—to be received by faith. He did this to demonstrate his righteousness" (Romans 3:25).* The merits of Christ's death are made over to us on condition of our believing, and we have the full benefit of all that Christ has suffered and done to honor the law. We now abandon all hope of justification from personally obeying the law, which is legalism, and we receive Christ as God's mode of making us right before the law. Christ is given to us as a Redeemer and Savior. Jesus Christ is treated in this transaction as if He had been the sinner and we were the ones who were righteous. So we now, "walk in the way of love, just as Christ loved us and gave himself up for us as a fragrant offering and sacrifice to God" (Ephesians 5:2). In this way we stand before God *in Christ*, as Paul said, "If someone else thinks they have reasons to put confidence in the flesh, I have more . . . as for righteousness based on the law, faultless. But whatever were gains to me I now consider loss for the sake of Christ. What is more, I consider everything a loss because of the surpassing worth of knowing Christ Jesus my Lord, for whose sake I have lost all things. I consider them garbage, that I may gain Christ and be found in him, not having a righteousness of my own that comes from the law, but that which is through faith in Christ—the righteousness that comes from God on the basis of faith" (Philippians 3:4-9). Thus by a governmental act, God merges *in Christ* the whole mass of believers—Christ having become our Surety, our Advocate, our Mediator and our King. In this wonderful arrangement, God turns the whole race around from looking to the law for justification to looking unto Christ for justification.

For the sinner to become personally righteous, he must submit to God. Submission to God's righteousness is the condition of salvation. So the apostle implies in our text: "For they, being ignorant of God's righteousness, and going about to establish their own righteousness, have not submitted themselves unto the righteousness of God" (Romans 10:3). In this verse you cannot fail to observe that God's method of gospel salvation is something to be submitted to. The will must yield its full assent to God's plan.

The constant effort of sinners is *to do something of their own* to be saved—some work of some sort; or, trying to get up some emotional or spiritual experience. This is the great idea which they aim to realize as soon as they are convicted of sin and know they are sinners. Hence, they cannot have peace of mind or real pardon, because they do not accept God's plan of salvation. They struggle against God's Spirit. They resist the Holy Spirit's influence. They turn and shift in all possible ways to get up some righteousness of their own or have some spiritual experience to save them. The seventh chapter in the Book of Romans is a picture of one who is struggling and floundering as in a spiritual quagmire—binding himself by promises and resolves and yet finding them all of no avail. Many of those who profess to be Christians are in precisely this condition! They

Men, Ignorant of God's Righteousness, Would Establish Their Own

make not a prayer in which they do not feel condemned. Their state is one of conviction of sin and condemnation and despair so deeply agonizing that they can have no peace. They are struggling to effect an impossibility—to establish, in some way, their own righteousness; and failing in this, they sink down into despair. Hence, it comes to pass that the last step a person takes before submission to God is usually a mighty effort to establish his own righteousness; which effort ends in despair, after which he consents to submit to God's plan of being made righteous through faith in Jesus Christ alone. How often have I seen this in those who thought they knew what Christian faith is, but in the clear light of these truths have seen their mistake! *If they come really to despair of help in themselves, and then cast their souls on God through faith in Jesus Christ, all is well.* Probably most ministers find cases of this sort. Great numbers of them have fallen under my observation. How many have I seen who struggle and struggle, long, and without relief, because they struggle in a wrong direction. They are ignorant of God's righteousness, and therefore they go about to establish a righteousness of their own.

A striking case now occurs to me of a lady who is now in mission work. She was a lady of many noble traits of character, but before her conversion, strong in her self-righteousness. Hearing of the great revivals in Oneida County, some thirty years ago, she came to see them. Her object was to learn what this new and strange movement might be. She heard sermon after sermon, but writhed under their pointed truths, often finding fault with the preaching as being too personal and full of wrong ideas. Conviction of sin, however, sank deeper and yet deeper. Soon a friend with whom she was boarding said to me, "We have a dreadful case at our house. You must come and see her." I went. I found she had decided to defend the idea that she did not deserve to be damned, for if she was a sinner, it was only because she was made a sinner, and because she was born a sinner, sin was not her fault. After these points were discussed and she was shown her error, she became more agonized and the struggle was fearful! At last she screamed at the top of her voice and yielded! Then a change came over her—a charming, glorious change, which no language can describe. Almost her first words, as she broke silence again, were, "I'll be a missionary!" Only a few months passed before she fulfilled her vow. She has served as a missionary to this day. Her former self-righteousness, like a mighty tower of strength, came down wonderfully. When Jesus Christ became her righteousness, she was a lamb at His feet. Such a change in a believer's whole being, manifest in every aspect, is truly wonderful.

Too often it happens that you see those who profess to be Christians moving heaven and earth by their legalistic and self-righteous efforts to get up some righteousness of their own. You will be struck in examining their belief system to see how utterly Jesus Christ is left out of it as a practical Savior. They think of their good and right doings—not of Christ—as really the basis or ground of their hope before God.

The gospel method of God's righteousness is exactly opposed to human pride. *Pride loves to do the work and have the honor* of it, but God's system of salvation has done all the meritorious work itself—*the gospel method leaves nothing for any person to do that he can be proud of or brag about.*

For this reason, conversion costs such a conflict. Very often, it seems indispensable that God should startle sinners with awful fears before they will yield submission to Him and trust in Christ alone for salvation. On Mt. Sinai and all around, the trumpet of God waxes louder and louder—the mountain is all ablaze and rocks quake under God's mighty voice long and loud until every nerve of the sinner trembles and he sees nothing but darkness until the atonement of Christ reveals a resurrected and living Christ to his agonized soul.

The gospel plan of salvation seems deep and dark as midnight to the sinner until the Holy Spirit reveals to him his selfishness, his self-righteousness, cleaves down his self-righteous spirit, knocks out his props, so that he falls and dies to his self-centeredness! Then, the cross of Jesus reveals life to him; he rejoices with exceeding joy in a salvation wrought of God through Christ's redeeming blood, and he begins to live *in Christ*.

The sinner must accept and *submit to* the righteousness of God. The sinner must submit to that righteous judgment of God that has sentenced him to hell. He must admit that God's judgment and God's sentence of him to hell is right and just. I often ask sinners, "Are you prepared to subscribe to that righteousness of God which dooms you to hell?" If I find him wavering on that point, I say to him, "You do not understand God's righteousness. You cannot be saved until you subscribe to God's

Men, Ignorant of God's Righteousness, Would Establish Their Own

righteousness in this, until you fully admit its justness and propriety. You must yield also to God's supreme authority and right to govern all of His creatures and consent to be saved wholly by God's grace—things which many fail to understand. In England, I found to my surprise that many ministers talked much about grace; and yet, they did not believe that people deserved damnation for their sins. I asked them, "What do you mean by this? You talk largely of grace, yet deny all need of it! For, grace is the antithesis of justice. How can there be grace shown the sinner, if it be not just to punish him?"

The point of greatest struggle with the sinner is in laying aside his own righteousness as worthless. You recollect the case of the poor Indian and his rich white neighbor, both awakened and convicted of sin at the same time, but the Indian came at once to Jesus, while the white man remained a long time in the most extreme darkness and distress. At last, he asked the Indian how it happened that he found Christ so soon, while himself had sought so long in vain. The Indian stammered his reply, "Indian poor; white man rich; poor Indian no clothes; white man good clothes, fine clothes; Indian throw his old rags right away, take Christ's robe at once; white man can't throw away his fine clothes."

Do you recollect the case of the poor woman in the gospel? Christ had been invited to a rich man's table. They sat reclined at their meal with their feet somewhat extended behind them when this woman came up gently, clasped His sacred feet, bathed them with her tears, and wiped them with the hair of her head. Blessed woman! She knew her position as a lost sinner, and she had tasted the grace of God that forgives freely. What an act was that! She did not seem to know or care if the whole world saw her! Her humility of spirit charms us, and we read in her case the feeling of those who discard all righteousness of their own and come to understand the righteousness of God (read Luke 7:36-50).

REMARKS

The ignorance of the Jews came from their great pride, and is not at all to be ascribed to the obscurity of the subject itself. The ignorance of sinners now, even under the gospel, is amazing. I have recently seen one who had been well instructed in the letter of these things, yet when he became deeply hungry for gospel life, seemed scarcely to know how to use one of the plainest truths it embraces. It was affecting to see him drink in a few of the simplest gospel truths, saying, "I am sure I never heard of that before! I never thought of that!" How common it is for sinners under the Holy Spirit's light to say, "All this is new to me! I wonder why I was never told of this before!"

Many feel the need of becoming truly religious. They mean to be, and they set themselves to work for it in some way. Perhaps they set themselves to serve God, but they have no right idea of what it is to be truly religious. Hence, we find so few who seem in their own experience to know the deep power of the gospel. Ah, the deep foundations of their selfishness are not broken up until they accept the gospel message of Jesus Christ. They have never been made conformable to Christ's death on the cross. Hence, the great difference between this class and those who are utterly cut down and slain by the law and then raised from the dead to a new life *in Christ*.

When the sinner is truly convicted of sin, the way opens before him, and the first conditions are fulfilled for his free pardon. Now, he has new apprehensions of God's law—of its great spirituality. But it is not enough to know this; another lesson yet remains. I am glad to see you cut down under thorough conviction of sin, but you must also learn not to fly in the face of that fiery law for salvation! Sinner, you who profess to be Christian, do you know how you are to be saved? You need not make any atonement; you need not suffer and toil to work up an atonement; no need of this at all. In my own first convictions, I said, under my great sorrow, "I shall have to bear a great deal of this, I have been a sinner so long. I shall have to be nearly killed before I can be saved." Ah, how mistaken! God wants no such atonement—no such suffering by you. *The atonement is all made by Jesus Christ, ready to your hands!* Do you understand that no works, or prayers, or tears of your own can do anything for you towards an atonement, and towards constituting a basis or ground of your acceptance before God? God himself has provided the Lamb for the offering. Now come, as the ancient Jew came, and lay your hand on that dear Sacrifice, and confess your sins to Jesus Christ. The veil of the

Men, Ignorant of God's Righteousness, Would Establish Their Own

great temple is rent away and you may enter the inner sanctuary. You may come to the mercy seat and lay your own hand on the head of the Victim, Jesus Christ, Who takes away the sin of the world. Will you come to Jesus Christ now for righteousness and salvation?*

---

*Also see Charles G. Finney, "On the Atonement" on Romans 3:25-26 in *Principles of Righteousness*, 53-65.
** Charles G. Finney, *The Oberlin Evangelist,* November 21, 1855; *Principles of Liberty,* 129–137. For Review: Answer the Study Questions on page 222, Cowles page 237.

Editor's Note: To assist your study, I have included some scripture quotations that use the word "joy" on pages 14, 26, 40, 76, 120, 142, 172, 200, and 220 in this book. Rather than just include blank even numbered pages when I wanted the new chapter page to begin on the right hand (odd numbered) page, I chose to add these Bible verses in these locations. One way to discover the Bible's meaning of a word is to study how the Bible uses that word, in context, in several locations in the Bible. I hope these verses expand your Biblical understanding of the word "joy" in your relationship with God in the Holy Spirit.

Food for Thought: In some sense, each of the three volumes in this series could have been titled: *Principles of Righteousness in the Holy Spirit*; *Principles of Peace in the Holy Spirit*, and *Principles of Joy in the Holy Spirit*, for people will not experience true righteousness, peace, and joy in this life apart from the atoning work of Jesus Christ and the indwelling guidance, power, and presence of the Holy Spirit in the heart of the believer according to the Bible's teachings.

The Psalms on Joy

Let all who take refuge in you be glad; let them ever sing for joy. Spread your protection over them, that those who love your name may rejoice in you. —Psalm 5:11

You make known to me the path of life; you will fill me with joy in your presence, with eternal pleasures at your right hand. —Psalm 16:11

The precepts of the LORD are right, giving joy to the heart. The commands of the LORD are radiant, giving light to the eyes. —Psalm 19:8

The LORD is my strength and my shield; my heart trusts in him, and he helps me. My heart leaps for joy, and with my song I praise him. —Psalm 28:7

You turned my wailing into dancing; you removed my sackcloth and clothed me with joy. —Psalm 30:11

May those who delight in my vindication shout for joy and gladness; may they always say, "The LORD be exalted, who delights in the well-being of his servant." —Psalm 35:27

Then I will go to the altar of God, to God, my joy and my delight. I will praise you with the lyre, O God, my God. —Psalm 43:4

You love righteousness and hate wickedness; therefore God, your God, has set you above your companions by anointing you with the oil of joy. —Psalm 45:7

Clap your hands, all you nations; shout to God with cries of joy. —Psalm 47:1

2

The Way to be Holy
1843

> *For Christ is the end of the law for righteousness to every one that believeth.* —Romans 10:4—KJV

> *Christ is the end of the law so that there may be righteousness for everyone who believes.* —Romans 10:4—NIV

To learn how the sinner can enter into a personal righteous relationship with God through faith in Jesus Christ and not by works of the law, we must discuss what Paul did not intend and what Paul intended by his assertion, "Christ is the end of the law for righteousness." Then, we must understand how Christ becomes the end of the law for righteousness to the believer.

What Paul did not intend by "the end of law for righteousness."

First, Paul did not mean that God in Christ abolished the law in respect to believers. I am aware that some antinomians in the Church affirm this, but it cannot be true for the following reasons:

1. The moral law of God is not founded in the *arbitrary* will of God. For if it were, God would have no rule of conduct, nothing with which to compare His own actions. But every moral agent must have some rule by which to act. If God had no moral rule by which to act, He would have no moral character at all, for moral character implies moral obligation, and moral obligation implies moral law. Unless the moral law is obligatory on God, benevolence in God is not virtue, for virtue must be compliance with moral obligation. Nor would we have any standard with which to compare God's actions, and by which to judge of them, so that we could know whether God is holy or unholy. Moreover, if God is capable of benevolence, it is impossible that He should not be under a moral obligation to act with benevolence; and if so, the law cannot of course be founded in His *arbitrary* will. Furthermore, God could, if the law were founded in His *arbitrary* will, by willing it, make benevolence vice, and malevolence virtue. He could will what is right to be wrong, and He could will what is wrong to be right. But this is absurd and impossible.

2. The moral law is founded in God's self-existent *nature*. He never made His own *nature*, and consequently never made the moral law, and it must therefore be obligatory upon God by virtue of His own *nature* which imposes it. The moral law is as really obligatory on God as on us.

3. God requires benevolence of us because it is *naturally* obligatory on us. He made us in His own image; that is, with a *nature* like His own; therefore, God could not discharge us from obligation to keep the moral law even if He wanted to do so, for our own reason would still reveal and impose it upon us. We would perceive our moral obligation by our *nature* as created in the image of God.

4. If God could and did abolish the moral law, then we could have no moral character. We could neither be sinful nor holy any more than the animals without reason can. Observe then, Christ cannot be the end of the law in the sense that Christ abolishes the law.

Second, Paul did not intend to mean that Christ abolishes the penalty of the law with respect to believers so they can sin without actual condemnation. Some have this view of justification; that, at the first act of faith, God so sets aside the penalty of the moral law so it never afterwards attaches to the individual. But this cannot be for the following reasons:

1. If the penalty is set aside, the moral law is repealed, for moral law consists of precept and penalty.

2. If the penalty were set aside, then Christians when they sinned would not need pardon. They could not, without folly and even wickedness, pray for God to forgive them. Praying for God to forgive them would be nothing else but sheer unbelief. But every Christian knows that when he sins he is condemned and must be pardoned or damned. Christ, therefore, is not the end of the law in this sense.

Third, Paul did not intend to mean that Christ was the end of the law for legal justification; for the reason:

Jesus Christ does not obtain a *legal justification* for believers. *Legal justification* is the act of pronouncing one just in the estimation of the moral law. Christ cannot do this with respect to any transgressor. Gospel justification is pardon and acceptance by God. It was never the goal or purpose of the moral law to pardon sinners. In this sense, then, it is impossible that Christ should be the end of the law, for the law never aimed at pardoning transgressors. The word *righteousness* sometimes means *justification*, but *righteousness* cannot mean *justification* here, as Christ never aimed at *legal justification*, and the law never aimed at pardon. Jesus Christ cannot, of course, then, be the end of the law in this sense.

Fourth, Paul did not mean that Christ is the end of the law in the sense of procuring a pardon for those who believe, for this was never the end proposed by the moral law. The law knows nothing of pardon.

Fifth, nor did Paul intend to mean that Christ imputes His own righteousness or obedience to believers. Some suppose that Christ was under no obligation to obey the moral law, and that He can, therefore impute His obedience to believers. However, consider these facts:

1. The moral law never aimed at imputation. This was no part of its object. Did the moral law require Christ's righteousness or personal holiness to be imputed?

2. The doctrine of *imputed righteousness* is founded on the absurd assumption that Christ owed no obedience to the moral law. But how can this be? Was Jesus Christ under no obligation to be benevolent, to love God and others? If He was not under this moral obligation, then His benevolence was not virtue. He certainly was just as much bound to love God with all His heart, and soul, and strength, and mind, and His neighbor as himself, as we are. How holy should God be? As holy as He can be. That is, He should be perfectly benevolent, and the Bible says He is.

3. The doctrine of *imputed righteousness* assumes that Christ's works were works of supererogation. Is this what the Apostle Paul meant when he says, "For such an high priest became us, who is holy, harmless, undefiled, separate from sinners, and made higher than the heavens" (Hebrews 7:26)?

4. The doctrine of *imputed righteousness* is a mere dogma of Popery, born, bred, and supported amid its darkness and superstitions. The sufferings and death of Christ were for us, and constitute the Atonement. His obedience was necessary to His making an atonement as a condition, since only a holy being could make it. Holiness is benevolence, and Christ must of necessity have been benevolent in order to make the Atonement which is a work of benevolence.

5. The doctrine of *imputed righteousness* represents God as requiring that Christ should render a perfect obedience for us; and then, that He should die just as if no such obedience had been rendered for us; that notwithstanding the debt is thus paid twice over by our substitute and we must repent as though it were unpaid; and then, that we must be forgiven. And after all this, that we must ourselves obey or be personally holy, and finally that we must count it all grace! What a jumble of nonsense is this! Is this the gospel of the blessed God? Impossible!

6. The doctrine of *imputed righteousness* utterly sets aside the true idea of the gospel. The true idea of pardon does not enter into it. It is rather a fivefold satisfaction of justice. According to this doctrine, we are not restored to the favor of God by a free pardon, but by *imputed righteousness*. It is not at all surprising that thinking men, when they hear such slang as this, say, "O, nonsense! If that be the gospel, we will have nothing to do with it."

Imputation is not and never was the end or object of the law. The end which the moral law seeks is righteousness or true obedience.

What Paul intended by "the end of law for righteousness."

Paul affirmed that Jesus Christ is the end of the law for righteousness. *Righteousness is obedience to the law*. Therefore, Christ is the end of the law for obedience. He secures the very goal aimed at by the moral law; that is, *Christ makes Christians holy!* As Paul wrote, "Therefore, there is now no condemnation for those who are in Christ Jesus, because through Christ Jesus the law of the Spirit who gives life has set you free from the law of sin and death. For what the law was powerless to do because it was weakened by the flesh, God did by sending his own Son in the likeness of sinful flesh to be a sin offering. And so he condemned sin in the flesh, in order that the righteous requirement of the law might be fully met in us, who do not live according to the flesh but according to the Spirit" (Romans 8:1-4).* What have we here? Why, an express assertion by the Apostle Paul that Christ by His Atonement and indwelling Spirit had secured in Christians the very obedience which the moral law required!

How Christ becomes the end of the law for righteousness.

Confidence or faith is essential to all hearty obedience to any law. Outward conformity to the requirements of a law may be secured by fear, but not by love. Christ, then, must secure love or true righteousness by inspiring confidence in the character and government of God. God had been slandered by Satan, and the world believed the slander. Satan represented to our first parents that God was insincere in forbidding them to eat of the tree of knowledge, and that the result of their eating of it would be just the reverse of what God had threatened. Satan said, "For God knows that when you eat from it your eyes will be opened, and you will be like God, knowing good and evil" (Genesis 3:5). This was a most taking temptation! For, "When the woman saw that the fruit of the tree was good for food and pleasing to the eye, and also desirable for gaining wisdom, she took some and ate it. She also gave some to her husband, who was with her, and he ate it. Then the eyes of both of them were opened, and they realized they were naked; so they sewed fig leaves together and made coverings for themselves" (Genesis 3:6-7). Now the thing to be done is to remove this prejudice which has existed in all ages, but how shall it be done?

Christ came to reveal the true God and the true character of God's government to remove the prejudice against Him. He came not only to teach, but by His example to give an illustration of what the law meant so the human mind could understand that God is love. Christ knew very well that we need confidence in God, and that to reveal the character of God so as to beget confidence He must hold out love in strong relief in a life of love before the human race. There was a great necessity for this at that time, because many of the dispensations of God toward the human race appeared severe. God had poured out the waters of the flood upon the old world and destroyed it. God had frowned upon the cities of the plain and sent them down to hell. In many other instances, God had been obliged to resort to such measures as were calculated in the circumstances to beget a dread and a slavish fear rather than to inspire confidence and love. Therefore, God adopted measures of a different nature, measures adapted to beget faith.

The nature of faith renders obedience certain so far as it is implicit. A wife, for example, is always perfectly under the influence of her husband just so far as she has confidence in him. Suppose her husband is a business man. If she has confidence in his business talents, she does not concern herself at all in his business transactions. So, if they are going on a journey, suppose she knows him to be careful and attentive to his affairs, she will not be in a fret. She will never ask whether he has taken care of their baggage and whether he has procured tickets and accommodations. She expects all this as a matter of natural course, and she is happy in her reliance on him. But suppose we turn this over and she has no confidence in his character. If he is a man of business, and she lacks confidence in his judgment, she will be all the time in distress for fear he will take some step which will ruin their affairs. If they are going on a journey, she will perhaps fear that he will start off without his pocketbook or forget some of his baggage or get lost on the way. It is easy to see that so far as this lack of confidence extends its tendency is to diminish her affection, and if it extends to his whole character, she cannot love him. I might illustrate this in a thousand ways. If you call in a physician and you have confidence in him, you will take any medicine which he may prescribe. I recollect a case when a certain king was sick and sent for his physician. The physician examined his symptoms and found his disease a dangerous one requiring a peculiar treatment. He told the king he would go home and prepare a certain medicine which would make him very sick while in its operation, but would remove the disease. While he was gone, the king received a letter warning him against the physician as though he designed to poison him. When the physician returned and presented him the medicine, he immediately swallowed it and then handed his physician the letter he had received. That was faith; and it placed him entirely under the control of his physician. Therefore, it is easy to see that if Christ could only restore faith among people, He would naturally secure obedience.

Faith in God's character is the foundation of faith in God's promises. Many people try to exercise faith in the promises of God without faith in His character. So, Christ takes the course of revealing the character of God as the foundation of faith in God's promises.

Christ baptizes those who believe in Him by His Spirit and actually works in them to will and to do. How wonderfully Christ works to get control of believers. Unless He gets their confidence, He cannot do this; but so soon as He inspires faith, He has them under His control. We see the same law among people. Observe a human pair. After securing mutual confidence, they wind imperishable cords around each other's hearts. Then, for one to know the will of the other is to do it. They do not need to be bound down or driven by the force of penalties or fear. Unfortunately, this is also the way of the seducer! The seducer can "smile and smile and be a villain still." He lays his foundation deep in the confidence of his victim until he may laugh at all her parents may say and do against him. He gains such an ascendency that he controls the will more absolutely than if he wielded it by his hand. Such is the natural result of getting into the confidence of another. They will and do at our bidding. Christ is no seducer, but Christ gains the heart and works in us to will and to do His good pleasure.

Principles of Joy in the Holy Spirit — Finney's Lessons on Romans

The way to be holy is to believe. In John 6:28-29, the people asked Jesus, "What must we do to do the works God requires? Jesus answered, "The work of God is this: to believe in the one he has sent." Those who believe in Jesus Christ will receive forgiveness of sins and a place among those who are sanctified by faith in Him (see Acts 20:32 and Acts 26:18). Paul wrote to the Galatians "I would like to learn just one thing from you: Did you receive the Spirit by the works of the law, or by believing what you heard? Are you so foolish? After beginning by means of the Spirit, are you now trying to finish by means of the flesh? Have you experienced so much in vain—if it really was in vain? So again I ask, does God give you his Spirit and work miracles among you by the works of the law, or by your believing what you heard? So also Abraham 'believed God, and it was credited to him as righteousness.' Understand, then, that those who have faith are children of Abraham. Scripture foresaw that God would justify the Gentiles by faith, and announced the gospel in advance to Abraham: 'All nations will be blessed through you.' So those who rely on faith are blessed along with Abraham, the man of faith. For all who rely on the works of the law are under a curse, as it is written: 'Cursed is everyone who does not continue to do everything written in the Book of the Law.' Clearly no one who relies on the law is justified before God, because 'the righteous will live by faith.' The law is not based on faith; on the contrary, it says, 'The person who does these things will live by them.' Christ redeemed us from the curse of the law by becoming a curse for us, for it is written: 'Cursed is everyone who is hung on a pole.' He redeemed us in order that the blessing given to Abraham might come to the Gentiles through Christ Jesus, so that by faith we might receive the promise of the Spirit" (Galatians 3:2-14).

When Paul wrote to the Romans about the unbelief of Israel, he declared, "What then shall we say? That the Gentiles, who did not pursue righteousness, have obtained it, a righteousness that is by faith; but the people of Israel, who pursued the law as the way of righteousness, have not attained their goal. Why not? Because they pursued it not by faith but as if it were by works. They stumbled over the stumbling stone. As it is written: 'See, I lay in Zion a stone that causes people to stumble and a rock that makes them fall, and the one who believes in him will never be put to shame'" (Romans 9:30-33).** Therefore, *in Christ* the believer is complete; that is, Christ is all we need. His offices and relations meet all our needs, and by faith we receive their redeeming influence.***

REMARKS

The gospel lays so much stress on faith because faith in Jesus Christ is the only way of salvation. The method of saving people through faith is perfectly philosophical; for Christ works himself into the very heart of believers.

Faith in Christ is the only possible way in the very nature of the case to secure love for God. God might command obedience and back up His command with threatening. But God's threats would only fill the selfish mind with terror, and leave its selfishness unbroken, and even leave it grasping for selfish goals amid the roar of its thunders. In the very nature of mind, to secure a hearty obedience God must secure confidence. Consider Eve. The moment she doubted, she fell into sin. And so would all heaven fall, if they lost confidence in God. Yes, they would fall into sin! They would no more retain their obedience than the planets would retain their places if the power of gravitation were broken. Everyone knows that if the power of attraction were destroyed, suns, stars, and planets would run lawless through the universe, and desolation would drive her plowshare through creation. So, break the power of confidence in heaven, and every angel there would fall like Lucifer, and universal anarchy would prevail.

What I have said does not represent virtue or holiness as consisting in mere emotions of complacency or in loving God merely for His favors. Rather, the exhibition of His moral character in Christ begets in us real benevolence. Christ shows us what benevolence is and He stimulates us to exercise it. Nearly all preachers and writers of the present day confuse Christianity with mere complacency in God for His favors. Both gratitude and complacency may, and often do, exist in the unrepentant mind. It must, therefore, be a fundamental mistake to confuse these values with true Christianity.

Christ, by exhibiting His benevolence, begets His own image in those who believe; that is, they are naturally led to yield themselves up to the transforming tendency of this view of Christ's character. The law could never secure this benevolence in a selfish mind.

I said the doctrine of *imputed righteousness* is another gospel, or no gospel at all. And here I would ask, "Is not this quite another way of salvation?" According to the true gospel, instead of imputing righteousness to believers, God actually makes them righteous through faith in Christ.

The gospel of Jesus Christ is not an evasion of the moral law. It comes in as an auxiliary to accomplish what the moral law aims to achieve, but cannot effect, because it is weak through the flesh.

Who are true believers? Those who love God supremely and their neighbor as themselves; and unless your faith begets this loving obedience, it is not the faith of the gospel.

We can see the sustaining power of faith. This is not well considered by many. If the head of a family secures its confidence, he controls it easily; but if not, there is a perpetual tendency to resist him. The same principle operates in local, state and national governments. These human governments are firm, just so far and no farther, than they are based upon the confidence of their citizens or subjects. So it is in the business world. Everything is prosperous, so long as confidence is secured. This gone, and the tide immediately sets forth the other way. Why are so many businesses and corporations in this country, which were once supposed to be perfectly stable, tumbling down around the heads of the merchants? Because confidence is destroyed. Restore that confidence, and immediately things will assume a different aspect. Every merchant in New York will feel the impulse; and ships from abroad will come freighted down with products to sell. This principle is equally efficient and necessary in the divine government. The devil well understood this fact; therefore, his first effort was directed to the overthrow of confidence. But ministers too often put confidence in the background, and hence the reason for so much failure in the work of reforming the world. Christ, on the other hand, always put confidence in God foremost, and His declaration, "Very truly I tell you, the one who believes has eternal life," is the unalterable law of God's government (John 6:47).

The Way to be Holy

Unbelievers cannot be saved, for their lack of confidence will necessarily keep their soul from hearty obedience.

Do you ask, "How can I believe?" I turn to you and ask, "How can you not believe?" Christ died for you to win your confidence. He stands at your door, offering blessings and assuring you of His good will. And you say you cannot believe! What! And with the Son of God at the door! But perhaps you stand away back, and say, "Christians can believe, but how can I? I am a poor, guilty wretch." And why not you? Come, let your anchor down upon the holy moral character of God, and then if the winds blow, let them blow; if the ocean tosses itself, and yawns till it lays bare its very bottom, you are secure, for God rules the wind and the waves. But I hear some one say, "I am such a backslider." Yes, and you are likely to be until you believe in Christ. Unless you believe, you will continue to go directly away from God. Come, instantly, and believe. Come, all you who think you are Christians! Come, all you sinners! Come now, and Christ will write His law in your hearts; and God's law will no longer be to you a law on tables of stone. You believe it! Let us come around the throne of grace and receive Christ as the end of the law for righteousness.****

---

*Also see Charles G. Finney, "Justification" on Romans 8:1 in *Principles of Peace*, 58-72.

** Also see Charles G. Finney, "Religion of the Law and the Gospel" on Romans 9:30-33 in *Principles of Peace*, 205-216.

*** Charles G. Finney described these offices and relations and their importance in *Principles of Union with Christ*, compiled and edited by L.G. Parkhurst, Jr., Minneapolis: Bethany House Publishers, 1985.

**** Charles G. Finney, *The Oberlin Evangelist*, March 29, 1843; *Principles of Liberty*, 139–146. For Review: Answer the Study Questions on page 223, Cowles page 237.

The Psalms on Joy

Restore to me the joy of your salvation and grant me a willing spirit, to sustain me. —Psalm 51:12

The whole earth is filled with awe at your wonders; where morning dawns, where evening fades, you call forth songs of joy. —Psalm 65:8

The meadows are covered with flocks and the valleys are mantled with grain; they shout for joy and sing. —Psalm 65:13

May the nations be glad and sing for joy, for you rule the peoples with equity and guide the nations of the earth. —Psalm 67:4

My lips will shout for joy when I sing praise to you— I whom you have delivered. —Psalm 71:23

Bring joy to your servant, Lord, for I put my trust in you. —Psalm 86:4

Satisfy us in the morning with your unfailing love, that we may sing for joy and be glad all our days. —Psalm 90:14

For you make me glad by your deeds, LORD; I sing for joy at what your hands have done. —Psalm 92:4

When anxiety was great within me, your consolation brought me joy. —Psalm 94:19

Light is sown on the righteous and joy on the upright in heart. —Psalm 97:11

Shouts of joy and victory resound in the tents of the righteous: "The LORD's right hand has done mighty things!" —Psalm 118:15

3

On Believing with the Heart
1856

For with the heart man believeth unto righteousness; and with the mouth confession is made unto salvation.—Romans 10:10—KJV

For it is with your heart that you believe and are justified, and it is with your mouth that you confess and are saved.—Romans 10:10—NIV

We need to carefully distinguish between *intellectual faith* and *heart-faith*. Several different states of mind are currently called *faith*, this term being obviously used in various senses. The term *heart* is also used in various senses; indeed, there are but few terms which are not used with some variety of definitions. Hence, it becomes very important to discriminate between these two types of faith. In regard to *faith*, the Scriptures affirm that the "devils also believe and tremble;" as the Apostle James wrote, "You believe that there is one God. Good! Even the demons believe that—and shudder" (James 2:19). But demons surely do not have *heart-faith*, for they do not "believe unto righteousness" (Romans 10:10). Demons cannot be justified by their *belief*. Demons persist in unrighteous living in spite of their knowledge.

Intellectual faith or faith in a person's intellect is a judgment—an opinion. The mind judges and becomes convinced that the facts are so. Whatever the nature of the things believed, *intellectual faith is an involuntary state of mind.* The things believed may be true. They may relate to God and may embrace the great fundamental facts and doctrines of religion; yet, intellectual faith may not result in righteousness. The intellectual faith of demons does not result in righteousness. It is often true that people have their judgments convinced, yet this conviction does not reach beyond their intelligence to their heart or will. Intellectual faith may go a little further and move their feelings and play on their emotions or sensibility; yet it may do nothing more, it may not influence them to make a decision based on the truth. Intellectual faith may produce no change in the will. It may result in no new moral purpose. It may utterly fail to reach the voluntary attitude of the mind; hence, it will make no change in the life.

On the other hand, *heart-faith is true confidence*. Heart-faith involves an earnest committal of one's self and interests to the demands of the truth believed. Heart-faith is precisely the trust we have in those to whom we cling in confidence—such as children feel in their friends and true fathers and mothers. They are naturally ready to believe what is said to them and to commit themselves to the care of those they love.

The *heart* is in *heart-faith*, which *is a voluntary state of mind*—always substantially and essentially *an act of the will*. Heart-faith will, of course, always affect the feelings, emotions, and sensibility, and it will also influence the person's way of life. Heart-faith naturally tends towards righteousness, and may truly be said to be, "unto righteousness." Heart-faith implies love, and it seems in its very nature to unify itself with the affections. The inspired writers of the Bible plainly did not hold faith to be so purely an act of the will as to exclude love and the affections. Obviously, they made heart-faith include the affections.

The conditions of intellectual faith.

Sometimes, but not always, the faith of the heart is essential to the faith

On Believing with the Heart

of the intellect. Thus, it may be necessary that we have heart-faith in a person before we are duly prepared to investigate the facts that relate to their character. So, in relation to God, if we lack heart-faith in God, we are in no state to deal fairly with the evidence of His works and ways. Here it is well to notice the vast difference between the irresistible assumptions of the mind respecting God, and those things which we arrive at by study and reasoning. Heart-faith seems essential to any candid investigation.

Heart-faith is also essential to our conviction as to the truth. I am not prepared to judge candidly concerning a friend unless I have some heart-faith in him. Suppose I hear a deeply scandalous rumor about my best friend. My regard for him forbids my believing this scandalous report unless it comes fully sustained by truthful testimony. On the other hand, if I had no heart-confidence in him, my intelligence might be thrown entirely off, and I might do both him and myself the greatest injustice.

Many of you have had this experience in regard to faith. Often, in the common walks of life, you have found that, if it had not been for your heart-confidence, you would have been greatly deceived. Your heart held on; at length, the evidence showed forth; you were in a condition to judge charitably, and thus you arrived at the truth.

Heart-faith is especially essential where there is mystery. Of course there are points in religious doctrine which are profoundly mysterious. This fact is not peculiar to religious truth, but is common to every part of God's works—which is equivalent to saying—it is common to all real science. Any child can ask me questions which I cannot answer. Without heart-confidence, it would be impossible for society to exist. Happily for us, we can often wisely confide, when we cannot by any means understand. In the nature of the case, there must be mysteries about God, for the simple reason that *God is infinite* and *we are finite*. Yet, God reveals enough of himself to authorize us to cherish the most unbounded confidence in Him. Therefore, let no one stumble at this as though it were something strange; for, in fact, the same thing obtains to some extent in all our social relations. In these, we are often compelled to confide in our friends where the case seems altogether suspicious. Yet, we confide, and by and by the truth comes to light, and we are thankful that our heart-faith held us from doing them injustice. Heart-faith is especially important where there is contradictory evidence.

It may seem to some that God shows partiality. If God seems partial, the mind needs the support of confidence in God. You go on safely if you maintain the deep conviction that God is and must do right. Think about a woman who has lost everything—husband, children, all—how can she give any account of this? I remember the case of a woman who traveled out to the West with her husband and family. On the way, she buried her husband and all but two little ones; and then, she made her weary way back with these on foot. Pinching want and weariness drove her into a stranger's dwelling at nightfall; and there a churlish man would have turned her into the street, but his wife had a human heart, and she insisted on letting them stay, even if she herself sat up all night. Think of the trying case of that lone widow. She did not sleep. Her mingled grief and faith found utterance in the words, "My heart is breaking, but God is good!" How could she make it out that God is good? Just as you would in the case of your husband, if one should tell you he had gone forever and proved faithless to his vows. You can set this insinuation aside, and let your heart rise above it. You do this on the strength of your heart-faith.

So the Christian does in regard to many mysterious points in God's character and ways. You cannot see how God can exist without ever beginning to exist; or how God can exist in three Persons, since no other beings known to you exist in more than one person. You cannot see how God can be eternally good, and yet allow sin and misery to befall His creatures. But, with heart-faith we do not need to have everything explained. With heart-faith, the believer says to his heavenly Father, "I do not need to teach You, nor ask impertinent questions, for I know it is all right. I know God can never do anything wrong." And so, the believer finds a precious joy in trusting, without knowing how the mystery is solved. Just as a wife, long parted from her husband and under circumstances that need explanation; yet when he returns, she rushes to meet him with her loving welcome without waiting for one word of explanation. Suppose she had waited for the explanation before she could speak a kind word. This might savor of the intellect, but certainly it would not do honor to her heart. For her heart-confidence, her husband loves her better than ever, and well he may!

On Believing with the Heart

You can understand this. You can apply this to your relationship to God. God may appear to be capricious, but you know He is not. God may appear unjust, but you know He cannot be. Ah, Christian, when you comprehend the fact of God's wider reach of vision, and of His greater love, then you will cry out with Job, "Though he slay me, yet will I trust in him" (Job 13:15). When you have trusted as Job trusted, you heart will be as dear to Christ as ever!

What are not and what are the conditions of heart-faith.

Comprehending the facts to be believed is not a condition of heart-faith. We may know something to be a fact, while being entirely unable to explain the fact. The reasons and the explanations are quite a different thing from the evidence which sustains the fact and commends it to our belief. It is not half as necessary to know all the reasons in the case of God's ways as in man's ways. The reason for the difference is this: we know that God is always right—a knowledge which we cannot have with regard to any human being. With respect to God, our deepest and most resistless convictions assure us that all is right. Our corresponding convictions in the case of human beings are far from being irresistible. Yet, even in regard to people, we often find that a conviction of their rectitude, which is far less than irresistible, lends us to trust them. How much more should our stronger convictions with respect to God always lead us to trust in Him!

Our ability to prove that God exists is not a condition of heart-faith. Many an earnest Christian has never thought of this, any more than he has thought of trying to prove his own existence. An irresistible conviction gives him knowledge of God's existence and his own existence without needing any other proof of either.

In order to acquire heart-faith or as a condition of heart-faith God must be revealed to your inner being so that you are conscious of His existence and presence. There is nothing in the universe, perhaps, of which we can be more certain of than God's existence. The mind may be more deeply acquainted with God than with any other being or thing. Hence, heart-confidence may be based on God's revelations to the inner soul of a human being. Such revelations may reach the very highest measure of certainty. I do not mean to imply here that we are not certain of the facts of observation. But this is a stronger assurance and certainty. The mind becomes personally acquainted with God and is conscious of this direct and positive knowledge.

Another condition of heart-faith is that our soul must be inwardly drawn to God. In our relations to each other, we are sometimes conscious of a peculiar sympathy which draws us toward a friend. This fact is a thing of consciousness that we may be quite unable to explain. A similar attraction draws us to God and seems to be a natural condition of the strongest form of heart-faith.

An essential condition of heart-faith is a genuine love for God. In the absence of goodwill toward God, there never can be this faith of the heart. The wife can have no heart-faith in her husband unless she loves him. Her heart must be drawn to him in real love or this heart-faith will draw back and demand more evidence.

In view of the principle that genuine love for God is a condition of heart-faith, God takes measures to win our love and draw our hearts to himself. As human beings do toward each other, so God manifests His deep interest in us. He pours out His blessings on us in lavish profusion, and, in every way, strives to assure us that He is truly our friend. These are His methods to win the confidence of our hearts. When it becomes real to us that we owe everything to God—our health, gifts, all our comforts—then we can bear many dark and trying things. Then, we know that God loves us even though He must punish us, just as children know their parents love them and mean their good even though they chastise them. Under these broad and general manifestations of love, children trust, even though there may not be a present manifestations of love. You may remember how Cecil taught his little daughter the meaning of gospel faith. One day, she came to him with her hands full of little beads and she greatly delighted to show them to him. He said to her calmly, "You had better throw them all into the fire." She almost refused; but, when she saw that he was in earnest, she trustfully obeyed and cast them into the fire. After a few days, he brought her a casket of jewels. He said, "There, my daughter, you had faith in me the other day, and you threw

On Believing with the Heart

your beads into the fire. That was faith! Now I can give you things much more precious. Are these not far better?" So you should always believe in God. He has jewels for those who will believe and cast away their sins.

Heart-faith leads to righteousness—real obedience. The trustful and affectionate state of heart naturally leads us to obey God. I have often admired the faith manifested by the old theologian philosophers who held fast to their confidence in God in spite of the greatest of absurdities. Their faith could laugh at the most absurd principles involved in their philosophy of religious truth. It is a remarkable fact that the greater numbers of people in the church have been in their philosophy necessitarians, holding not the freedom but the bondage of the will. Their doctrine being that the will is determined necessarily by the strongest motive. President Edwards held these philosophical views; but in spite of them, he believed that God is supremely good. The absurdities of this philosophy did not shake his faith in God. All of the Old School Theologians hold the absurdities of Hyper-Calvinism; for example, that God absolutely and supremely controls all the moral actions of all His creatures.

Dr. Beecher, in a controversy with Dr. Wilson some years ago, held that obligation implied ability to obey. Dr. Wilson flatly denied this fact. Whereupon Dr. Beecher remarked that few men could march up and face such a proposition without winking. It is often the case that men have such heart-confidence in God that they will trust Him in spite of the most flagrant absurdities. There is less superstition in this than I used to suppose and more faith. Men forget their dogmas and philosophy, and in spite of both love and trust God.

Some theologians have held monstrous doctrines—even that God is the author of sin and puts forth His divine efficiency to make people sin, as truly as by His Spirit to make people holy. This view was held by Dr. Emmons. In spite of his view, he was eminently a pious man of childlike trustful spirit. It is indeed strange how such men could hold these absurdities at all, and scarcely less so, how they could hold them and yet trust sweetly in God. Their heart must have been fixed in their faith in God by some other influence than that of these monstrous notions in philosophy and theology. For, these views of God, we absolutely know, were contrary to their reason, though not to their reasonings—a very wide and essential distinction—which is sometimes overlooked. The intuitive affirmations of their reason were one thing; the points which they reached by their philosophical reasonings were quite another thing. The former could not lie about God, the latter could. The former laid that sure foundation for heart-faith; the latter went to make up their intellectual notions, the absurdities of which never seemed to shake their Christian faith. While these reasonings pushed them on into the greatest absurdities, their reason held their faith and piety straight.

The faith of the heart is proof against all forms of infidelity. Without this nothing is proof. For if people without piety drop the affirmations of their intuitive reason, and then attempt, philosophically, to reason out all the difficulties they meet with, they almost inevitably stumble.

Heart-faith carries one over the manifold mysteries and difficulties of God's providence. In this life there must be difficulties, for no human vision can penetrate to the bottom of God's providential plans and purposes.

The faith of the heart also carries one over the mysteries of the atonement. It is indeed curious to notice how the heart gets over all these mysteries. It is generally the case that the atonement is accepted by the heart unto salvation before its philosophy is understood. It was manifestly so with the apostles; so with their hearers; and so, even with those who heard the Lord Jesus Christ himself. The Bible says but very little indeed on the point of *the philosophy* of the atonement.

So, also, of the doctrine of the Trinity; and so of other doctrines generally. They were known and taught as practical truths, and were accepted as such, long before their philosophy was specially investigated. If any difficulties arose in minds specially inquisitive, they were overcome by heart-faith or settled by the intuitive affirmations of the reason and not by speculative reasoning.

It is not unreasonable for God to require us to have heart-faith in Him. Properly considered, God does not require us to believe what we do not know to be true. God does not ask us to renounce our commonsense and exercise a groundless credulity. When we trust in God's general character and accept certain dark dispensations of His providence as doubtless right, what is it that we believe? Not the special reason for this mysterious dispensation, but we believe that in spite of its dark aspect to us God's hand in it is both wise and good. We believe this because we have abundant ground to confide in God's general character. It is as if you were to tell me that a known and tried friend of mine had told a lie. I would say, "I cannot believe it. I know him too well." But if you say, "Here is the evidence. It looks very dark against him." "Very likely," I might reply, "but yet I cannot believe it. There will be some explanation of this. I cannot believe it." Now, I consider myself fully authorized to reject at once all surmises and rumors against my known friend. I am bound to do so until the evidence against him becomes absolutely conclusive. This is altogether reasonable. How much more so in the case of dark things in God's doings!

We should consider that a person may deceive us; but God never will. We do not always know a person's heart to the very core; and even if we did, his heart may change. What once was true of a person may become false. But not so with God! Our intuitive convictions affirm that God is always good, always wise; and moreover, that there can never be any declension in His love or any revolution or change in His moral character or nature. Consequently, Christians are often called on to believe God, not only without, but against, present evidence.

For example, God called Abraham out of his home and country to go into a strange land. He obeyed, not knowing where he went (Genesis 12:1-5). He might have asked God many questions about His reasons, but he does not appear to have asked any. God commanded Abraham to offer up Isaac. He might, with apparent propriety, have earnestly questioned God and argued with Him. Abraham might have argued, "Lord, that would be murder! It would outrage the natural affection which You have planted in my bosom. It would encourage the heathen around us in their horrid abominations of making their children pass through the fire of Moloch." All this and more, Abraham might have argued; but it appears, he said nothing except this: "The Lord commands, and I obey. If He pleases, God can raise up Isaac from the dead" (see Genesis 22:1-19). So he went and virtually offered up his son Isaac, and in a figure, "received him again from the dead" (see Hebrews 11:19). And God fixed the seal of His approbation on this act of faith, and held it out before all ages as a model of faith and obedience in spite of darkness and objections.

Likewise, Christians are often called to believe without present evidence, other than what comes from their knowledge of God's general character. For a season, God lets everything go against them; yet, they believe. A woman passing through great trials with great confidence in God said, "O Lord, I know You are good; for You have shown me this; but, Lord, others do not understand this; they are stumbled at it. Can You not show them so that they shall understand this?"

REMARKS

The demand for reasons often embarrasses our faith. This is one of the tricks of the devil. He would embarrass our faith by telling us we must understand all of God's ways before we can believe. Yet, we ought to see that this is impossible and unreasonable. Abraham could not see the reasons for God's command to offer Isaac a bloody sacrifice. He might have argued with God, but he did not. The simplicity and beauty of his faith appears all along in this very thing—he raised no questions. He had a deep insight into God's character. He knew too much of God to question God's wisdom or love. A person might understand all the reasons for God's ways; yet, this knowledge might do him no good and his heart might rebel even then.

In the light of this truth, you may see why the Bible says so much about Abraham's faith. His heart-faith was gloriously trustful and unquestioning! What a model! No wonder God commends it to the admiring imitation of the world!

True, faith must often go forward in the midst of darkness. Who can read the histories of believing saints as recorded in scripture without seeing that faith often leads the way through trials. It would be but a sorry development of faith if at every step God's people must know everything before they could trust Him, and must understand all His reasons before they could obey Him. Most ample grounds for faith lie in God's general character; so, we do not need to understand His special reasons for His particular acts.

We are mere infants—miserably poor students of God's ways. His dealings on every side of us appear to us mysterious. Hence it should be expected that we shall fail to comprehend His reasons; consequently, we must confide in Him without this knowledge. Indeed, here lies the virtue of faith—it trusts God on the ground of His general character, while the mind can by no means comprehend His reasons for particular acts. Knowing enough of God to assure us that He must be good, our faith trusts Him, although the special evidence of goodness in particular cases may be wanting. This is a kind of heart-faith which many do not seem to possess or to understand. Plainly they do not confide in God's dealings.

It is obviously needed that God should train Christians to exercise faith here and now; since in heaven we shall be equally unable to comprehend all God's dealings. The holy in heaven will no doubt believe in God; but they must do it by simple faith—not on the ground of a perfect knowledge of God's plans. What a trial of faith it must have been to the holy in heaven to see sin enter our world! They could see few, perhaps none, of the reasons before the final judgment, and must have fallen back upon the intuitive affirmations of their own minds. The utmost they could say was, "We know God must be good and wise; therefore we must wait to see the results, and humbly trust."

It is not best for parents to explain everything to their children. They should not take the position of requiring nothing of their children except that which they can explain by giving all their reasons. Some profess to take this ground. It is for many reasons unwise. God does not train His children so.

Faith is really natural to children. Yet some will not believe their children converted until they can be real theologians. This assumes that they must have all the great facts of the gospel system explained so that they can comprehend their philosophy before they can believe them. Nothing can be further from the truth. It sometimes happens that those who are converted in childhood become students of theology in more advanced years, and then, getting proud of their philosophy and wisdom, they lose their simple faith and relapse into disbelief and infidelity. No, I do not object to their studying the philosophy of every doctrine up to the limits of human knowledge; but, I do object to their casting away their faith in God, because there is no lack of substantial testimony to the great doctrines of the gospel. The philosophy of the great doctrines may stagger the wisest man; but the evidence of their truth ought to satisfy all alike, the child and the philosopher. Last winter I was struck with this fact, which I mention because it seems to present one department of the evidences of Christianity in a clear light. One judge of the court said to another, "I come to you with my assertion that I inwardly know Jesus Christ, and as truly and as well as I know you. Can you reject such testimony? What would the people of this State say to you if you rejected such testimony on any other subject? In your court, do you not let people testify to their own experience?" The judge replied, "I cannot answer you." "Why, then," replied the other, "do you not believe this testimony? I can bring before you thousands who will testify to the same thing."

It is of great value to study the truths of the gospel system theologically and philosophically, for thus you may reach a satisfactory explanation of many things which your heart knows, grasps, and will hold fast till the hour of your death. It is a great satisfaction to see the beautiful harmony of the gospel truths with each other and with the known laws of mind and of all just government.

Unfortunately, some theological students decline in their piety, and for a reason which it is well for them to understand. One enters upon the study of theology simple-hearted and trusting; but, by-and-by, study expands his views. He begins to be charmed with the explanations he is able to give of many things not understood before. He becomes opinionated and proud. He becomes ashamed of his former simple heart-faith, and thus stumbles fearfully if not fatally. If you will hold on with all your simple heart-confidence to the immutable love and wisdom of God, all will be well. But it never can be well to put your intellectual philosophy in the place of the simplicity of gospel faith.

Do you see the reason some students do not become pious? They determine that they will understand everything before they will become Christians. Of course they are never converted. Quite in point, here is a case I saw a few years ago. Dr. B. was intelligent, but not pious. He had a pious wife who was leading her little daughter to Christ. The Dr. seeing this, said to her, "Why do you try to lead that child to Christ? I cannot understand these things myself, although I have been trying to understand them these many years. How then can she?" But some days later, as he was riding out alone, he began to reflect on the matter. The truth flashed upon his mind, and he saw that neither of them could understand God perfectly—not he anymore than his child; but, either of them could know enough to believe and be saved.

Gospel faith is voluntary—a will-trust. I remember a case in my own circle of friends. I could not satisfy my mind about one of them. At length, after long struggling, I said, "I will repel these things from my mind, and rule out these difficulties. My friend is honest and right. I will believe it, and will trust him none the less for these slanders." In this I was right.

Toward God, this course is always right. It is always right to cast away from your mind all those dark suspicions about Him Who can never make mistakes, and Who is too good to purpose wrong. I once said to a sister in affliction, "Can you not believe all this is for your good, though you cannot see how it is?" She brightened up, saying, "I must believe in God, and I will."

Who of you have this heart-faith? Which of you will not commit yourself to Christ? If you required *intellectual-faith*, I could explain to you how it is reached—by a through searching of the evidence in the case. But *heart-faith* must be reached by simple effort—by a voluntary purpose to *trust*. You who say, "I cannot do this," bow your knees before God and commit yourself to His will; say, "O, my Savior! I take You at Your word." This is a simple act of will.*

---

* Charles G. Finney, *The Oberlin Evangelist*, December 3, 1856, *Sermons on the Way of Salvation*, 313-331, *Principles of Victory*, 146–155. For Review: Answer the Study Questions on page 224, Cowles page 237.

The Psalms on Joy

Your statutes are my heritage forever; they are the joy of my heart. —Psalm 119:111

Our mouths were filled with laughter, our tongues with songs of joy. Then it was said among the nations, "The LORD has done great things for them." —Psalm 126:2

The LORD has done great things for us, and we are filled with joy. —Psalm 126:3

Those who sow with tears will reap with songs of joy. —Psalm 126:5

Those who go out weeping, carrying seed to sow, will return with songs of joy, carrying sheaves with them. —Psalm 126:6

May your priests be clothed with your righteousness; may your faithful people sing for joy. —Psalm 132:9

I will clothe her priests with salvation, and her faithful people will ever sing for joy. —Psalm 132:16

Our captors asked us for songs, our tormentors demanded songs of joy; they said, "Sing us one of the songs of Zion!" —Psalm 137:3

May my tongue cling to the roof of my mouth if I do not remember you, if I do not consider Jerusalem my highest joy. —Psalm 137:6

They celebrate your abundant goodness and joyfully sing of your righteousness. —Psalm 145:7

Let his faithful people rejoice in this honor and sing for joy on their beds. —Psalm 149:5

4

Conformity to the World
1837

And be not conformed to this world: but be ye transformed by the renewing of your mind, that ye may prove what is that good, and acceptable, and perfect, will of God.—Romans 12:2—KJV

Do not conform any longer to the pattern of this world, but be transformed by the renewing of your mind. Then you will be able to test and approve what God's will is — his good, pleasing and perfect will.—Romans 12:2—NIV

If we want to live godly, we must not be conformed to this world; therefore, I will show what "Be not conformed to this world" *does not mean*, what the command *does mean*, and some reasons why all who will live a godly life must obey this command. Finally, I will answer some objections.

What "Be not conformed to this world" does not mean.

Briefly, the command does not mean that Christians should refuse to benefit by the useful arts, improvements and discoveries of the world. It is not only the privilege but the duty of the friends of God to avail themselves of these, and to use for God all the really useful arts and improvements that arise among mankind.

What "Be not conformed to this world" means.

The command means that Christians are obligated to refuse conformity to the world in business, fashion, and politics. I mention only these three departments of life, *not because there are not many other areas in which conformity to the world is forbidden*, but because these three classes are all that I have time to examine and these three are especially necessary to discuss at this time. In all these departments, Christians should not do as the world does. Christians should neither receive the maxims, nor adopt the principles, nor follow the practices of the world.

Some reasons for the command, "Be not conformed to this world."

Christians must never act on the same principles, on the same motives, or pursue their objectives, in the same manner that the world does in the pursuits of business, fashion, or politics. I shall examine these separately.

Of Business

The first reason you must not conform to *this world* in business is because *the principle of this world is that of supreme selfishness*, and this is true universally in the pursuit of this world's business. The whole course of this world's business is governed and regulated by the maxims of supreme and unmixed selfishness. *This world* is regulated without the least regard to the commands of God, or the glory of God, or the welfare of others. The maxims of business generally current among those in business, and the habits and usages of those in business, are all based upon supreme selfishness. In making bargains, business people of this world consult their own interest. They seek their own benefit; not the benefit of those they deal with. Who has ever heard of a worldly man of business making bargains and doing business for the benefit of those he dealt with? No, they always do business for their own worldly benefit. Now, are Christians to do as the worldly do in business? No! The Bible teaches that Christians should act on the very opposite principle. The Bible says: "Let no man seek his own, but every man another's wealth" (1 Corinthians 10:24). God requires Christians to copy the example of Jesus Christ. Did Jesus ever make bargains for His own advantage? Would Jesus want His followers to adopt a principle of the world—a principle that contains in it the seeds of hell? If Christians adopt the principles of this world, how is the world ever going to be converted to the gospel?

The second reason Christians should not conform to the world is because conformity to the world is totally inconsistent with the love of God or others. The whole system of this world recognizes only the love of self. Go through all the ranks of those in the business of this world, from the person who sells candy on the sidewalk at the corner of the street, to the greatest wholesale merchant or importer, and you will find that one maxim runs through the whole: BUY AS CHEAP AS YOU CAN AND SELL AS HIGH AS YOU CAN—LOOK OUT FOR NUMBER ONE! Those who do business on the principles of this world always look out first for themselves, sometimes more or less as far as the rules of honesty will allow. They will do all that will advance their own interest. It does not matter to them what becomes of the interest of others. Even those who live ungodly will not deny that these are the maxims on which business is done in the world. The person who pursues this selfish course is universally regarded as doing business on business principles. Now, are these business maxims consistent with holiness, with the love of God and the love of others, with the spirit of the gospel and the example of Jesus Christ? Can a person conform to this world in these principles and still love God? Impossible! No two things can be more unlike! By no means should Christians conform to the business maxims of the world!

These selfish maxims, and the rules by which business is done in the world, are directly opposite to the gospel of Jesus Christ, the spirit He exhibited, the maxims He inculcated, and the rules which He enjoined that all of His followers should obey on pain of hell.

Principles of Joy in the Holy Spirit — Finney's Lessons on Romans

What was the spirit that Jesus Christ exemplified on earth? It was the spirit of self-denial, of benevolence, of sacrificing himself to do good to others. He exhibited the same spirit that God does, Who enjoys His infinite happiness in going out of himself to gratify His benevolent heart in doing good to others. For those who do trust in Jesus Christ, one goal of the gospel is to be like God and act as God acts; not only by doing good, but by actually enjoying it and joyfully going out of oneself to do good. This is the gospel maxim: "It is more blessed to give than to receive" (Acts 20:35). And again, "Look not every man on his own things, but every man also on the things of others" (Philippians 2:4). What says the businessman of this world? "Look out for number one." These very maxims were made by people who knew and cared no more for the gospel than the heathen do. Why should Christians conform to such maxims as these?

To conform to the world in the pursuits of business is a flat contradiction of the commitments that Christians make when they become members of the church. What is the commitment that you make when you join the church? Is it not to renounce the world and live for God, to be actuated by the Spirit of Jesus Christ, to possess supreme love to God, to renounce self, to give yourself to glorify God and do good to others? You profess that you will not love the world, its honors or its riches. Around the communion table, with your hand on the broken body of your Savior, you solemnly declare these to be your principles, and you pledge yourself to live by these maxims. And then what do you do? Do you go away and follow maxims and rules gotten up by those whose avowed principle is the love of the world, and whose avowed object is to get as much from the world as they can? Is this your way? Then, unless you repent, let me tell you, you will be damned. It is no more certain that any infidel or any profligate wretch will go to hell than that all who claim to be Christians will go there if they conform to the world. They have double guilt. They have sworn before God that they intend to live a different way of life, a life according to Christian principles, but when they pursue the business principles of this world, they show that they are lying, perjured wretches.

Conformity to the world is such an obvious contradiction of the principles of the gospel that sinners, when they see Christians conforming

Conformity to the World

to the world, do not and cannot understand from observing their way of life the true nature and object of the gospel itself. How can they understand that the object of the gospel is to raise people above the love of the world and above the influence of the world, and place them on higher ground to live on totally different principles, when they see professing Christians acting on the same principles as others? How can they understand the true principles of the gospel, or know what it means to be heavenly minded, to deny self, to practice benevolence, when they see Christians conforming to this world?

Conformity to the world has already eaten out the love of God from the church. Show me a young convert while his heart is warm and the love of God glows out from his lips. What does he care for the world? Call up his attention to it, point him to its riches, its pleasures or its honors, and try to engage him in their pursuit, and he loathes the thought. But let him now go into business, and do business on the principles of the world for one year, and you no longer find the love of God glowing in his heart. He now has a religion of conscience, which is dry, meager, and not influential. He has lost the glowing love of God, which once moved him to acts of benevolence. I ask you, and would ask every person in the church if I could, is not this true? If anyone objected, I would regard it as proof that he never knew what it was to feel the glow of a convert's first love.

Conformity to the world in business is one of the greatest stumbling blocks in the way of converting sinners to love Christ. What do wicked people think when they see professing Christians, with professions on their lips and pretending to believe what the Bible teaches, pursuing after the world as eager as anybody; making the most selfish bargains and dealing as hard as the most worldly person? What do they think? I can tell you what they say. They say, "Christians do just as the rest of us. They act on the same principles as we do. They look out as sharp for number one as we do. They drive as hard a bargain and get as high an interest on their loans as anybody." And it must be said that these are not things of which the world accuses Christians slanderously. It is a notorious fact that most church members pursue the world in the same spirit, by the same maxims, and to the same degree, that the ungodly do who maintain a character for uprightness and humanity. The world says, "Look at the church! Those in the church are not any better than I am. They go the full length after the world the same as I do." If those who claim to be Christians act on the same principles as worldly men and women, as the Lord lives, they shall have the same reward. They are set down in God's book of remembrance as black hypocrites, pretending to be the friends of God while they love the world; for whosoever loves the world is the enemy of God. They profess to be governed by principles directly opposite to the world, and if they do the same things with the world, they are hypocrites.

Another reason for the requirement "Be not conformed to this world" is the immense, salutary and instantaneous influence it would have if every body would do business on the principles of the gospel. Just turn the tables over, and let Christians do business one year on gospel principles. It would shake the world. It would ring louder than thunder. Let the ungodly see true, professing Christians consulting the good of the person they are trading with in every bargain—seeking not their own wealth, but every man another's wealth—living above the world—setting no value on the world any further than it can be a means of glorifying God—what do you think would be the effect? What effect did it have in Jerusalem when the whole body of Christians gave up their business and began to pursue the salvation of the world? They were only a few ignorant fishermen and a few humble women, but they turned the world upside down. Let the church live so now, and it would cover the world with confusion of face and overwhelm them with convictions of sin. Only let them see the church living above the world, doing business on gospel principles, seeking not their own interests but the interests of others too, and infidelity would hide its head, heresy would be driven from church, and this charming, blessed spirit of love would go over the world like the waves of the sea.

Of Fashions

Following the fashions of the world is directly at war with the spirit of the gospel and is *minding earthly things*. What is *minding earthly things* if it is not following the fashions of the world that like a tide are continually setting to and fro and fluctuating in their forms and keeping the world continually changing? There are many people managing large businesses in the world and people of wealth who think they care nothing for the fashions. They are occupied with something else. They trust the fashions altogether with their tailor and take it for granted that he will make all things right. But notice, if their tailor made a garment unfashionable, you would see that they do care about the fashions, and they never would employ that tailor again. Still, at present, their thoughts are not much on the fashions. They have a higher object in view. And they think it beneath the dignity of a minister to preach about fashions. They overlook the fact that with most people fashion is everything. Most of those in a community are not rich, and they never expect to be; however, they look to the world to enable them to make a respectable appearance and to bring up their families in a respectable manner; that is, to follow the fashions. Nine-tenths of the population never set a higher purpose than to do as the world does or to follow the fashions. For this they strain every nerve. This is what they set their hearts on, and this is what they live for.

Merchants and rich men deceive themselves if they suppose that fashion is a little thing. Most people set their minds on staying in fashion. The things they look for in life are having their dress, equipage, furniture, and so on like other people of fashion, to be "respectable" as they call it.

Conforming to the world is contrary to a profession of faith in Jesus Christ. When people join the church, they profess to give up the spirit that gives rise to the fashions. They profess to renounce the vanities of the world, to repent of their pride, to follow the meek and lowly Savior and live for God. But what do they do? You often see those who profess to be Christians going to the extremes of fashion. Nothing will satisfy them that is not in the height of fashion. Furthermore, a Christian female dressmaker, who is conscientiously opposed to following fashions, cannot make a living. She cannot get employment even among those who profess to be Christian ladies, unless she follows the fashions in all their countless changes. God knows it is so, and they must give up their business if their conscience will not permit them to follow the fashions.

Conformity to the world is a broad and complete approval of the spirit of the world. What is it that lies at the bottom of all this shifting scenery?

Principles of Joy in the Holy Spirit — Finney's Lessons on Romans

What is the cause that produces all this gaudy show and dash and display? It is the love of applause. And when Christians follow the changes of fashion, they pronounce all this innocent. All this waste of money and time and thought, all this feeding and cherishing of vanity and the love of applause, the church approves when she conforms to the world.

By following the fashions of the world, professing Christians show that they do in fact love the world. They show it by their conduct, just as the ungodly show it by the same conduct. As they act alike, they give evidence that they are actuated by one principle, the love of fashion. When those who profess to be Christians do this, they show most clearly that they love the praise of others. It is evident that they love admiration and flattery, just as sinners do. Is not this inconsistent with Christian principles, to go right into the very things that are set up by the pride and fashion and lust of the ungodly?

When you conform to the world in fashion, you show that you do not hold yourself accountable to God for the manner in which you lay out money. You practically disown your stewardship of the wealth that is in your possession. By laying out money to gratify your own vanity and lust, you take off the keen edge of that truth which ought to cut that sinner in two who is living to himself. It is practically denying that the earth is the Lord's, with the cattle on a thousand hills, and all is to be employed for His glory.

By conforming to the world in fashion, you show that reputation is your idol. When the cry comes to your ears on every wind, from the ignorant and the lost of all nations, "Come over and help us, come over and help us," and every week brings some call to send the gospel, to send tracts and Bibles and missionaries to those who are perishing for lack of knowledge, if you choose to expend money in following the fashions, it is demonstration that reputation is your idol. Suppose now, for the sake of argument, that it is not prohibited in the word of God to follow the fashions, and that professing Christians, if they will, may innocently follow the fashions. I deny that it is innocent, but suppose it were, does not the fact that they do follow them when there are such calls for money and time and thought and labor to save souls prove conclusively that they do not love God nor the souls of the saved or the perishing?

Conformity to the World

Consider the case of a woman whose husband is in slavery and she is trying to raise enough money for his redemption. There she is, toiling and saving, rising up early and sitting up late, and eating the bread of carefulness, because her husband, the father of her children, the friend of her youth, is in slavery. Now go to that woman and tell her that it is innocent for her to follow the fashions, to dress and display herself like her neighbors. Will she follow the fashions? Why not? Because she does not desire the fashions. She will scarcely buy a pair of shoes for her feet. She almost hates to spend money on the bread she eats, so intent is she on her great object of freeing her husband from slavery to bring him home.

Now suppose a person loved God and souls and the kingdom of Christ, does he need an express prohibition from God to prevent him from spending his money and his life in following the fashions? No indeed, he will rather need a positive injunction to take what is needful for his own comfort and the support of his own life. Consider Paul's companion, Timothy. Did he need a prohibition to prevent him from indulging in the use of wine? No! Instead, Timothy was so cautious that he required an express injunction from God through Paul to make him drink a little wine as a medicine. Although Timothy was sick, he would not drink a little wine until he had a word from God that it was alright under the circumstances. Timothy saw the evils of wine so clearly that he would not touch it otherwise (see 1 Timothy 5:23). Now, show me a man or a woman, I care not what they profess to be, who follows the fashions of the world, and I will show you what spirit they have.

Now, don't ask me why Abraham and David and Solomon, who were so rich, did not lay out their money in spreading the kingdom of God. Ah, tell me, did they enjoy the light that Christians now enjoy? Did they even know so much as this, that the world can be converted, as Christians now see clearly that it can? But suppose it were as allowable in you as it was in Abraham or David to be rich, and to lay out the property you possess in display and pomp and fashion. Suppose it were perfectly innocent; who that loves the Lord Jesus Christ would wish to lay out money in fashion when they could lay it out to gratify the *all-absorbing* passion to do good to others?

By conforming to the world in fashion, you show that you differ not at all from ungodly sinners. Ungodly sinners say, "Christian men and women love to follow the fashions as well as I do." Who does not know, that this leads many to infidelity? By following the fashions you are tempting God to give you up to a worldly spirit. There are many now that have followed the world and the fashions until God seems to have given them over to the devil for the destruction of the flesh. They have little or no Christian feeling, no spirit of prayer, no zeal for the glory of God or the conversion of sinners, and the Holy Spirit seems to have withdrawn from them. They tempt the church to follow the fashions. Where the principal members, the elders and leaders in the church, and their wives and families, are fashionable Christians, they drag the whole church along with them into the train of fashion, and every one apes them as far as they can, down to the lowest servant. Only let a rich Christian lady come out to the house of God in full fashion, and the whole church are set agog to follow as far as they can, and it is a miracle if they do not run into debt to do it.

When you follow the fashions, you tempt yourself to pride and folly and a worldly spirit. Suppose someone had been intemperate and was reformed. Suppose he should go and surround himself with wine and brandy and every seductive liquor, keeping the provocatives of appetite always under his eye, and from time to time tasting a little; does he not tempt himself? Now, consider a woman who has been brought up in the spirit of pride and show, and who has been reformed and has professed to abandon them all. If she keeps all the trappings of fashion and continues to follow the fashions, pride will drag her backwards as sure as she lives. She tempts herself to sin and folly.

When you follow the fashions, you are tempting the world. You are setting the world into a more fierce and hot pursuit of these things. The very things that the world loves, and that they are sure to have scruples about their being right, those who only profess to be Christians fall in with and follow, and thus they tempt the world to continue in the pursuit of what will destroy their souls in hell.

By following the fashions, you are tempting the devil to tempt you. When you follow the fashions, you open your heart to him. You keep it for him, empty, swept, and garnished. Every woman who allows herself to follow the fashions may rely upon it, she is helping Satan to tempt her to pride and sin.

By following the fashions, you lay a great stumbling block before most people. There are a few persons who are pursuing greater objects than fashion. They are engaged in the scramble for political power, or they are eager for literary distinction, or they are striving for wealth. And they do not know that their hearts are set on fashion at all. They are following selfishness on a larger scale. But most people are influenced mostly by these fluctuating fashions. To this class of persons it is a great and sore stumbling-block when they see professing Christians just as prompt and as eager to follow the changing fashions as themselves. They see, and say, "What does their professing to be a Christian amount to, when they follow the fashions as much as anybody?" Or, "Certainly it is right to follow the fashions, for see, Christians do it as much as we do."

Another reason professing Christians are not to conform to the world in fashion is the great influence that their disregarding fashion would have on the world. If professing Christians showed their contempt for these things rather than following them or regarding them, it would shame the world and convince the world that Christians were living for another object; that is, for God and eternity! How irresistible it would be! What an overwhelming testimony in favor of our Christian faith! Even the apparent renunciation of the world by many orders of monks has doubtless done more than anything else to put down the opposition to their religion and give it currency and influence in the world. Now suppose all this were hearty and sincere, and coupled with all that is consistent and lovely in Christian character, and all that is zealous and bold in labors for the conversion of the world from sin to holiness. What an influence it would have! What thunders it would pour into the ears of the world, which would wake people up to follow after God!

In Politics

As Christians, we are not to be conformed to the world in politics, because the politics of the world are perfectly dishonest. Who does not know this? Who does not know that it is the purposed policy of every political party to cover up the defects of their own candidate and the good qualities of the opposing candidate? Is not this dishonest? Every party holds up its candidate as a piece of perfection, and then aims to elect him into office by any means, fair or foul. A person cannot be honest if they are committed to going along with a political party no matter what it does. Can a Christian do this and keep a conscience void of offense? No!

To conform to the world in politics is to tempt God. By falling in with the world in politics, Christians are guilty of setting up rulers over them by their own vote who do not fear or love God. These rulers set the law of God at defiance, break the Sabbath, gamble, commit adultery, fight duels, swear profanely, ignore laws at their pleasure, and care not for the wellbeing of their country as long as they can remain in office. I say Christians should do this: where political parties are divided, as they are in the United States, there are enough Christians to turn the balance and decide any election. Now, Christians should take the position that they will not vote for a dishonest candidate (a Sabbath breaker, gambler, whoremonger, or duellist); then, no party could ever nominate a candidate with such an immoral character with any hope of success. In the present system of government, where politicians do not enforce the laws (but give full swing to mobs, lynch-murders, robbing the mails, or anything else), so they can elect the candidates who will benefit them, any voter who does this is dishonest, whether he professes to be a Christian or not. Can a Christian do dishonest things in politics and be blameless?

By engaging with the world in politics, Christians can grieve the Spirit of God. Ask any politician who professes to be a Christian if he ever carried the Spirit of God with him into a political campaign. Never. I would by no means be understood to say that Christians should refuse to vote and exercise their lawful influence in public affairs. But they ought not to follow a political party.

By following the present course of politics, you are contributing your aid to undermine all government and order in the land. Who does not know that this great nation now rocks and reels, because the laws are broken and trampled under foot, and the executive power refuses or dares not act? Either the magistrate does not wish to put down disorder, or he temporizes and lets the devil rule. And so it is in all parts of the country, and all political parties. And can a Christian be consistent with his profession and vote for such people who seek office?

When you follow the present course of politics, you lay a stumbling-block in the way of sinners. What do sinners think when they see professing Christians acting with them in their political measures, which they themselves know to be dishonest and corrupt? They say, "We understand what we are about. We want our party elected to office. We are determined to carry our party into power. We are pursuing our own interest. But these Christians! They profess to live for another and a higher end; and yet, here they come and join with us, just as eager for the loaves and fishes as the rest of us." What greater stumbling-block can they have?

You prove to the ungodly that those who profess to be Christians are actuated by the same spirit as themselves. Who can wonder that the world is incredulous as to the reality of Christianity? If the world does not look for themselves into the scriptures, and there learn what Christianity is; if the world were governed by the rules of evidence, from what they see in the lives of professing Christians, they ought to be incredulous. They ought to infer, so far as this evidence goes, that those who profess to be Christians do not themselves believe in it. It is a fact. I myself doubt whether most of those who claim to be Christians really believe the Bible to be true.

As far as the evidence can go, many who profess to be Christians show that they have no change of heart. What is a change of heart? Is a change of heart going to the communion table once in a month or two, and sometimes to a prayer meeting? Is it a change of heart when they are just as eager in the scramble for political office as anyone else? The world must be fools to believe a "Christian" has had a change of heart on such little evidence.

Christians ought to cease from conformity to the world in politics, and from the influence which such a course would have on the world. Suppose Christians were to act perfectly conscientious and consistent in this matter, saying, "We will not vote for anyone unless he fears God and will rule the people in righteousness." Then, the ungodly would not set anyone as a candidate who defied the nation's laws or God's laws. No. Every candidate would be obliged to show that he was prepared to act from higher motives, and that he would lay himself out to make the country prosperous, and to promote virtue, and to put down vice and oppression and disorder, and to do all he can to make the people happy and HOLY! It would shame the dishonest politicians to show that the love of God and man is the motive that Christians have in view. And a blessed influence would go over the land like a wave.

OBJECTIONS

In regard to business

"If we do not transact business on the same principles on which the ungodly do it, we cannot compete with them, and all the business of the world will fall into the hands of the ungodly. If we pursue our business for the good of others, if we buy and sell on the principle of not seeking our own wealth, but the wealth of those we do business with, we cannot sustain a competition with worldly men, and they will get all the business."

Answer: Then let them have it. You can support yourself by your industry in some humbler calling and let the worldly do all the business.

"But then, how should we get money to spread the gospel?"

Answer: A holy church that acts on the principles of the gospel will spread the gospel faster than all the money that ever was in New York City or ever will be. Give me a holy church, a church that will live above the world, and the work of salvation will roll on faster than with all the money in Christendom.

"But we must spend a great deal of money to bring forward an educated ministry."

Answer: Ah! If we had a holy ministry, it would be far more important than an educated ministry. If the ministry were holy enough, they would do without so much education. God forbid that I should undervalue an educated ministry. Let ministers be educated as well as they can, the more the better, if they are only holy enough. But it is all a farce to suppose that a literary ministry can convert the world. Let the ministry have the spirit of prayer, let the baptism of the Holy Spirit be upon them, and they will spread the gospel. Only let Christians live as they ought, and the church would shake the world. For example, if Christians in New York City would do it, the report would soon fill every ship that leaves the port, and waft the news on every wind, till the earth was full of excitement and inquiry, and conversions would multiply like the drops of morning dew.

Suppose you were to give up your business, and devote yourselves entirely to the work of extending the gospel. The church once did so, and you know what followed. When that little band in Jerusalem gave up their business and spent their time in the work of God, salvation spread like a wave. And, I believe, if the whole Christian church were to turn right out, and convert the world, it would be done in a very short time.

The fact is, you would not be required to give up your business. If Christians would do business in the spirit of the gospel, they would soon capture the business of the world. Only let the world see that if they go to a Christian to do business, he will not only deal honestly, but benevolently, that he will actually consult the interest of the person he deals with, as if it were his own interest, and who would deal with any body else? What merchant would go to an ungodly man to trade, who he knew would try to get the advantage of him and cheat him, when he knew that there were Christian merchants to deal with that would consult his interests as much as they do their own? Indeed, it is a known fact that there are now Christian merchants who regulate fairly and honestly the prices of the articles they sell. Merchants come in from the country and inquire around to see how they can buy goods, and they go to these men to know exactly what articles are worth at a fair price, and they govern themselves accordingly.

Therefore, the advantage is all on one side. True Christians can make it in the interest of the ungodly to do business on right principles. The true Christian can regulate the business of the world just by practicing honesty and benevolence in their business dealings with their customers and competitors, and woe to them if they do not.

In regard to Fashion

"Is it best for Christians to be different or unusual?"

Principles of Joy in the Holy Spirit — Finney's Lessons on Romans

Answer: Certainly, Christians are bound to be different from others. They are called to be peculiar people; that is, an unusual people, essentially different from those who do not follow Jesus Christ. To maintain that we are not to be different is the same as to maintain that we are to be conformed to the world. "Be not different" means "Be like the world." In other words, "Be ye conformed to the world." This is the direct opposite to the command in the text.

But the question now regards fashion, in dress, equipage, and so on. And here I will confess that I was formerly in error. I once believed and taught that the best way for Christians was to dress so as not to be different; to follow the fashions and changes so as not to appear unusual; so no one would think of Christians as being different from others in these particulars. But I have seen my error and now wonder very much at my former blindness. It is your duty to dress so plain as to show to the world that you place no sort of reliance in the things of fashion, and set no value at all on them, but despise and neglect them altogether. But unless you are different, unless you separate yourselves from the fashions of the world, you show that you value them. There is no way in which you can bear a proper testimony against the fashions of the world except by dressing plainly. I do not mean that you should study being unusual. You should consult convenience and economy, although it may be unusual.

"But if we dress plain, the attention of people will be taken with it."

Answer: The reason is this: so few do it that it is a novelty, and everybody stares when they see a professing Christian so strict as to disregard the fashions. Let them all do it, and the only thing you show by it is that you are a Christian, and do not wish to be confounded with the ungodly. Would it not tell on the pride of the world, if all the Christians in it were united in bearing a practical testimony against its vain show.

"But in this way you carry Christianity too far away from the multitude. It is better not to set up an artificial distinction between the church and the world."

Answer: The direct reverse of this is true. The nearer you bring the church to the world, the more you annihilate the reasons that ought to stand out in view of the world for their changing sides and coming over to the church. Unless you go right out from them, and show that you are not of them in any respect, and carry the church so far as to have a broad interval between saints and sinners, how can you make the ungodly feel that so great a change is necessary.

"But the change which is necessary is a change of heart."

Answer: True; but will not a change of heart produce a change of life?

"You will throw obstacles in the way of persons becoming Christians. Many respectable people will become disgusted with the church, and if they cannot be allowed to dress as they want and be Christians, they will take to the world altogether."

Answer: This is just about as reasonable as it would be for a temperance man to think he must get drunk now and then to avoid disgusting the intemperate and to retain his influence over them. The truth is, people ought to know and see in the lives of professing Christians that if they embrace Christianity, they must be weaned from the world, and must give up the love of the world with its pride and show and folly, and live a holy life in watchfulness and self-denial and active benevolence.

"Is it not better for us to disregard this altogether and not pay any attention to such little things and let them take their course? Is it not better to let the dress designer and the hatter do as they please, and follow the usages of society in which we live, and the circle in which we move?"

Answer: Is this the way to show contempt for the fashions of the world? Do people ordinarily take this course of showing contempt for a thing to practise it? Why, is the way to show your abhorrence of ardent spirits to drink it! Is the way to show your abhorrence of the world to follow along in the customs and the fashions of the world! What reasoning is this?

"It does not matter how we dress, if our hearts are right."

Answer: Your heart right! You say your heart may be right when your conduct is all wrong? Just as well might the profane swearer say, "No matter what words I speak, if my heart is right." No, your heart is not right, unless your conduct is right. What is outward conduct, but the acting out of the heart? If your heart were right, you would not wish to follow the fashions of the world.

"What is the standard of dress? I do not see the use of all your preaching, and laying down rules about plain dress, unless you give us a standard."

Answer: This is a mighty stumbling-block with many. But to my mind the matter is extremely simple. The whole can be comprised in two simple rules. One: Be sure in all your equipage, dress, and furniture to show that you have no fellowship with the designs and principles of those who are aiming to set themselves apart and gain the applause of others Two: Let economy be first consulted; then convenience. Follow Christian economy; that is, save all you can for Christ's service. And then let things be as convenient as Christian economy will admit.

"Would you have us all become Quakers and put on their plain dress?"

Answer: Who does not know that the plain dress of the Quakers has won for them the respect of all the thinking part of the ungodly in the community? Now, if they had coupled with their plain dress, a zeal for God, separation from the world, contempt for riches, and self-denying labor for the conversion of sinners to Christ (which the gospel enjoins), and clear views of the plan of salvation (which the gospel inculcates), they would long ago have converted the world. And if all Christians would imitate them in their plain dress (I do not mean the precise cut and fashion of their dress, but in a plain dress, throwing contempt upon the fashions of the world), who can doubt that the conversion of the world would hasten on apace?

"Would you make us all Methodists?"

Answer: Who does not know that the Methodists, when they were noted for their plain dress and for renouncing the fashions and show of the world, used to have power with God in prayer? They had the universal respect of the world as sincere Christians. And who does not know that since they have laid aside this peculiarity and have conformed to the world in dress and other things, and seemed to be trying to lift themselves up as a denomination and gain influence with the world, that they are losing the power of prayer? Would to God they had never thrown down this wall. It was one of the leading benefits of Wesley's system to have his followers distinguished from others by a plain dress.

"We may be proud of a plain dress, as well as of a fashionable dress. The Quakers are as proud as we are."

Answer: So may any good thing be abused. But that is no reason why it should not be used, if it can be shown to be good. I put it back to the objector: "Is that any reason why a Christian female, who fears God and loves souls, should neglect the means which may make an impression that she is separated from the world, and pour contempt on the fashions of the ungodly, in which they are dancing their way to hell?"

"This is a small thing, and ought not to take up so much of a minister's time in the pulpit."

Answer: This is an objection often heard from worldly people who profess to be Christians. But the minister who fears God will not be deterred by this objection. He will pursue the subject until such professing Christians are cut off from their conformity to the world or cut off from the church. It is not merely the dress, as dress, but it is the conformity to the world in dress and fashion that is the great stumbling-block in the way of sinners. How can the world be converted while professing Christians are conformed to the world? What good will it do to give money to send the gospel to the heathen, when "Christians" live like heathens at home? Well might the heathen ask, "What profit will it be to become Christians, when those who are Christians are pursuing the world with all the hot-haste of the ungodly?" The great thing necessary for the church is to break off from conformity to the world, and then they will have power with God in prayer, and the Holy Spirit will descend and bless their efforts, and the world will be converted.

"But if we dress so, we shall be called fanatics."

Answer: Whatever the ungodly may call you, fanatics, Methodists, or anything, you will be known as Christians, and in the secret consciences of men, you will be acknowledged as such. It is not in the power of unbelievers to pour contempt on a holy church that is separated from the world. How was it with the early Christians? They lived separate from the world, and it made such an impression that even infidel writers say of them, "These men win the hearts of the masses, because they perform deeds of charity and pour contempt on the world." If Christians would live so now, the last effort of hell would soon be expended in vain to defeat the spread of the gospel. Wave after wave would flow abroad, till the highest mountain tops were covered with the waters of life.

In regard to politics

"In this way, by acting on these principles, and refusing to unite with the world in politics, we could have no influence in government and national affairs."

Answer: First, it is so now. Christians, as such, have no influence. There is not a Christian principle adopted because it is Christian, or because it is according to the law of God. Second, if there is no other way for Christians to have an influence in the government, but by becoming conformed to the world in their habitual principles and parties, then let the ungodly take the government and manage it in their own way, and you go and serve God Third, no such result would follow. Directly the reverse of this would be the fact. Only let it be known that Christian citizens will on no account assist bad people into office; only let it be known that the church will go only for those who will aim at the public good, and both parties will be sure to set up such candidates. And in this way, the church could legitimately exert an influence, by compelling all parties to bring forward only those who are worthy of an honest person's support.

"In this way the church and the world will be arrayed against each other."

Answer: The world is too selfish for this. You cannot make political parties so. Such a line can never be a permanent division. For one year, the ungodly might unite against the church and leave Christians in a small minority. But in the end, the others would form two parties, each courting the votes of Christians by offering candidates such as Christians can conscientiously vote for.

REMARKS

By non-conformity to the world, you may save much money for doing good. In one year a greater fund might be saved by the church than all that has ever been raised for the spread of the gospel.

By non-conformity to the world, a great deal of time may be saved for doing good that is now consumed and wasted in following the fashions, and obeying the maxims, and joining in the pursuits of the world.

Conformity to the World

At the same time, Christians in this way would preserve their peace of conscience, would enjoy communion with God, would have the spirit of prayer, and would possess far greater usefulness.

Is it not time something was done? Is it not time that some church struck out a path that should be not conformed to the world, but should be according to the example and Spirit of Christ?

You profess that you want to have sinners converted. But what avails it, if they sink right back again into conformity with the world? Brethren, I confess, I am filled with pain in view of the conduct of the church. Where are the proper results of the glorious revivals we have had? I believe they were genuine revivals of Christian faith and outpourings of the Holy Spirit that the church has enjoyed the past ten years. I believe the converts of the past ten years are among the best Christians in the land. Yet, after all, the great body of them are a disgrace to the church. Of what use would it be to have a thousand members added to the church, if they remain just as they are now? Would the church be more honored by the ungodly? One holy church, believers that are really crucified to the world, and the world crucified to them, would do more to recommend Christianity than all the churches in the country living as they now do. O, if I had strength of body to go through the churches again, instead of preaching to convert sinners I would preach to bring up the churches to the gospel standard of holy living. Of what use is it to convert sinners and make them worldly "Christians"? Of what use is it to try to convert sinners and make them feel there is something in Christianity, if when they go to trade with you or meet you in the street, you contradict it all and tell them by your conformity to the world that there is nothing in Christianity?

Where shall I look, where shall the Lord look for a church like the first church, that will come out from the world and be separate, and give themselves up to serve God? O, if every church would do so. But it is of little use to make Christians, if they are not better. Do not understand me as saying that the converts made in our revivals are spurious conversions. But they live so as to be a disgrace to Christianity. They are so stumbled by old professors that many of them do more hurt than good. The more there are of them, the more occasion infidelity seems to find for her jeers and scoffs.

Now do you believe that God commands you not to be conformed to the world? Do you believe it? DARE YOU obey it, let people say what they will about you? Do you dare separate yourself from the world, never again to be controlled by its maxims, and never again to copy its practices, and never again to be whiffled here and there by its fashions? I know a man that lives so. I can mention his name. He pays no attention to the customs of the world in this respect. And what is the result? Wherever that man goes, he leaves the impression behind that he is a Christian. O, if one church would disregard the customs of the world and practice what the Bible teaches with all the energy that the men of the world practice in their business, they would turn the world upside down. Will you do so? Will you break off from the world now? Will you enter into a covenant with God and declare that you dare to be different enough to be separate from the world, and from this time forth you will set your face as a flint to obey God and let the world say what it will? Dare you do it? Will you do it? Will you do it now?*

---

* Charles G. Finney, *Lectures to Professing Christians,* 128-154, *Principles of Victory,* 156-171. For Review: Answer the Study Questions on page 225, Cowles page 240.

5

How to Prevent Our Employments from Injuring Our Souls
1839

Not slothful in business; fervent in spirit; serving the Lord.—Romans 12:11—KJV

Never be lacking in zeal, but keep your spiritual fervor, serving the Lord.—Romans 12:11—NIV

Idleness is inconsistent with living the Christian faith, and God requires everyone to pursue some lawful employment and be diligent in their calling (whatever it is). In addition, we need to prevent our employments (secular or spiritual) from becoming snares to our souls.

Idleness is inconsistent with living the Christian faith.

Idleness (escaping employment or work) is wholly inconsistent with loving God. Whoever loves God with all his heart will certainly set himself to do the will of God. Neither God nor he will be slothful.

Idleness is wholly inconsistent with loving others. The love we have for the human race will certainly lead us to exert ourselves to promote the happiness of others.

Idleness is one result of selfishness. A man must love his own ease supremely to be idle in a world like this.

Idleness is sponging off the community in which we live. A person who refuses to earn his bread—who will not contribute as much to the happiness and good things of the world as he consumes—who chooses to live upon the common stock without contributing his share, is a drone. If he is not engaged in some employment that promotes the well-being of others, he is subtracting continually from the common stock of blessings. He is sponging off the universe of God.

Idleness is injustice. This follows from what has just been said. A person has no more right to live by sponging than he has to live by stealing. Indeed it involves the same principle.

Idleness is absolute and downright disobedience to God. God forbids idleness just as much as He forbids theft or murder. If able, a man or woman can no more be Christians without pursuing some employment by which God may be glorified and the world benefited than an habitual drunkard can manifest Christian faith and virtue before the world.

God requires everyone to pursue some lawful employment.

The fact that God requires everyone to pursue lawful employment is a plain inference from what I have already said. But what is a lawful employment? This is an all-important question.

To be lawful, an employment must not be injurious to our own best interests or the best interests of humankind. Speculation is not a lawful employment. To embark in uncertain speculations involves in it the principle of gambling, and is eminently the spirit of gambling. It is a game of chance, where one of the parties must gain and the other lose, and where selfishness stalks abroad naked to grasp everyone's wealth without shame.

To be lawful, an employment must not be selfish. All selfishness is sin. Every employment however lawful it may be in itself is rendered unlawful if it is selfishly pursued.

How to Prevent Our Employments from Injuring Our Souls

To be lawful, there must not be too much or too little of it. A business lawful in itself may become unlawful when too much is undertaken or too little is performed, so that on the one hand a man is crushed, or on the other he is idle or slothful.

To be lawful, a business must be useful. It must be such an employment as is calculated in its nature to benefit humankind.

To be lawful, a business must be suited to your capacity. You cannot lawfully employ yourself in that for which you are not fitted. By this I do not mean that you are to be perfectly qualified for the transaction of any business before you can lawfully engage in it. I mean that you should be as well or better fitted for that particular employment than any other.

To be lawful, your employment must be employment to which you are called to by God. You are to be wholly the Lord's. You are to consult His will in all things and never be engaged in any employment to please yourself alone or to promote your own separate or private interest apart from God. Therefore, you are obligated to submit yourself to the direction of the Lord in all things, and to select no employment for life, or for any length of time, except under the direction of God.

People generally admit that ministers especially are to be called by God to the work of the ministry. But everyone is to be equally devoted to God, and all employments are to be pursued equally for the glory of God. Every faculty of every human being, and every day and moment of every person, are to be devoted to the Lord. Every person is as equally obligated to consult the will of God in the selection and pursuit of their employments as is every minister. No person should give himself up to any employment to which God has not called him, or to which he does not really believe himself to be called of God; otherwise, his service of God is apostate and he has abandoned true faith. Now, everyone would say that if a minister selected the ministry simply to please himself, he would lose his soul. This is equally true of every other employment.

To be lawfully employed, you must engage in that in which you can be the most useful. It is not enough that you should render yourself useful in some degree. You are obligated to be engaged in that employment in which you can (all things considered) do the most good. A man might render himself useful as a pedlar, but if he can be more useful in some other employment he is obligated to prefer it.

The only lawful employment is that which can be honestly and reasonably pursued for the glory of God. Every kind and degree of business that cannot with an enlightened conscience be solemnly engaged in and transacted for the glory of God carries its own condemnation.

No business is lawful that is not, as a matter of fact, engaged in and pursued with the supreme desire to know and glorify God.

No business is lawful which is inconsistent with the highest degree of spirituality. I mean this: to be lawful, the business or employment in which you are engaged must be consistent with entire holiness of heart and life. Any employment that Jesus Christ or an apostle would not engage in under the circumstances is really unlawful for everyone.

Everyone should be diligent in their calling.

The scripture text implies that everyone should be diligent in their calling. The scripture text is commonly quoted as if it read, "Be diligent in business." This is not the way in which it reads; although, diligence in business is plainly implied in the scriptures.

Diligence is also plainly implied in the law of God. The needs of the world require diligence. There is enough for everyone to do. And no one has any right to be idle or dilatory in their calling. Every degree of slothfulness is injurious to yourself in many ways, and it is also injurious to those with whom you are immediately connected. They have a right to expect the diligent use of your powers in promoting their common interests. Every degree of slothfulness in you is injurious to the world at large, and to the universe inasmuch as there is just so much less of real good in the universe for every moment's idleness or negligence in which you indulge.

You set a bad example when you remain negligent or slothful in your employment for a day or an hour. The tendency toward negligence can produce universal idleness which would ruin the universe. You are bound to do all the good you can in every way to the bodies and souls of others, and this obligation is entirely inconsistent with any degree of slothfulness.

How to Prevent Our Employments from Injuring Our Souls

How to prevent our employments from becoming snares to our souls.

It has come to be a subject of almost universal complaint that our employments lead us away from God, but this should not be. People complain of their cares, and of having so much business on their hands as to secularize their spirit, blunt the edge of devotional feeling, and more or less insensibly but certainly to draw off their hearts from God. And those who are engaged in intellectual and even spiritual occupations, such as teachers of science and teachers of religion, are by their employments apt to fall into an intellectual and hardened frame of mind and to wander far from God. It seems to be understood that there is a kind of necessity in the case, and that we are naturally unable to attend to the various duties and callings incidental to our relations in this world without secularizing our spirit and annihilating a devotional state of mind. However, to suppose there is any necessity for this result is to charge God foolishly. God did not place us in the world and surrounded us with these necessities so our employments would be a snare and a curse to us. On the contrary, all the employments that are strictly lawful, instead of being a snare, are indispensable to the highest development of our powers and to the growth and consummation of our piety. The whole difficulty lies in the abuse of something eminently wise and good. That the facts are according to the general complaint cannot be doubted. People really are ensnared by their employments. But why? Many seem to suppose that the only way to maintain a spiritual frame of mind is by a total abstraction from those employments in which it seems to be necessary for people to engage in this world. It was this conceit that led to the establishment of nunneries and monasteries, and to all those fanatical and odious seclusions from society that have abounded among the Papists. The truth is, the right discharge of our duties to God and others is indispensable to holiness. Voluntary seclusion from human society and abstracting ourselves from those employments by which people may be benefited are wholly inconsistent with the principles and spirit of the Christian faith. Neither Christ nor the Apostles secluded themselves from human society. They were eminently active, zealous, and useful in promoting the glory of God and the good of others in every way in their power. It is absolutely essential for Christians to understand the secret of making their employments, whatever they are, the means of increasing instead of destroying their spirituality. A great deal needs to be said upon this subject, but with the time that I have, I can only explain the following ideas.

If you would not have your employments be snares to your soul, see to it that it is not unlawful; see to it that it is not an injurious employment—that you are not engaged in anything of which the natural tendency is to injure yourself or anyone.

See to it that you do not introduce some unlawful ingredient into a business otherwise lawful, and thus vitiate the whole and render it a curse to you and those around you. Consider this example. A man can be lawful and useful as an innkeeper. But, if he tries to increase his profits or seeks to please all classes of people by selling ardent spirits, this is absolutely unlawful and an abomination in the sight of God. By selling ardent spirits, he introduces an element into his business which vitiates the whole and renders his business a curse to others and himself. A merchant will sometimes do the same thing. In order to increase his profits or please his customers, he sells tobacco and other fashionable but injurious narcotics. While he deals in many things that are useful and important, he does not hesitate to buy and sell almost anything upon which he can make a profit. Now, if he admits into his business any ingredient that is injurious to the interests of others, he renders the whole an unlawful business. He demonstrates that he is not and cannot be pursuing his employment from right motives. He cannot possibly pursue a business of this kind and be acceptable to God. In other words, his business is a falling away from faith in God. God has said, "For whosoever shall keep the whole law, and yet offend in one point, he is guilty of all" (James 2:10) The principle involved is this: when a person allows any form of sin whatever to be habitual in his employment, it is rendering all obedience for the time being wholly impossible. He is in the exercise of a spirit which is in itself disobedience to the whole law and a setting aside the authority of God.

Be sure that you do nothing selfishly. If you allow selfishness in any of its forms to have a place in your employments, you are already departed from God, and your business, whether spiritual, intellectual or whatever it may be, has become an abomination to God.

How to Prevent Our Employments from Injuring Our Souls

See that your business is strictly and properly a lawful one. If it be not in the most proper sense a lawful employment, it will, if persevered in, certainly ruin your soul. To be lawful, as I have already said, it must be some employment that is useful—suited to your capacity—that to which you are called of God—that in which you can become useful—that which *can be* truly, honestly, and solemnly dedicated to and performed for God—that which *as a matter of fact is* dedicated to and performed for God—that which is consistent with the highest degree of spirituality, with perfect holiness of heart and life—and an employment such as Christ and the Apostles would engage in under the same circumstances.

See that your eye is single; that is, that you have but one great leading motive, and that is to glorify God and serve your generation.

Consult God at every step of your employment. Do everything with prayer. Let every day and every hour bear witness that you are transacting everything for God, and consulting God at every step of your progress. You would no doubt feel shocked if you knew that a minister went about his preparation for the pulpit without prayer to God. If he did not, on going out to visit his people, pray for divine direction, and when he returned from such visits, he did not spread the whole matter and what he had done before the Lord; in short, if he did not take counsel of God in all the departments of his employment. You would feel shocked. And should he become exceedingly hardened and reprobate in his work, and should his employment be the snare and ruin of his soul, you would not be surprised or amazed, for this would be the very natural result that under the circumstances you would anticipate. And it is to be feared that this is the very course and the very result with multitudes of ministers. Now, as everything is God's, and every person is God's, and every employment is to be pursued just as much for God's glory as the employment of a minister, it naturally follows that every person is obligated to have as single an eye, to consult God at every step, and to make his employment a subject of daily prayer, just as much as a minister. And if he does not, he will surely apostatize from God.

Be sure to do everything in a spirit of entire consecration to God. Maintain perpetually, in everything, a spirit of entire consecration, as you know and feel that you ought to maintain in the exercises of the Sabbath day.

Until people understand that the business of every day is to be as sacredly devoted to God and performed in a spirit of entire consecration to God's service as the holy exercises of the Sabbath, they will not pursue their employments without ensnaring their souls, This must not only be understood in theory, but must be reduced to practice. The Sabbath must be distinguished from other days only in the peculiarity of its employments as a day of worship and rest. You must cease to suppose that the Sabbath is God's day and that the weekdays are your days—that you may serve God one day and serve yourself six days in the week. The Sabbath has its specific and appropriate duties, and so have other days. But every day and every hour and every employment and every thought are to be wholly consecrated to God. And until you have habituated yourself to go to your farms, to your shops, or to your merchandise, as to a business that belongs wholly to God and is to be performed in a spirit of as true devotion as are the duties of your closet or of the sanctuary, your whole employment will be an everlasting snare and the final ruin of your soul.

In short, do nothing, be nothing, buy nothing, sell nothing, possess nothing, do not marry nor decline marriage, do not study nor refrain from study, but in a spirit of entire devotion to God. Consecrate your sleep, your rest, your exercise, your all to God. Learn to do this; practice this, or your employment, whatever it may be, will be the snare and ruin of your soul.

But that without which all else will be in vain is yet to be mentioned. And mark what I say. You must abide in Christ. "Without me," says Christ, "you can do nothing" (John 15:5) Only as you abide in Christ, by faith, and Christ in you, will you do in a right spirit any one of the things that have been mentioned. Christ is your life. Christ is the bread and water of life. Faith in Christ is the grand and universal condition of all true virtue and obedience to God.

REMARKS

God will not call you to any employment in kind or amount that is inconsistent with entire holiness of heart and life. Therefore, if you find that your employment really prevents your walking wholly with God,

How to Prevent Our Employments from Injuring Our Souls

something is certainly wrong. Either your employment is unlawful in itself, or if in itself a lawful employment, it is that to which you are not called, or you have taken too much upon yourself, or too little, or your motives have become wrong. There is surely some fault in you. Make a solemn pause as on the very brink of eternity, and inquire after and remove the stumbling blocks out of the way. If it be a right hand or a right eye, give it up in a moment, as you love the ways and dread the wrath of God.

God will never call you to any business and withhold the necessary grace for the perfect discharge of your obligations. If grace is sought as it ought to be and constantly will be while your motives are right, it will not be withheld.

If God calls you to a business and you become selfish in your business, it will no longer be acceptable to Him, and your pursuing it with a selfish heart is an utter abomination to God. I fear it is not an uncommon thing for young men who suppose themselves to be called to the gospel ministry, in the course of their preparation, to become cold, ambitious, and anything but holy. And yet they persevere, because they dare not go back and relinquish their course. They are sensible that they are away from God, but believing themselves to have been called to the work of the ministry, they feel as if they must go forward, partly lest they should lose their reputation, and partly because they fear the displeasure of God, while they know that as a matter of fact, their hearts are not right with Him. And thus, they go through their classical studies hoping that when they enter upon theology their studies will be of such a character as to make them holy. But coming as they do in such a state of heart to the study of theology, they are only hardened more rapidly than before. But finding this to be the case does not deter them from going forward. They think that now they must make up their opinion on various points of doctrine, and that when they have settled all these things and entered upon the active duties of the ministry, then they shall be aroused to a better state of feeling. But the hardening process still goes on. So that by the time they are through their course of ministerial studies their hearts are like the nether millstone. They are all head and no heart—all intellect and no emotion. In this state they come to the active duties of the ministry, and woe to the Church that shall employ one of them. They might as well place a skeleton in their pulpit, for he is but the shadow of a minister and not the substance. He has the bones, but not the marrow, the life, or the spirit of the Gospel.

No one has a right to undertake so much business, for any compensation whatever, as to interfere with his hours of devotion. In cases where people labor by the day, month, or year, allowance should always be made in the prices they receive for sufficient time and opportunity for devotional exercises. They have no right to exact or receive such wages as to render it necessary for them to give up all their time to labor nor ought their employers to expect them to encroach under any pretense whatever, upon those hours appointed to secret communion with God. There is great danger of a diligence in business which is inconsistent with fervency of spirit in serving the Lord.

From my own observation, I am persuaded that there is a great error in requiring too much study of young men who are preparing for the ministry. There is such a great cry for a learned ministry—so much stress is laid upon a thorough education—and so much competition among colleges and seminaries, as to present a great temptation to instructors to push the intellectual pursuits of young men to the utmost, and even beyond the utmost limit of endurance.

Now, while I am in favor of a thorough education, with the facts as they exist before me, I do not and cannot believe that the great difference in the usefulness of ministers depends on their being learned men in the common acceptance of that term. Studying human science by itself never made a useful minister, and wherever the study of human science is pushed beyond its proper limit and made to encroach upon the hours and spirit of devotion—wherever the spirit of human science, instead of the Spirit of God, comes to be that fountain at which a man drinks, he may become in the language of men, a great man, but he will never be a good minister. Until there is a great change upon this subject—until the great effort of teachers is to make their pupils pious as well as learned, and teachers are more anxious and take more pains to effect the former than the latter, our seminaries can never send out efficient ministers. To require diligence in study, without requiring fervency of spirit—to concern

How to Prevent Our Employments from Injuring Our Souls

ourselves more that our students have their lessons than that they walk with God—that they commune with Cicero, Horace, and Demosthenes, rather than with God—for us to satisfy ourselves everyday in relation to their intellectual progress and pay little or no attention to the state of their hearts is an utter abomination; and teachers who do so, whatever other qualifications they may have, are unfit to have the care of young men.

When you find yourselves proceeding in any employment without prayer for direction, support, and guidance, you may rest assured that you are selfish, and however diligent you may be, you may know that you are not fervent in spirit serving the Lord.

The financial speculations of the last few years have so secularized the Church as to annihilate her power with God. She has in reality been engaged in gambling under the pretense of making money for God. In doing this multitudes of leading Church members have involved themselves and the cause of Christ in great embarrassment and disgrace. And it does seem as if they were deranged in their spasmodic efforts to enrich themselves through speculation.

No amount of money can save or even benefit the world in the hands of a secular Church. If professors of religion had made all the money they have endeavored to make, and did they possess a universe of gold, it would do nothing towards converting the world while the very spirit and life of the Church is secular, earthly, sensual and devilish.

No idle or slothful person can enjoy communion with God for the plain reason that his idleness is perpetual disobedience to God.

The Apostle has commanded that those who will not work (i.e. who are idle or slothful) shall not eat (2 Thessalonians 3:10). If someone is able to pursue and can find any employment by which they can benefit others, yet they refuse to work, it is no enlightened charity to feed them.

If idle persons eat, they cannot digest their food. It is an unalterable law of God that people shall perform some kind of labor. This is essential to the well-being of their body and mind. Idleness is as inconsistent with health as it is with good morals. So, if someone chooses to be slothful, they must suffer the penalties of both the physical and moral law.

Principles of Joy in the Holy Spirit — Finney's Lessons on Romans

You see from this subject the great importance of training children to habits of industry, and of early imbibing their minds with the spirit of continually doing something that is useful.

Everyone can do something to glorify God and in some way benefit the human race. He can labor with his hands or his head or his heart—he can work or teach or pray or do something to contribute his share to the common stock of good in the universe. It is the language of a sluggard to complain that you can do no good. The truth is that if you have a spirit to do good, you will certainly be trying to do good.

If we do all we can do, however little, it is just as acceptable to God as if we could do a thousand times more. "If there be first a willing mind, it is accepted according to what a man hath and not according to what he hath not" (2 Corinthians 8:12). Christ said of the poor widow who gave her two mites into the Lord's treasury, she has cast in more than the rich, who of their abundance cast in much (Mark 12:41-44). It is well if you have a heart to do a great deal more than you are able to do. Christ gives you credit for doing what you really would do for Christ if you were able. He does not just give you credit for what you are actually physically, materially, or spiritually able to do. God will reward you according to the largeness of your heart in serving Him, not according to the weakness of your hands.

None of the employments that are essential to the highest good of others has any natural or necessary tendency to alienate the heart from God. By this statement I do not mean that *the perverted state* of the human heart is not such that it is natural for it, *being in a state of selfishness*, to take occasion to depart from God in these essential employments. What I mean is this: the real tendency of all these employments *to a mind not given up to selfishness* is to increase and perpetuate the deepest communion with God. There is no excuse for a secular spirit. Whenever your spirit is secular, your heart is selfish.

If you have been called by God to any employment, and have become selfish in it, your employment has become an abomination to God and you are obligated to abandon it instantly or to renounce your selfishness and diligently pursue your employment for God. By this, I do not mean that you would do right to abandon the employment to which God has

How to Prevent Our Employments from Injuring Our Souls

called you, but that if you will not repent and be "fervent in spirit serving the Lord," you are as far as possible from pleasing Him in pursuing your business selfishly (Romans 12:11). If God is not with you in any employment, whether it be study, the ministry, merchandise, farming, or anything else; if God does not go with you in it, you have certainly strayed out of the Lord's way, and you are obligated to reform, to turn instantly and wholly to the Lord, and not go a step forward until you have evidence of Divine acceptance.

Lastly, beloved, let me ask you solemnly, "Do you have some employment in which you are endeavoring, honestly and fervently to glorify God? What is your employment—in what manner do you pursue it—with what design—in what spirit—and what is the effect? Do you as a matter of fact find yourself walking with God and does the peace of God rule in your heart? Or is there some ingredient in your business that vitiates the whole? Are you dealing in some article of death—do you think you can poison your fellowmen for the glory of God? Are you a real estate or stock speculator? Are you pursuing some scandalous traffic for some selfish purpose?"

O that the Lord may search you, and pour the gaze of His eye through and through your inmost soul. And if your hands are clean, may the blessing of the Lord that makes rich and adds no sorrow be multiplied to you a thousand fold. But, if you are out of the Lord's will, may Christ lay His reclaiming, sanctifying hand upon you, and not allow you to rest until you have wholly devoted to the Lord all that you have and are.*

---

* Charles G. Finney, *The Oberlin Evangelist*, November 6, 1839, *Principles of Liberty*, 147-156. For Review: Answer the Study Questions on page 226, Cowles page 242.

The Proverbs on Joy

Deceit is in the hearts of those who plot evil, but those who promote peace have joy. —Proverbs 12:20

Each heart knows its own bitterness, and no one else can share its joy. —Proverbs 14:10

Folly brings joy to one who has no sense, but whoever has understanding keeps a straight course. —Proverbs 15:21

A person finds joy in giving an apt reply—and how good is a timely word! —Proverbs 15:23

To have a fool for a child brings grief; there is no joy for the parent of a godless fool. —Proverbs 17:21

When justice is done, it brings joy to the righteous but terror to evildoers. —Proverbs 21:15

The father of a righteous child has great joy; a man who fathers a wise son rejoices in him. —Proverbs 23:24

6

Being in Debt
1839

Owe no man any thing, but to love one another: for he that loveth another hath fulfilled the law.—Romans 13:8—KJV

Let no debt remain outstanding, except the continuing debt to love one another, for he who loves his fellowman has fulfilled the law.—Romans 13:8—NIV

In discussing this verse, I will first explain the meaning of the scripture text, then show that being in debt is sin, and finally the duty of those who are in debt:

The meaning of the scripture text.

As with most scripture texts, the meaning of this text must be learned from a careful examination of the verse in context. The Apostle begins the chapter by enforcing the duty of obedience to civil magistrates.

Principles of Joy in the Holy Spirit — Finney's Lessons on Romans

"Let every soul be subject unto the higher powers. For there is no power but of God; the powers that be are ordained of God. Whosoever, therefore, resisteth the power, resisteth the ordinance of God, and they that resist shall receive unto themselves damnation. For rulers are not a terror to good works, but to the evil. Wilt thou then not be afraid of the power? Do that which is good, and thou shalt have praise of the same. For he is the minister of God unto thee for good. But if thou do that which is evil, be afraid; for he beareth not the sword in vain; for he is the minister of God, a revenger to execute wrath upon him that doeth evil. Wherefore ye must be subject not only for wrath, but also for conscience sake. For, for this cause pay ye tribute also, for they are God's ministers, attending continually upon this very thing" (Romans 13:1-6).

Rulers are the servants of God, employed for your benefit. You are therefore to pay them tribute; which means, give them the support which their circumstances require. In the light of these verses and various other passages of scripture, I have often wondered how it was possible that any person could call into question the duty of obeying civil magistrates. Or how they could call in question the right and duty of magistrates to inflict civil penalties, and even capital punishment, where the nature of the case demands it. Certainly, this passage recognizes the right and duty of magistrates, as the servants and executioners of God's vengeance, "to execute wrath" upon transgressors.

"Render therefore to all their dues; tribute to whom tribute is due; custom to whom custom; fear to whom fear; honor to whom honor. Owe no man any thing, but to love one another; for he that loveth another hath fulfilled the law. For this, Thou shalt not commit adultery, Thou shalt not kill, Thou shalt not bear false witness, Thou shalt not covet, and if there be any other commandment, it is briefly comprehended in this saying, namely, Thou shalt love thy neighbor as thyself. Love worketh no ill to his neighbor, therefore love is the fulfilling of the law" (Romans 13:7-10).

From the context, it is evident that the Apostle designed to teach that whenever we owe someone we should immediately pay them. We should not allow any debt or obligation to rest upon us without making payment.

Being in Debt

"Owe no man any thing, but to love one another" (Romans 13:8). Here the Apostle recognizes the truth that love is a perpetual obligation. The obligation to love can never be so canceled or discharged as to be no longer binding. He recognizes no other obligation except love, with the natural fruits of love being in its own nature of perpetual obligation. With respect to this obligation, all we can do is fulfill it every moment, without the possibility of so fulfilling it as to set aside the continued obligation to love. We are to owe no man any thing else but love. We are to "render to all their dues, tribute to whom tribute is due, honor to whom honor."

I understand the scripture text to mean this: "Let no obligation but that of love with its natural fruits, which is from its very nature a perpetual obligation, rest upon you unpaid or unfulfilled."

I am aware that some modern critics maintain that this passage should have been rendered indicatively. But such commentators as Doddridge, Henry, Barnes, and Stuart, are of the opinion that its imperative rendering is correct. [Editor's Note: Albert Barnes quoted Hodge as agreeing, "Acquit yourselves of all obligations except love, which is a debt that must remain ever due."] All are agreed that the doctrine of this text as it stands is plainly a doctrine of the Bible.

Now, the question arises, "What does it mean to owe someone in the sense of this text?"

It means that if you employ a laborer, and do not stipulate the time and terms of payment, it is taken for granted that he is to be paid when his work is done. If you hire him for a day, and nothing is said to the contrary, he cannot demand his pay till his day's work is done. Till then, you owe him nothing. The same is true if you hire him for a week or a month or a year, if you do not stipulate the time and terms of payment. When the time which he is to labor is stipulated, and nothing is said about the time and terms of payment, you owe him nothing until his time has expired. Then you owe him; and you are obligated to pay him, and pay him the money that is owed. But, if the time was not specified which he was to labor, he may break off at any time and demand pay for what he has done. Or, if the time of payment was expressed or understood, whenever it arrives you, owe him, and you are obligated to pay him agreeably to the understanding.

The same is true if you hire a horse or any other piece of property. If you hire it for a specified time, and nothing is said of the conditions of payment, the understanding is that you are to pay when the time for which the property was hired has expired. It then becomes a debt. Then you are to pay and pay in money. If there were any other understanding fixing the time and terms of payment, you do not owe the man until the specified conditions are complied with.

The same is true if you purchase any piece of property. If nothing is stipulated to the contrary, the understanding is that you are to pay in cash at the time you receive the property. At that time, and neither before nor after, you are expected to pay the purchase amount in money.

We do not properly owe an individual until we are under an obligation to pay him. Whenever he has a right to demand payment, we have no right to withhold it.

There may be such a thing as contracting a prospective debt; that is, giving your obligation to become due at a certain time. But then you do not properly owe, because you are under no obligation to pay until it becomes due. But whenever it becomes due, you are bound immediately to pay the obligation.

Being in debt is sin.

To be in debt is sin because it is a direct violation of the command of God. This text is just as binding as any of the ten commandments. And a violation of this text is a setting aside of the command of Jehovah, just as much as to commit adultery or murder. It is not to be regarded merely as a piece of advice given by the Apostle Paul, because it is a direct, positive, and authoritative command of God.

To be in debt is unjust. If your creditor has a right to demand payment, you certainly have no right to withhold it. If it is due, it is a contradiction to say that it is not unjust for you not to pay. It is a contradiction, both in terms and in fact, to say that you owe someone and at the same time are guilty of no injustice in refusing or neglecting to pay him. It is as much an injustice as stealing, and involves the same principle. The sin of stealing consists in the appropriating to ourselves that which properly belongs to

Being in Debt

another. Therefore, whenever you withhold from anyone his due, you are guilty of an absolute injustice, just as if you had stolen his property.

To be in debt is sin, because it is falsehood. I have already shown that you do not properly owe a man until payment becomes due. It becomes due when and because there is a promise on your part expressed or implied that you will pay it at the time it is due. Now, you cannot violate this promise without being guilty of falsehood.

If what has just been said is true, it follows that people should meet their contracts, just as they would avoid the grossest sins. They are bound to avoid being in debt. They are obligated to meet and fulfill their engagements, just as much as they are bound to avoid blasphemy, idolatry, murder, or any other sin. A person who does not pay his debts is no more to be accounted an honest person than one who is guilty of any other heinous crime.

If a person who claims to be a Christian is in debt, he is a moral delinquent and should be accounted and treated as a subject of church discipline.

Someone may object that they cannot avoid being in debt, but I say that if you cannot pay as you contracted, then you could have and should have avoided contracting the debt. If you reply, I really needed the thing which I purchased, I ask, were your necessities so great that you would have been justified in your estimation in lying or stealing to supply them? If not, why have you resorted to fraud? The same authority that prohibits lying or stealing also prohibits owing a debt that you will not pay. Why do you violate this commandment of God any more than any other command? Is it not because a corrupt public sentiment has rendered the violation of this commandment less disgraceful than violating the other commands of God? Why did you not resort to begging instead of running into debt? Better far to beg than to run into debt. Begging is not prohibited by any command of God, but being in debt is prohibited. True, it is disgraceful to beg, but a God-dishonoring public sentiment has rendered it far less so than to be in debt. And does not this account for your shameless violation of this command of God?

Do you say that you cannot avoid being in debt because you were disappointed in your expectations, that you expected to have the money, that you made the contract in good faith, that you expected to meet it at the appointed time; but others owe you and did not pay you; therefore, you are unable to pay your debts. To this I reply that you should have contracted with that expressed condition. You should have made known your circumstances, and the ground of your expectation in regard to being able to pay at the time appointed. In that case, if your creditor was willing to run the risk of your being disappointed, the fault is not yours, as you have practiced no injustice or deception. But if your contract was without condition, you have taken upon yourself the risk of disappointment and are not guiltless.

But here again, someone may say that nearly the whole Church are in debt, and if subject to discipline, who shall cast the first stone? I reply that if it is true that the Church is so extensively in debt, no wonder that the curse of God is upon her. It may be true that a Church may be so generally involved in any given sin as to make that sin a difficult subject of discipline, because each person knows that he himself is guilty and must in his turn submit to the same discipline. But when this is true of any Church, it is a shameless abomination for the members of that Church to attempt to hide themselves under the admitted fact that nearly all the Church are involved in the guilt of it. Now rest assured, when any sin becomes so prevalent that it cannot and is not made in that Church a subject of discipline, God himself will sooner or later take up the rod and find the means to discipline, and that effectually, such a Church.

The duty of those who are in debt.

Those who are in debt are obligated to make any sacrifice of property, time, or any other sacrifice that it is possible for them to make to pay their debts. Someone may object: "Does the law of love permit my creditor to demand a sacrifice of me? If he loves me as he does himself, why should he require or even allow me to make a sacrifice of property to pay what I owe him?" Surely, if anyone is to make a sacrifice or suffer loss, it is the debtor and not the creditor. There will almost certainly be some damage to the creditor when he does not receive what is owed him. It may so disarrange his affairs, and break in upon his calculations as to occasion

Being in Debt

him great damage. Of this he is to be the judge and not the debtor. Your sacrifice may be necessary not only to prevent his loss, but to enable him to meet his contractual duties and thus prevent his sin of being in debt. His confidence in your veracity may have led him to contract prospective debts, and by not paying him you not only sin yourself but cause him to sin. The refusal of a debtor to make a sacrifice to pay his debts may involve many others in both loss and sin. Suppose A owes B, B owes C, and C owes D, and so on in a long chain of mutual dependencies. Now, what if there is a failure in the first or any other link of this chain of dependencies; then, everyone below it is involved in loss and sin. Consider, how can this evil be stopped? Suppose you hold the place of C and A refuses to make a sacrifice to pay B; then, B refuses to make a sacrifice to pay you. Will you sin because they do? Will you involve your creditor in loss and sin? No! Whatever others may do, you are obligated to pay your debts. Unless your creditor voluntarily consents to defer the time of payment, you are obligated to pay him at any sacrifice.

People who are in debt should not contract new debts to pay old ones. It is the practice of some to keep up their credit by borrowing from one to pay another. Their meeting and canceling the last debt depends altogether upon the presumption that they shall be able to borrow the money from someone else. After they have borrowed from one, they will keep from paying him as long as possible without losing their credit. And then, instead of making a sacrifice of property sufficient to discharge the obligation, they borrow from B to pay A and from C to pay B and thus, perhaps, disappoint and disoblige a dozen people by not paying them exactly at the time agreed upon; instead, they should have stopped short and parted with what property they have at any sacrifice to pay the debt.

I am not saying that someone should never in any case borrow from one person to pay another. But I do say this as a general rule, such practices are highly reprehensible. Still, if a debt becomes due and you do not have the money, but are certain that at a given time you shall have it, I do not suppose it is wrong for you to borrow and pay this debt with the understanding that you pay this borrowed money at the time specified. But to borrow money with no other prospect of an ultimate payment than that you can borrow again and thus keep up your credit from time to time is wicked.

Those who are in debt have no right to give away the money which they owe. If you are in debt, the money you have belongs to your creditor, not to you. You have no right to be generous until you are just. You have strictly no more right to give that money away than you have to steal money to give away. But here it should be particularly understood what is and what is not to be accounted as giving money away. For example, it is not giving away your money to pay the current expenses of the congregation to which you are attached. Your proportion of the current expenses of the congregation or church to which you belong is impliedly, if not expressly, contracted by you. You cannot withhold it any more than the payment of any other debt.

The same may be said of the support of ministers and foreign missionaries and all for whose support the faith of the Church is pledged. It seems to be a common misunderstanding of some church members that what are more generally called their secular debts or obligations are binding and of course to be paid; but, that their obligations expressed or implied to the Church are not so absolutely binding. They make the excuse that they can give nothing to Christian institutions until their debts are paid. Now, beloved, you ought to know that you are pledged to support the institutions of the Church both virtually and actually by your profession of Christian faith; these are your most sacred debts and are thus to be considered and discharged by you. I beseech you not to consider the meeting and canceling of such demands as these in the light of a gift, as if you were making a present to God instead of discharging a solemn debt. I have been astonished to find that the pecuniary embarrassments of the few past years have so far crippled the movements of the great benevolent societies for lack of funds; and that missionaries for whose support the faith and honor of the Church were pledged should be so far cut short of their necessary supplies under the pretense that the Church must pay her secular debts before she could discharge her high and sacred obligations to them and the work in which they are engaged.

A person who is in debt has no right to purchase for himself or for his family things not absolutely essential for their subsistence. Things that might lawfully be purchased and used under other circumstances

Being in Debt

become unlawful when you are in debt and not paying your obligations. A creditor has no right to deprive you of necessary food, indispensable clothing, or your liberty. To do so would put it out of your power ever to pay him. But, while your debts are unpaid, you have no right to indulge in anything more than the necessaries of life. To do so is as unlawful as it would be to steal to purchase unnecessary articles.

REMARKS

From what has been said, it is clear that the whole credit system, if not absolutely sinful, is nevertheless so highly dangerous that no Christian should embark upon it. After I preached this sermon and prior to its publication, some censured this particular remark as a rash one. A rash remark! Let the present history and experience of the Church say whether the credit system is not so highly dangerous that the person who will venture to embark upon it is guilty of rashness and presumption. Look back over the centuries, when has the Church been so generally disgraced (as it has been within the last few years) by the bankruptcy of those who profess to be Christians? How many millions of dollars are now owed by Church members to the ungodly, who will never be repaid? Rash! Why this is the very plea of church members, that they can do nothing for the support of the gospel because they are so much in debt. Is there no danger of anyone's getting in debt when they try to trade using borrowed capital? Indeed it is highly dangerous, as universal experience shows. What is the necessity for Christians to embark in so dangerous an enterprise, and one that so highly jeopardizes the honor or religion? Is it because the necessities of life can be procured in no other way? Is it because the institutions of the Church demand it? Christianity sustains a greater loss through the debts and bankruptcies of church members than it ever gains by their prosperity.

The credit system as it now prevails and has prevailed is useless and worse than useless. For example, suppose the consumers of merchandize (instead of anticipating their yearly crops and yearly income and running in debt with the expectation of paying from these) were to take a little pains to reverse this order of things and be a year ahead, paying down for what they purchase and having the income of each year beforehand, so as to contract no debts. In this case the country merchants, giving no credit, but receiving ready pay, would be able to pay down on the purchase of their goods from the wholesale dealer. The wholesale dealer would pay down to the importer, and the importer to the manufacturer, and the manufacturer to the producer. Now, anyone can see that many millions of dollars a year would be saved to this country in this way. The manufacturer could afford an article cheaper for ready pay, and so could the importer, and the wholesale dealer, and each one in his turn down to the consumer. Everyone could sell cheaper for ready pay, since no risk would be run, and business could be done with much greater convenience and safety. Thus, an entire rejection of the credit system in its present form, and an adoption of the system of ready pay would afford to the consumer every article so much cheaper as to save millions of dollars every year. And I do not apprehend that there is in reality any serious difficulty in so reversing the whole order of business.

At another time I may more particularly examine the credit system in its foundation and various ramifications, and the nature and tendencies of the prevailing system of doing business on borrowed capital. But at present I can only say, as I have said, that, waiving the question whether it is absolutely sinful in itself, it is too highly dangerous to be embarked in by those who feel a tender solicitude for the honor and cause of Christ.

If in any case the present payment of debts is impossible, your duty is to regard your indebtedness as a sin against God and your neighbor, to repent, and set yourself with all practicable self-denial to pay as fast as you can. Unless you are laying yourself out to pay your debts, do not imagine that you repent either of your indebtedness or any other sin. For you are impenitent and a shameless hypocrite rather than a Christian, if you allow yourself to be in debt and are not making all practicable efforts to do justice to your creditors.

If payment is possible by any sacrifice of property on your part, sin is upon you until you pay your debt. There is a wicked custom among many, and to a considerable number in the Church, of putting property out of their hands and into someone else's in order to avoid a sacrifice in the payment of their debts. I remember talking to an elder in a church who confessed to me that "he was avoiding the sacrifice of his property in the payment of his debts by finesse of law." The lax notions and practices of the world and of the Church upon this subject are truly abominable. It has come to pass that a person may not only be considered a respectable citizen, but a respectable member of the Church, who allows himself to be in debt, and who has judgments and executions against him, and who resorts not only "to finesse of law to avoid the payment of his debts," but who also practices the most palpable frauds against both God and his creditors by putting his property out of his hands and into someone else's hands in order to avoid meeting his just responsibilities.

O shame on the Church and on those who claim to be Christians! Some in the Church will even go to an unconverted lawyer for advice in this iniquitous business and lay open before his unconverted heart their shameless iniquity. Alas, how many lawyers are thus led to call in question the whole truth of the Christian faith; and over these dishonest "Christians", they stumble into hell. Until the Church will rise up and wash her hands and cleanse her garments from this iniquity by banishing such persons from her communion, the cause of Christ will not cease to bleed at every pore.

Some people take the ground that not to meet their contracts and pay their debts when they become due is not sinful on account of the general understanding of those in business upon such subjects. To this I answer that there is no understanding among business people that debts are not to be paid when they become due. Among those in business, the nonpayment of a debt always involves a disgrace and a wrong. Let the public sentiment be what it might among those doing business, still the law of God cannot be altered; and by this unchanging law of God, it is a sin to be in debt. "Righteousness exalts a nation: but sin is a reproach to any people;" it is both a sin and a shame to be in debt (Proverbs 14:34).

The rule laid down in this text is applicable to individuals, corporations, nations, and all bodies of people assuming pecuniary responsibilities.

It is dishonest and dishonorable to hire or purchase an article and say nothing about payment until afterwards.

The violation of this law is working immense mischief in the Church and in the world. It is truly shocking to see to what an extent the Church is involved in debt, and church members are engaged in collecting debts of each other by force of law. The heart-burning and bitterness that exist among Church members on account of not paying their debts to each other are awfully great and alarming. Besides all of this, in what light does the Church appear before the world—as a mass of money-makers, speculators, and bankrupts—shuffling and managing through finesse of law to avoid the payment of their debts? I could relate many additional facts from my own observations that would cause the cheek of piety to blush. Alas, for the rage and madness of a speculating, money-making, fraudulent Church!

There is great reason to believe that many young people in the course of their education involve themselves in debts that so far eat up their piety as to render them nearly useless all the rest of their lives. I would rather be twenty-five years in getting an education and paying my own way than involve myself in debt to the Education Society or in any other way. How many young men there are, who are in debt to the Education Society, and who are dealing very loosely with their consciences on the subject of payment. Because the Education Society does not press them for immediate payment, they let the matter ride along without payment; they increase their expenditures as their income increases, instead of practicing self-denial and honestly discharging their obligations to the Society.

I cannot have confidence in the piety of anyone who is not conscientious in paying their debts. I know some who are in debt, and who spend their time and their property in a manner wholly inconsistent with their circumstances, and who still make great pretensions to piety. They are active in prayer meetings. They take a conspicuous place at the communion table. They even hold a responsible office in the Church, and yet they seem to have no conscience about paying their debts. I believe it is right, and the duty of all churches and ministers, to exclude such people from the communion of the Church. And were it generally done, it would go far to wipe away the stains that have been brought by such people upon the gospel of Jesus Christ. I do not see why they should be allowed to come to the communion table any more than whoremongers, murderers, drunkards, Sabbath breakers, or slave-holders.

Being in Debt

There must be a great reformation in the Church upon this subject before the business class of ungodly men will have much confidence in the Christian faith. This reformation should begin immediately and where it ought to begin, among the leading members of the Church. Ministers and Church Judicatories should speak out upon the subject—should "Cry aloud and spare not, but lift up their voice like a trumpet and show Israel his transgressions and the house of Jacob their sins" (Isaiah 58:1).

And now, beloved, are you in debt? Then sin is upon you. Rise up and show yourself clean in this matter, I beseech you. Make every effort to meet and discharge your responsibilities. And beware that in attempting to pay your debts, you do not resort to means that are as highly reprehensible as to be in debt.

Let no one complain and say that instead of preaching the gospel I am discussing mere business transactions. The truth is that the gospel is to regulate the business transactions of the world. Christian faith is practical. The practice of true Christian faith does not consist in austerities, prayers, masses, and monkish superstitions, as Papists vainly dream.

If the gospel of Jesus Christ does not take hold of a person's business operations, if it does not reform his daily life and habits, of what avail is it? Until in these respects your practice is right, you cannot expect to enjoy the influences of the Holy Spirit. You cannot grow in holiness any further than you reform your practice.

The Christian faith requires that the preceptive part of the gospel should be spread out in all its detail before the Church. And if you find that this gospel message convinces you of sin, I beg you not to turn around and say that this sermon is just about business and not about Christianity. Business is but one part of exercising your faith. A person who does not consider their business practices has no faith at all.

And now, dearly beloved, instead of allowing your heart to rise up and resist what I have said, will you not as I have often requested, go down upon your knees and spread this whole subject before the Lord? Will you not inquire wherein you have erred, if you have, and sinned, if you have, and make haste to repent, and reform your life?*

Principles of Joy in the Holy Spirit — Finney's Lessons on Romans

---

* Charles G. Finney, *The Oberlin Evangelist*, July 31, 1839, *Principles of Liberty*, 157-166. For Review: Answer the Study Questions on page 227, Cowles page 242.

7

Nature of True Virtue
1843

Owe no man any thing, but to love one another: for he that loveth another hath fulfilled the law. For this, Thou shalt not commit adultery, Thou shalt not kill, Thou shalt not steal, Thou shalt not bear false witness, Thou shalt not covet; and if there be any other commandment, it is briefly comprehended in this saying, namely, Thou shalt love thy neighbour as thyself. Love worketh no ill to his neighbour: therefore love is the fulfilling of the law.—Romans 13:8-10—KJV

Let no debt remain outstanding, except the continuing debt to love one another, for he who loves his fellowman has fulfilled the law. The commandments, "Do not commit adultery," "Do not murder," "Do not steal," "Do not covet," and whatever other commandment there may be, are summed up in this one rule: "Love your neighbor as yourself." Love does no harm to its neighbor. Therefore love is the fulfillment of the law.—Romans 13:8-10—NIV

Principles of Joy in the Holy Spirit — Finney's Lessons on Romans

In discussing these verses, I will show what is intended by the term "love," and that "love" is the whole of virtue. As the Apostle Paul wrote, "For all the law is fulfilled in one word, even this, Thou shalt love thy neighbor as thyself" (Galatians 5: 14).

What is intended by the term "love".

It is of the utmost importance to understand the biblical meaning of the term *love*. It is represented in the text, and in the Bible generally, as the substance of all Christian faith, and the only preparation for heaven. What can be more important than love?

The love required in the text is not what is generally called *natural affection* or the love of kindred. This is obvious from the fact that natural affection is involuntary. True, the will is employed in acting out this type of love, but what is generally intended by natural affection is the strong constitutional impulses experienced by parents towards their children, brothers and sisters towards one another, and other family relationships. This natural affection is common to both saints and sinners, and certainly nothing can be Christian faith which is common to both the ungodly and the saints. Natural affection may also be participated in by animals.

Christian love is not *complacency* or esteem. Complacency is that pleasant emotion or state of the sensibility which is experienced when we see anything which, from the laws of our constitution, is naturally pleasing to us. For example, if you contemplate beautiful natural scenery, you experience a pleasing emotion or delight from the very nature of your constitution. It is precisely the same in contemplating moral beauty. People are so constituted that whenever they contemplate a virtuous character, provided it does not in any way conflict with their selfishness, they delight in it—a pleasurable emotion always springs up naturally. Now this complacency, or esteem of virtuous character, is perfectly involuntary; therefore, it can have no virtue in it. This we know by consciousness which I defined in my last lecture to be the mind's knowledge of its own existence, acts, and states, and of the liberty or necessity of these acts and states.* By consciousness then we know that this complacency in the character, either in God or any other virtuous being, is involuntary, and the natural and

Nature of True Virtue

necessary result of the mental constitution when brought into certain relations to such characters. This complacency cannot be true virtue, or the love required in the Bible, because it can with propriety be exercised only towards the virtuous, whereas the love which the Bible requires is to be exercised towards all. We are not required to exercise complacency towards sinners, and it would plainly be unjust and absurd if we were, since to delight in a sinful character is impossible. But the text requires universal love. Therefore, the love which the Bible requires and complacency cannot be identical. Complacency is common to real saints, to the self-deceived, and to the unrepentant. Much evil is done by denying that sinners have this feeling of complacency towards God and His law when the fact is they know that they have. Whenever they see the character of God apart from His relationship with themselves, they cannot avoid complacency; it arises by a natural necessity from their mental constitution. The most wicked devil in hell would experience complacency, if he could view the character of God apart from God's relations to himself. It is absurd to deny that mind would feel complacency, for if it would not, it must be inconsistent with itself, which cannot be. Furthermore, complacency in virtuous character is consistent with the highest degree of wickedness. It is related of a certain infidel that he would go into ecstasies in contemplating the character of God. Who has not heard those who act wickedly insist that they love God? Have you not found it almost impossible to convince them that they do not love God with a virtuous love? Why? Because they are conscious of the emotions of complacency towards God and they mistake these feelings for real benevolence.

The love required in the text is not what is commonly called *fondness*, for this is a mere emotion and therefore involuntary. I do not know what to call this development of the mind towards God except *fondness*. People often exhibit a fondness towards God, the same as towards any other being. They feel fondness towards God, because God loves them, just as sinners feel fondness towards those who do them a good turn. They do not distinguish between fondness and true Christian love; but immediately after the strongest exhibition of fondness towards God, they will take advantage of a neighbor in trade or exhibit selfishness in some other form.

Principles of Joy in the Holy Spirit — Finney's Lessons on Romans

Truthfully, fondness towards God often includes the most fiendish wickedness and the highest irreverence. When conversing about God and in their prayers to God, people in this state of mind often seem in every way to regard and treat God merely as an equal. I have often thought how infinitely insulting to Him their conduct must be. Fondness for God can coexist with self-indulgence. While exercising fondness for God, people often show themselves to be the perfect slaves of their appetites and passions. They undoubtedly feel their fondness for God, but they do not love God as God intends. They say they love God, but is their love benevolence? Is it true Christianity? Can that be Christian faith which puts no restraint on the appetites and passions, or only curbs some of them, while it cleaves the more tenaciously to others? Impossible!

Love is a virtue, and the love intended in the text is not synonymous with *desire*. People say they desire to love God. They desire to love their neighbor as themselves. No doubt they do have this desire, but there is no Christian virtue in this, since desire is constitutional and has no moral character. Sinners may have the desire to love and remain sinners still, and everyone knows that desires can be consistent with the highest wickedness. Besides, as it is mere desire, it may exist forever and do no good. Suppose God had from all eternity merely desired to create a universe and make it happy. If He had never gone any further than that, what good would His desire have done? So, it will not do for us to say to our neighbors, "Go in peace; keep warm and well fed," while refusing to give them those things which are essential to their well-being (James 2:16). Unless we really will what we desire, it will never effect any good.

The love required in the text is not *pity* or compassion to individuals. This is wholly constitutional, the way we were created, and people are strongly exercised with pity in spite of themselves because this is natural. It is related of Whitefield that he often appealed to people with such power in behalf of his orphanage as to induce those to give liberally who had beforehand determined not to give or be influenced by him. Truthfully, his mighty appeals aroused the constitutional susceptibility of pity to such a pitch that they had to give out of self defense. They were wrought up to such an agony that they had to give to relieve their feelings, but this mere excitement was far from being virtuous. After their excitement subsided, perhaps those people whose pity induced them to give called themselves a thousand fools for having given!**

The love required in the text in not *delight* in the happiness of others. God created us to naturally delight in the happiness of others, whenever there is no selfish reason to prevent it. This same constitutional tendency produces abhorrence of whatever is unjust and injurious. For example, think of how people's feelings of indignation swell and boil on witnessing acts of injustice! Suppose, in a court of justice, a judge perverts justice, shamefully wronging the innocent and clearing the guilty. How would the spectators feel? I remember a case where a man had been guilty of a flagrant outrage, but the court of justice so insulted and abused the sufferer and showed such a disposition to clear the guilty that the indignation of the spectators became aroused to such a degree that they could hardly be restrained from seizing and wreaking their vengeance upon the guilty man. These people made no pretensions to being Christians. Universally, whether they are virtuous or not, people abhor a liar and the character of the devil. Whoever contemplated the character of the devil, as it really is, without abhorring it? On the contrary, universally, whether virtuous themselves or not, people admire and delight in virtuous characters. For example, consider the Jews in Christ's time. How they admired and manifested their delight in the character of the prophets, who had formerly perished by the violence of their contemporaries. Now how was this? Why, they now saw the true character of those prophets, without its sustaining such a relation to their selfishness as to annoy them, and their constitutional delight was naturally awakened in this way. But at the same time, they were treating Christ in the same manner that their fathers treated those prophets and for the same reason. So today, multitudes admire and praise such preachers as Whitefield, Wesley, and Edwards; however, if they preached today, these same multitudes would cry as loud as their contemporaries did, "Away with them!" Now, why is this? Because the relations of the characters of these preachers to the world are now changed. They do not directly cross the track of people's selfishness, as they did of the people who heard them preach. The same principle is manifested in respect to human freedom. For example, some years ago, during the struggle of the Greeks for their freedom, what enthusiasm prevailed, what earnestness to go and help them! The government could scarcely control the waves of excitement in their favor. But those very men, who were so enthusiastic in behalf of the Greeks, would now hiss at any effort to remove slavery from this country! Now why is this? Because, I say again, human beings are so created that when no selfish reason exists to prevent it, they naturally delight in the happiness of others and sympathize with those who suffer. But there is no virtue in this. It is mere natural emotion which is consistent with the highest wickedness.

The love required in the Bible is not good will to only some individuals. Jesus said, "If you love those who love you, what credit is that to you? Even sinners love those who love them" (Luke 6:32). People love their friends and partisans, and so do fallen spirits for ought I know, but there is no benevolence in only loving those who love you.

Twelve attributes of benevolence.

Benevolence is willing the good of being. Twelve attributes of benevolence are the following:

1. *Voluntariness.* Voluntariness belongs to the will. Voluntariness does not belong to the sensibility, emotions or feelings.

2. *Disinterestedness.* Disinterestedness is willing the good of being for its own sake, and not for the sake of oneself. Disinterestedness is recognizing the good of being as valuable in itself and willing the good of being for that reason. The ultimate goal of the willing is the good that is willed, not the potential benefits to oneself supremely, which is selfishness.

3. *Universality.* Universality goes out towards all beings. Benevolence is impartial and admits no exceptions. Wherever there is a being capable of happiness, benevolence wills its happiness according to its perceived value and for its own sake. Such is God's benevolence, which is universal, embracing in its infinite bosom all beings from the highest archangel to the sparrow which falls to the ground. God views and really wills the happiness of every being as a good. Indeed, universality is essential to the very nature of benevolence, for if good is willed on its own account, benevolence will of course cover all good known.

4. *Unity.* Benevolence is a simple principle. Benevolence is the whole

heart, an unmixed general choice, as the good of being is a unity. Benevolence is a single end, and benevolence is the choice of this one end.

5. *Choice.* Benevolence is a choice as distinguished from a volition. The choice of an end always naturally necessitates volitions to accomplish the end, but these executive volitions have no character in themselves, and all virtue or vice belongs to the choice or intention which they are designed to execute. We know this by consciousness. Benevolence is a choice as distinguished from desire, emotion, or feeling. We are conscious that all the states of the sensibility—all desires, emotions, and passions whatever—are involuntary, and therefore without moral character. Benevolence cannot consist either wholly or partly in these desires or feelings.

7. *Efficiency.* Benevolence is active and efficient. Since benevolence is a choice, it must be efficient. Choice necessitates volition. For example, suppose I intend to go to the post office as soon as possible. While this choice remains—to go as soon as possible—it naturally necessitates all the volitions necessary to its execution. The very nature of benevolence involves activity to achieve its goal in the most direct way.

8. *Aggressiveness.* Benevolence will involve aggressiveness. If benevolence is willing the good of being, then benevolence wills the destruction of whatever prevents that good. Benevolence will continually make encroachments in every direction upon every form of wickedness however fortified. Benevolence will not only fight against such sins as licentiousness, intemperance, and profanity, but against every form of selfishness however popular it may be with selfish people.

9. *Ultimate Intention.* Benevolence must be an ultimate intention. An intention is the choice of an end. Benevolence is the choice of an ultimate end, which must be the highest good of being. Being the ultimate choice, it is a disposition to promote good to the utmost.

10. *Supreme to God.* Benevolence is willing the good of being for its own sake. It follows that benevolence is willing the good of every being, according to its perceived value. The correct definition of virtue includes a disposition to regard things according to their perceived relative value. Now, everyone must perceive that the happiness of God is the greatest good in the universe; therefore, benevolence must naturally will the supreme happiness of God.

11. *Equality*. Benevolence must be equal toward all people. I do not mean to say that the happiness of every person *is* equal to the happiness of every other person, or that the happiness of every person is equally valuable. The happiness of a person is of more value than the happiness of an animal. It would be unjust to regard persons and animals as equals. In some circumstances, some people are of more value than others. For example, the life and leadership of George Washington was of more value in the Revolutionary War than that of a private soldier. Therefore, if George Washington or the private *must* be sacrificed for the good, it should be the least valuable to the good. What I mean to say is this: *the good of every being is to be regarded according to its relative value as you understand it.*

12. *Impartiality*. Benevolence must regard the good of enemies as well as friends. The Savior insists on this as essential to virtue.

The love God requires must be benevolence.

God requires benevolence. Benevolence is the only form of love which is voluntary, or can reasonably be commanded. Benevolence, and no other kind of love, is voluntary, and everyone knows this fact by their own consciousness. We are conscious that our emotions are all produced indirectly and not directly. For example, if a parent wishes to feel about his family, he must direct his attention to them. The result will be that he will feel about them by a natural necessity, and his feelings will take the type of whatever aspect he views them in. And while his attention is fixed upon them, he cannot help but feel. So with every form of love except benevolence. Hatred is produced and perpetuated in the same way. An individual conceives himself injured by another, and he keeps his attention focused upon it. The more he views it, the more he feels emotions of hatred or indignation, so that when urged to give it up, he says he cannot. And it is true that while he keeps his eye upon that particular thing—while his mind broods over it, he cannot—but he can turn his attention off and thus indirectly remove his feelings of hatred or indignation.

God requires benevolence towards all beings, which is obvious from what I have already said. God's love to us must be benevolence. It could not be complacency, for instead of feeling complacent towards sinners,

Nature of True Virtue

God must abhor their character. God's benevolence made the Atonement and all the provisions of salvation. No other kind of love would do any real good. Without benevolence, God would never have made the Atonement or have done anything else to secure the salvation of sinners, nor would any other moral being. In the nature of things, no other love can be universal except benevolence, which consists in willing universal good for its own sake.

Benevolence is naturally and universally obligatory, and therefore must be virtue. The good of being is valuable, and therefore to will it must be virtue. To deny this is to talk stark nonsense. It is to deny that we are to treat things as they are, or according to their nature. Therefore, the law of God must require benevolence, and God's law would be unjust if it did not. It would be unjust if God did not require all moral beings to act according to the nature and relations of things as He created them.

Nothing else except benevolence needs to be required of moral beings, since everything else possible to us follows the exercise of benevolence of necessity. This follows from the fact that benevolence consists in choice. If I will right, my right willing secures the corresponding volitions, muscular movements, desires, and feelings as a matter of course, and whatever my willing will not secure is impossible to me. To produce the right emotions, I have only to fix my attention on the right objects. Therefore, if a person wills right, of course the whole person will be right. By our consciousness, we know this is the influence of the will.

In short, nothing more nor less than benevolence can be justly required of a person. That nothing less can be required is a certain intuition of every moral being in the universe. Ask anyone you will if everyone ought not to be required to will the universal good of being, and if he understands the terms of your proposition, from the deepest recesses of his soul he will immediately cry out, "Yes! Yes!" That nothing more can be required is equally intuitive. If someone asserts that a person can be required to do anything beyond the power of their will, the nature of every moral being cries out against it as false.

Benevolence is the whole of virtue.

We have seen that this love, benevolence, is disposition or intention. We know that intention necessitates corresponding states and acts. Virtue cannot consist in the outward act or in necessitated mental acts. Therefore, virtue must consist in benevolence, and this the Bible teaches in many ways.

In the text, Paul asserts that love is the fulfilling of the law; all the law is fulfilled in one word "love." In the Old Testament, God commands, "Love your neighbor as yourself. I am the LORD" (Leviticus 19:18). Jesus Christ taught and lived as the perfect example of the spirit of the whole law, summarized in one word "love." When answering an expert in the law, who tested Him regarding the greatest commandment in the law, "Jesus replied: 'Love the Lord your God with all your heart and with all your soul and with all your mind.' This is the first and greatest commandment. And the second is like it: 'Love your neighbor as yourself'" (Matthew 22:37-39). Benevolence is the spirit of every precept of the Bible. Paul asserts, "For if the willingness is there, the gift is acceptable according to what one has, not according to what one does not have;" that is, a right intention obeys the very spirit of the Bible (2 Corinthians 8:12). If we intend right, the will is taken for the deed. Suppose my intention is to do all the good I possibly can, but I am confined to a sick bed so that I can accomplish but little; nevertheless, I am virtuous because of my intention. So, on the other hand, the Bible teaches that if people intend wrong, their moral character is as their intention, whatever they may do. Even if good should result from their wrong actions, no thanks to them, because they did not intend to do good. *All the moral attributes of Christian character are only modifications of benevolence.*

REMARKS

Strictly speaking, the Bible makes all virtue consist in love, and it cannot be inconsistent with itself. Words, thoughts, and outward actions are and can be virtuous only in the sense of their being manifestations of benevolence. The same may be said in regard to words, thoughts, and actions that are called wicked. The Bible says, "the plowing of the wicked is sin" (Proverbs 21:4). *Words, thoughts, and actions are holy or sinful in no other sense than that they indicate the state of the will.* A word! What is a word? A breath, a motion of the atmosphere on the drum of the ear. Can this have moral character in itself? No, but it may be an index of the state of mind of the person who utters it.

Do you see the infinite importance of understanding that benevolence always and necessarily manifests itself in choice, and it is naturally impossible that it should not?

See the spurious nature of any religion which does not manifest itself in efforts to do good. Such religion is mere antinomianism. It may be some kind of happiness, but it is not Christianity.

All the attributes of Christian character must belong to the will, just as all God's moral attributes are only modifications of benevolence. They are not modifications of emotion, but of will. His justice in sending the wicked to hell is as much a modification of benevolence as is His mercy in taking the virtuous to heaven. He does both for the same reason, because the general good equally demands both. So with all that the true Christian does.

Some definitions of Christian love involve attributes that are false and dangerous! For example, some speak of love of as a mere feeling; therefore, they represent the Christian faith, at one time, like smothered embers, scarcely in existence; and at another time, in a slight glow, which may be fanned till it breaks out into flame. Now, this is not the love which the Bible requires, since it is nothing except mere feeling, and even if legitimately produced, it is only the natural and constitutional result of Christianity, and not the same as living the Christian faith itself.

Repentance is often spoken of as mere sorrow for sin, but true repentance does not consist in feeling at all. *True repentance is a change of mind.* When we have made up our mind to do one thing, and then change it, and do the opposite, we say in popular language, "I changed my mind." *Changing our mind is the simple idea of repentance. It is an act of the will; therefore, sorrow follows it as a result.* Some represent faith as the conviction of the intellect; but this cannot be faith, for *the Bible everywhere represents faith as a virtue, and it must, therefore, be an act of the will, and no mere belief.* Faith is committing the soul to God. The Bible says Christ did not commit himself to certain persons, for He knew what was in them; that is, He did not trust or exercise faith in them. The word rendered *commit* here, is the same as that rendered *faith*. Peter says, "Commit the keeping of your souls to Him in well doing as to a faithful Creator" (1 Peter 4:19). When the mind apprehends the true meaning of the characteristics and relations of Christ to the world, this is often mistaken for faith. But the devil may have as good a faith as that. This is a mere perception of truth by the intellect, and is, *as a condition*, indispensable to faith, but it is no more faith itself than an act of the intellect is an act of the will.

Some represent humility as having a sense of guilt and unworthiness. Now, by a natural necessity, if this is humility, then Satan is doubtless humble, and so is every convicted sinner. But *humility is a willingness to be known and esteemed according to your true character*. These illustrations show how prevalent these dangerous mistakes are respecting the attributes of Christian character.

There is no such thing as a Christian faith that is not exercised. People often talk as though they had some true faith, although they are conscious of exercising no faith. They say they have a good enough religion, but it is not in operation just now. Now this is a radical mistake.

How many are living on frames and feelings, while remaining perfectly selfish. Many are satisfied with no preaching except what fans into existence certain happy emotions. These are a kind of religious epicures. Whenever we preach so as to lay bare the roots of selfishness and detect its secret workings, they say they are not fed. They say this is not "the gospel". "Let us have the gospel," they cry. But what do they mean by "the gospel"? Why, they simply want to hear what will create and fan their emotions into a flame. And those who most need to be searched are often most unwilling to endure the probing of sound preaching. They make their religion to consist in emotions, and if these are taken away what have they left? Hence, they cling to their emotions with a death grasp. Now, let me say that these emotions have not one particle of Christianity in them, and those who want simply that class of truths which fan their feelings into existence are mere religious epicures, and their view of the gospel is sheer antinomianism. If the world were full of such religion it

Nature of True Virtue

would be none the better for it.

True Christian faith is the cause of happiness, but it is not identical with it. Happiness is a state of the sensibility, and of course involuntary. *Christianity is benevolence and powerful action.*

People may work without benevolence, but they cannot be benevolent without works. Many persons wake up occasionally, and bluster about, get up protracted meetings, and make mighty efforts to work themselves into a right state of feeling by dint of mere friction. But they never get a right spirit this way, and their working is mere legality. I do not mean to condemn protracted meetings, nor special efforts to promote Christianity, but I do condemn a legal engaging in these efforts in a selfish attempt to merit favor with God. *While persons may work without benevolence, it is also certain that if they are benevolent they will work.* It is impossible that benevolence should be inactive.

All virtue consists in the ultimate intention; therefore, we can be conscious of our spiritual state. We certainly can tell what we are aiming at. Character consists in ultimate intention. We can be conscious of what our intention is. We can know our own character. Therefore, we can see what we are to inquire after in our hours of self-examination. Our inquiry should not be how we feel, but for what end we live—*what is the aim of our life, what is our ultimate intention.*

How vain is religion without love! Those who have such a religion are continually lashed up by conscience to the performance of duty. Conscience stands like a task-master, scourge in hand, points to the duty, and says it must not be omitted. The heart shrinks back from its performance, but still it must be done or worse evil endured. The hesitating soul drags itself up by resolution to fulfill the letter of the requirement, while there is no acquiescence in its spirit, and thus a miserable slavery is substituted for the cheerful obedience of the heart.

I must close by saying *benevolence naturally fills the mind with peace and joy*. God made the human mind to exercise benevolence, and whenever it is benevolent it is in harmony with itself, with God, and with the universe. *Benevolence wills just as God wills; therefore, it naturally and cheerfully acts out His will.* This is its choice. It is like some heavenly instrument whose chords are touched by some angelic hand which makes music for the ear of God.

But on the contrary, a selfish person is necessarily, from the very nature of mind, a wretched man. His reason and conscience continually affirm his obligations to God and His universe, to the world and the Church. But he never wills in accordance with it, and thus a continual warfare is kept up within him. His mind is like an instrument untuned and harsh. Instead of harmony, it renders only discord, and makes music only fit to mingle with the wailing of the damned.***

---

* Charles G. Finney, "Prove All Things" on 1 Thessalonians 5:21, *The Oberlin Evangelist,* January 4, 1843, *Principles of Holiness,* 54-62.

** This was the experience reported of Benjamin Franklin according to his autobiography: *Benjamin Franklin, His Autobiography,* in *The Harvard Classics* (New York: P. F. Collier & Son, 1909), Volume I, pp. 101-104.

*** Charles G. Finney, *The Oberlin Evangelist,* January 18, 1843, *Principles of Holiness,* 63-75. For Review: Answer the Study Questions on page 228, Cowles page 242.

8

Love is the Whole of Religion
1837

Love worketh no ill to his neighbour: therefore love is the fulfilling of the law. —Romans 13:10—KJV

Love does no harm to its neighbor. Therefore love is the fulfillment of the law. —Romans 13:10—NIV

From this text, I will make some remarks on the nature of love, show that love is the whole of true Christianity, show some things that are not essential to perfect love, show some things that are essential to perfect love, and show some of the effects of perfect love.

Remarks on the nature of love.

So far as religion is concerned, the two principal forms under which love may exist are benevolence and complacency. Benevolence is an affection of the mind or an act of the will. Benevolence is willing good, or a desire to promote the happiness of its object. Complacency is esteem or approbation of the character of its object. Benevolence should be exercised towards all beings irrespective of their moral character. Complacency is due only toward good and holy beings.

Love may exist as an affection or as an emotion. When love is an affection, it is voluntary or consists in the act of the will. When love is an emotion, it is involuntary. What we call feelings or emotions are involuntary. They are not directly dependent on the will or controlled by a direct act of will. Mostly, love is virtuous when love is in the form of an affection. On the other hand, the happiness of love is mostly when it is in the form of an emotion. If the affection of love is very strong, it produces a high degree of happiness; however, the emotion of holy love is happiness itself.

I said that the emotion of love is involuntary. I do not mean that the will or choice has nothing to do with the emotion of love, but that the emotion of love is not the result of a mere or direct act of the will. No one can exercise the emotion of love by merely willing it. The emotion of love may often exist in spite of the will. Individuals often feel emotions rising in their minds which they know to be improper, and they try by direct efforts of will to banish them from their minds. Finding that impossible, they therefore conclude that they have no control over these emotions. But the emotions may always be controlled by the will in an indirect way. The mind can bring up any class of emotions it chooses by directing the attention sufficiently to the proper object. These emotions will be certain to rise in proportion as the attention is fixed, provided the will is right in regard to the object of attention. Regarding those emotions which are improper or disagreeable, the mind may be rid of them by turning the attention entirely away from the object and not allowing the thoughts to dwell on that object.

Ordinarily, the emotions of love towards God are experienced when we exercise love towards Him in the form of affection. But this is not always the case. We may exercise good will towards any object, and yet at times feel no sensible emotions of love. It is not certain that even the Lord Jesus Christ exercised love towards God *in the form of emotion* at all times. As far as our understanding of the nature of the mind goes, we know that a person may exercise affection and be guided and governed by it constantly in all his actions without any felt emotion of love towards its object at the time. For example, a husband and father may be engaged in laboring for the benefit of his family. His very life is controlled by affection for them, while his thoughts are not so engaged upon them as to make him feel any sensible emotions of love to them at the time. The things about which he is engaged may take up his mind so much that he has scarcely a thought of them; therefore, he may have no felt emotion towards them, and yet he is all the time guided and governed by affection for his family. Observe, I use the term *affection* in the sense of President Jonathan Edwards as explained by him in his celebrated *Treatise on the Will*. In his treatise, an affection is an act of the will or a volition.*

Love to our neighbor naturally implies the existence of love to God, and love to God naturally implies love to our neighbor. The same is declared in the eighth verse, "Owe no man any thing, but to love one another: for he that loveth another hath fulfilled the law. For this, Thou shalt not commit adultery, Thou shalt not kill, Thou shalt not steal, Thou shalt not bear false witness, Thou shalt not covet; and if there be any other commandment, it is briefly comprehended in this saying, namely, Thou shalt love thy neighbor as thyself." Here it is taken for granted that love to our neighbor implies the existence of love to God; otherwise, it could not be said that "he that loveth another hath fulfilled the law." The Apostle James recognizes the same principle when he says, "If ye fulfill the royal law according to the scripture, Thou shalt love thy neighbor as thyself, ye do well" (James 2:8). Here love to our neighbor is spoken of as constituting obedience to the whole law. Benevolence, that is, *good will to our neighbor*, naturally implies love to God. It is love to the happiness of being. So the love of complacency towards holy beings naturally implies love to God, as a Being of infinite holiness.

Love is the whole of true Christianity.

In other words, all that God requires of us consists in love in various modifications and results. Love is the sum total of all. The first proof I offer is that this sentiment is taught in the scripture text and in many other passages of scripture.

Principles of Joy in the Holy Spirit — Finney's Lessons on Romans

The scriptures fully teach that love is the sum total of all the requirements of both the law and the gospel. Our Savior declares that the great command, "Thou shalt love the Lord thy God with all thy heart, soul, mind and strength, and thy neighbor as thyself," is the sum total of all the law and the prophets, or implies and includes all that the whole scriptures, the law and the gospel require (Matthew 22:37-40).

God is love, and to love is to be like God, and to be perfect in love is to be perfect as God is perfect. All of God's moral attributes consist in love acting under certain circumstances and for certain ends. God's justice in punishing the wicked and His anger at sin and the like are only exercises of His love to the general happiness of His kingdom. So it is in us. All that is good in us is some modification of love. Hatred of sin is only love to virtue acting itself out in opposing whatever is opposed to virtue. True faith implies and includes love, and faith which has no love in it, or that does not work by love, is no part of Christianity. The faith that belongs to the Christian religion is an affectionate confidence in God. There is a kind of faith in God which has no love in it. The devil has that kind of faith. The convicted sinner has that kind of faith. But there is no Christian religion in it. Faith might rise even to the faith of miracles, and yet if there is no love in it, it amounts to nothing. In the thirteenth chapter of 1 Corinthians, Paul writes, "Though I have the gift of prophecy, and understand all mysteries, and all knowledge; and though I have all faith, so that I could remove mountains, and have not charity, I am nothing." Just so with repentance, the repentance that does not include love is not "repentance towards God." True repentance implies obedience to the law of love and consequently opposition to sin.

Some things that are not essential to perfect love.

The highest degree of emotion is not essential to perfect love. Obviously, the Lord Jesus Christ seldom had the highest degree of emotion of love; yet, He always had perfect love. Generally, He demonstrated very little emotion or excitement. Excitement is always proportioned to the strength of the emotions as it consists in them. In general, the Savior seemed remarkably calm. Sometimes His indignation was strong or His grief for the hardness of people's hearts; and sometimes, we read that He rejoiced in spirit. But He was commonly calm, and He manifested no high degree of emotion. Plainly, it is not essential to perfect love that the emotion of love should exist in a high degree.

Perfect love does not exclude the idea of an increase in love or a growth in grace. I suppose that the growth of the mind in knowledge to all eternity naturally implies growth in love to all eternity. In His human nature, the Lord Jesus Christ grew in stature and in favor with God and man. Without a doubt, as a child He grew in knowledge, and as He grew in knowledge, He grew in love towards God as well as in favor with God. His love was perfect when He was a child, but it was greater when He became an adult. As a human being, Jesus probably always continued to increase in love to God as long as He lived in this world. From the nature of mind, we see that it may be so with all the saints in glory; their love will increase to all eternity, and yet always be a perfect love.

It is not essential to perfect love that love should always be exercised towards all individuals alike. We cannot think of all individuals at once. You cannot even think of every individual of your acquaintance at once. The degree of love towards an individual depends on the fact that the individual is present to the thoughts.

It is not essential to perfect love that there should be the same degree of the spirit of prayer for every individual or for the same individual at all times. The spirit of prayer is not always essential to pure and perfect love. The saints in heaven have pure and perfect love for all beings, yet we know not that they have the spirit of prayer for any. You may love any individual with a very strong degree of love, and yet not have the spirit of prayer for that individual. That is, the Spirit of God may not lead you to pray for the salvation of that individual. You do not pray for the wicked in hell. The spirit of prayer depends on the influences of the Holy Spirit leading the mind to pray for things agreeable to the will of God. You cannot pray in the Spirit with the same degree of fervor and faith for all humanity. Jesus Christ said expressly that He did not pray for all the world, "I pray not for the world" (John 17:9). In this, there has been a great mistake in regard to the spirit of prayer. Some suppose that Christians have not done all their duty if they have not prayed in faith for every individual as long as there is a sinner on earth. If this were true, then Jesus Christ never did all His duty, for He never did this. God has never told us that He will save every person, and He has never given us any reason to believe He will do so. How then can we pray in faith for the salvation of all? On what scripture truth has that belief that we must pray for the salvation of all rest?

Perfect love is not inconsistent with those feelings of languor or constitutional debility which are the necessary consequence of exhaustion or ill health. We are so constituted that excitement naturally and necessarily exhausts our powers. But love may be perfect, notwithstanding. Though one may feel more like lying down and sleeping, than he does like praying, yet his love may be perfect. The Lord Jesus Christ often felt this weariness and exhaustion, when the spirit was still willing, but the flesh was weak.

Some things that are essential to perfect love.

Perfect implies that there is nothing in the mind inconsistent with love. A perfect love excludes hatred, malice, wrath, envy, or any other malignant emotions that are inconsistent with pure and perfect love. Perfect implies that there is nothing in the life inconsistent with love. All the actions, words, and thoughts are continually under the entire and perfect control of love.

Essential to perfect love is loving God supremely. The love to God is completely supreme, and so entirely above all other objects, that in comparison with God nothing else is loved. A love for God that is disinterested is a perfect love. The characteristic of a disinterested love for God is this: God is loved for Who He is and not because of His relation to us. God is loved for the excellence of His character.

A perfect love includes equal love to our neighbors. Our neighbors interests and happiness should be regarded by us as of equal value with our own interests and happiness, and the interests of our neighbor are to be treated accordingly by us.

Love is the Whole of Religion

Some of the effects of perfect love.

One effect of perfect love to God and others will certainly be delight in self-denial for the sake of promoting the interests of God's kingdom and the salvation of sinners. Consider affectionate parents; see how they delight in self-denial for the sake of promoting the happiness of their children. Consider a father; see how he gives himself up to exhausting labor, day by day and year to year through the whole of a long life, rising early, and eating the bread of carefulness continually, to promote the welfare of his family. And he counts all this self-denial and toil not a grief or a burden, but a delight, because of the love he bears to his family. Consider a mother; she wishes to educate her son at college. And now, instead of finding it painful it is a joy to her to sit up late and labor incessantly to help him. That is because she really loves her son. Such parents rejoice more in conferring gifts on their children than they would enjoy the same things themselves. What parent does not enjoy a piece of fruit more in giving it to his little child, than in eating it himself? The Lord Jesus Christ enjoyed more solid satisfaction in working out the salvation of sinners than any of His saints can ever enjoy in receiving favors at His hands. Christ testified that "It is more blessed to give than to receive" (Acts 20:35). This was the joy set before Him for which He "endured the cross, despising the shame" (Hebrews 12:2). His love was so great for us that it constrained Him to undertake this work and sustained Him triumphantly through it. The Apostle Paul did not count it a grief and a hardship to be hunted from place to place, imprisoned, scourged, stoned, and counted the offscouring of all things for the sake of spreading the gospel and saving souls (1 Corinthians 4:13). It was his joy. The love of Christ so constrained Paul that he had such a desire to do good, that it was his highest delight to lay himself on that altar as a sacrifice to the cause. Other individuals have had the same mind with the apostle. Some have said that they would be willing to live a thousand years, or to the end of time, if they could be employed in doing good, in promoting the kingdom of God, in saving the souls of sinners, and be willing to forego even sleep and food to benefit the objects they so greatly love.

Principles of Joy in the Holy Spirit — Finney's Lessons on Romans

Perfect love to God delivers a person from the power of legal motives. Perfect love leads a person to obey God, not because he fears the wrath of God or hopes to be rewarded for doing this or that, but because he loves God and loves to do the will of God. There are two extremes on this subject. One class of thinkers make virtue to consist in doing right, simply because it is right, without any reference to the will of God or any influence from love to God. Another class of thinkers make virtue to consist in acting from love to the employment, but without reference to God's authority as a Ruler and Law-giver. Both of these classes of thinkers are in error. To do a thing simply because he thinks it right, and not out of love to God, is not virtue. Neither is it virtue to do a thing because he loves to do it with no regard to God's will. A woman might do certain things because she knew it would please her husband, but if she did the same thing merely because she loved to do it, and with no regard to her husband, it would be no virtue as it respects her husband. If a person loves God, as soon as he knows what is God's will, he will do it because it is God's will. Perfect love will lead to universal obedience, to do God's will in all things, because it is the will of God.

The individual who exercises perfect love will be dead to the world. I mean by this that he will be cut loose from the influence of worldly considerations. Perfect love will so annihilate selfishness that he will have no will but the will of God, and no interest but God's glory. He will not be influenced by public sentiment or what this and that person will say or think. Consider a woman and what she will do from natural affection to her husband. She is willing to cut loose from all her friends as much as if she was dead to them. She will not pay the least regard to what they say, and leave all the riches, honors, and delights they can offer to join the individual whom she loves, and to live with him in poverty, in disgrace, and in exile. Her affection is so great that she does it joyfully, and she is ready to go with him from a palace to any cottage or cave in earth and be perfectly happy. And all that her friends can say against the man of her affection has not the least influence on her mind except to make her cling the more closely to him. This one ALL-ABSORBING affection has actually killed all the influences that used to act on her. To attempt to influence her by such things is in vain. There is only one avenue of approach to her mind; only one class of motives move her, and that is through the object of her affection.

So far as the philosophy of mind is concerned, the perfect love of God operates in the same way. The mind that is filled with perfect love cannot be diverted from God, while love continues in exercise. Take away his worldly possessions, his friends, his good name, his children, send him to prison, beat him with stripes, bind him to the stake, fill his flesh full of pine knots and set them on fire; and then leave him his God and he is happy. His strong affection can make him insensible to all things but God. He is as if he were dead to all the world but God. Cases have been known of martyrs who, while their bodies were frying at the stake, were so perfectly happy in God as to lose the sense of pain. Put such a one in hell, in the lake of fire and brimstone, and as long as he enjoys God, and the love of God fills his soul, he is happy.

Who has not witnessed or heard of cases of affection, approaching in degree to what I have described, where a person is in fact dead to all other things and lives only for the loved object. How often do you see fond parents who live for an only child, and when that child dies they wish themselves dead. Sometimes a husband and wife have such an absorbing affection for each other that they live for nothing else; and if the husband dies, the wife pines away and dies also. The soul-absorbing object for which she lived is gone, and why should she live any longer? So, when an individual is filled with the perfect love of God, he wishes to live only to love and serve God. He is dead to the world, dead to his own reputation, and has no desire to live for any other reason, here or in heaven, or anywhere else in the universe, except to glorify God. He is willing to live, here or anywhere else, and suffer and labor a thousand years, or to all eternity, if it will glorify God.

I recollect hearing a friend often say, "I don't know that I have one thought of living a single moment for any other purpose than to glorify God, any more than I should think of leaping right into hell." This was said soberly and deliberately, and the whole life of that individual corresponded with the declaration. He was intelligent, sober-minded, and honest, and I have no doubt expressed what had been the fullest conviction of his mind for years. What was this but perfect love? What more does any angel in heaven do than this? The angel's love may be greater in degree, because his strength is greater. But the highest angel could not love more perfectly than to be able to say in sincerity, "I should as soon think of leaping into hell, as of living one moment for any other object but to glorify God." What could Jesus Christ himself say more than that?

It is hardly necessary to say that perfect joy and peace are the natural results of perfect love. But I wish to turn your attention here to what the apostle says in the thirteenth chapter of 1 Corinthians, speaking of charity or love. You will observe that the word here translated *charity* is the same that is in other places rendered *love*. In the Bible, *charity means love*. "Though I speak with the tongues of men and of angels, and have not charity, I am become as sounding brass, or a tinkling cymbal. And though I have the gift of prophecy, and understand all mysteries, and all knowledge; and though I have all faith, so that I could remove mountains, and have not charity, I am nothing." He might have even the faith of miracles, so strong that he could move mountains from their everlasting foundations, and yet have no love. "And though I bestow all my goods to feed the poor, and though I give my body to be burned, and have not charity, it profiteth me nothing." You see how far he supposes a person may go without love! "Charity suffereth long." *Long-suffering is meekness under opposition or injury.* This is one of the effects of love, to bear great provocations and not retaliate or revile again. Love "is kind," or affectionate in all relationships with others, never harsh or rude, or needlessly giving pain to any. Love "envieth not," never dislikes others because they are more thought of or noticed, more honored or useful, or make greater attainments in knowledge, happiness or piety. "Is not puffed up" with pride, but always humble and modest. "Doth not behave itself unseemly," but naturally begets a pleasant and courteous deportment towards all. However unacquainted an individual may be with the ways of society, if he is actuated by perfect love, he always appears well; it is natural for him to be kind, gentle, and courteous. "Seeketh not her own," or has no selfishness. "Is not easily provoked," this is always the effect of love. Consider a mother; see how long she bears with her children, because she loves them. If you see an individual that is testy, or crusty, easily flying into a passion when anything goes wrong—he is by no means perfect in love, if he has any love. To be easily provoked is always a sign of pride. If a person is full of love, it is impossible to make him exercise sinful anger while love continues. He exercises such indignation as God exercises, and as holy angels feel, at what is base and wrong, but he will not be provoked by it. Love "Thinketh no evil." Show me someone who is always suspicious of the motives of others; who is always putting the worst construction on the words and actions of others; he has the devil in him, not the Holy Spirit. He has that in his own mind which makes him think evil of others. If an individual is honest and simple-hearted himself, he will be the last to think evil of others. He will not be always smelling heresy or mischief in others. On the contrary, such persons are often liable to be imposed on by designing men, not from any lack of good sense, but from the effect of love. They do not suspect evil where the exterior appears fair, nor without the strongest proof.

Love "rejoiceth not in iniquity, but rejoiceth in the truth." See a person who exults at his neighbor's fall, or cries out, "I told you so;" and I tell you, that man is far enough from being perfect in love. "Beareth all things," all provocations and injuries, without revenge. "Believeth all things," instead of being hard to be convinced of what is in favor of others, is always ready to believe good wherever there is the least evidence of it. "Hopeth all things;" even where there is reason to suspect evil, as long as there is room for hope, by putting the best construction upon the thing which it will bear. Where you see an individual that has not this spirit, rest assured, he is by no means perfect in love. Nay, he has no love at all.

I might pursue this course of thought further, but have no time. "Love worketh no ill to his neighbor." Mark that, NO ILL! Perfect love never overreaches, nor defrauds, nor oppresses, nor does any ill to a neighbor. Would a man under the influence of perfect love sell his neighbor rum? Never! Would a man who perfectly loved God with all his heart hold his neighbor as a slave? "Love worketh no ill to his neighbor!" Slavery denies a person the wages that they have earned, and perhaps sells him, and tears him away from his family, deprives him of the Bible, and endeavors as far as possible to make him an animal. There cannot be greater falsehood and hypocrisy than for a man who will do that to pretend that he loves God! Now that light is shed upon this subject, and the attention of people turned upon it. Will a man hate his own flesh? How can he love God while he hates or injures his neighbor?

Perfect love uniformly shows itself in great efforts for the sanctification of the church and the salvation of souls. Where a person is negligent or deficient in either of these, he is by no means perfect in love, whatever may be his pretensions.

REMARKS

When you understand the meaning of true Christian love, you can see that this is true: "If any man among you seem to be religious, and bridleth not his tongue, but deceiveth his own heart, this man's religion is vain" (James 1:26). A person who professes to be a Christian, and who thinks he loves his neighbor as himself, and who allows himself to speak against his neighbor with an unbridled tongue to injure his neighbor deceives himself. Strange love!

There may be much light or truth in a mind concerning the Christian religion, but without love. You often see individuals who understand a great deal intellectually about Christianity; they can spread it out before others, while it is plain that they are not actuated by the spirit of love. They have not the law of kindness on their lips. Those individuals who have much religious knowledge and zeal, but without love, are most unlovely and dangerous persons. They are always censorious, proud, heady, high-minded. They may make a strong impression, but do not produce true Christian faith. They zealously affect you, but not well!

The drift of a person's zeal will determine the character of his religion. It will show whether the light in his mind is accompanied with love. If it is, his zeal will not be sectarian in its character. A person who is full of jealously towards all those who do not belong to his sect or party is far from perfect love.

True love is never denunciatory or harsh. If it has occasion to speak of the faults of others, it does it in kindness and with sorrow. Perfect love cannot speak in a rough or abusive manner, either to or of others. It will not lay great stress on the mere circumstantial aspects of Christianity, nor be sticklish for particular measures or forms in the Church. Many

Love is the Whole of Religion

will contend fiercely either for or against certain things, as for or against new measures; but if they were full of love they would not do it. The zeal that is governed by perfect love will not spend itself in contending for or against any minor forms of Christian practices, nor attack minor errors and evils. Love leads to laying stress on the fundamental teachings in the Bible and Christian faith. Christian zeal cleaves to warm-hearted Christians, no matter of what denomination they may be, and loves them and delights to associate with them.

The zeal of Christian love is never disputatious or full of controversy. Find a person who loves to attend ecclesiastical meetings and enter into all the janglings of the day, that person is not full of love. To a mind filled with holy love, it is exceedingly painful to go to such meetings and see ministers dividing into parties and maneuvering and caucusing and pettifogging and striving for the mastery. Find an individual who loves controversy in the newspapers, he is not full of love. If he were full of love, he would rather be abused and reviled and slandered, either in person or by the papers, than turn aside to defend himself or to reply. He would never return railing for railing, but contrariwise return blessing for railing. And as much as possible, he would live peaceably with all people.

Much of what people call *Christianity* has no love! How much of what passes for works of faith is really only motivated by outward causes and influences instead of the inward power of love. Christianity ought to be better understood than it is! Unless love is the mainspring, no matter what the outward action may be, whether praying, praising, giving, or anything else, there is no Christian faith in it. Much of what causes excitement and passes for Christianity has no love. How much zeal has no Christian faith and love in it? Consider a person who is always full of bitter zeal; if you reprove him for it, he immediately makes an excuse and refers you to the example of Paul, when Paul said to Elymas, "Thou child of the devil" (Acts 13:10). If he was under the influence of perfect love, he would see that his circumstances are so different from those of the Apostle Paul, who was filled with the Holy Spirit when he spoke, that he cannot justify the exercise of such a bitter spirit.

Religious excitements that do not consist in the spirit of love are not revivals of religion. Perhaps the church may be much excited, and bustle about with a great show of zeal, and boisterous noise, but no tenderness of spirit. Perhaps those who go about may show a spirit of insolence, and rudeness, and pick a quarrel with every family they visit. I once knew a young man who acknowledged that he aimed at making people angry, and the reason he assigned was, that it often brought them under conviction, and so issued in conversion. And so it might if he should go in and utter horrid blasphemies in their presence, until they were frightened into a consideration of their own character. But who would defend such a conduct on the ground that such was now and then the result? And if this is the character of the excitement, it may be a revival of wrath and malice and all uncharitableness, but it is not a revival of practicing true Christian faith and love. I do not mean to say that when some or many are "filled with wrath," it is certain evidence that there is no revival of the Christian faith. But when a religious excitement has this prevailing character, it is not a true revival. Some in the revival may have the spirit of love, but certainly those who are filled with a bitter disputatious zeal are not truly practicing Christianity. Christian faith and practice may be revived in some individuals; but in the main in such cases, it is a revival of irreligion.

When people profess to be converted, if love is not the ruling feature in their character, they are not truly converted. However well they may appear in other respects, no matter how clear their views, or how deep their feelings, if they have not the spirit of love to God and love to neighbor, they are deceived. Let no such converts be trusted.

Do you see what the world will be like, when everyone is actuated by a spirit of love. In the Bible, we learn that the time will come when there shall be nothing to hurt or destroy, and when the Spirit of love will universally prevail. What a change in society! What a change in all the methods of doing business, and in all relationships, when each shall love his neighbor as himself and seek the good of others as his own! If any of the saints who now live were to revisit the earth after that change, they would not know the world in which they lived. Everything will be so changed that they will exclaim, "Is it possible that this is the earth; the same earth that used to be so full of jangling and oppression and fraud?"

The Lord Jesus Christ is determined to bring humanity under the influence of love. Is it not a worthy object? He came to destroy the works of the devil. And this is the way to do it. Suppose the world was full of such men as Jesus Christ was in His human nature. Compare it with what it is now. Would not such a change be worthy of the Son of God? What a glorious goal, to fill the earth with love!

Now, it is easy to see what makes heaven. It is love, perfect love. And it is easy to see what makes heaven begun on earth, in those who are full of love. How sweet their temper, what delightful companions, how blessed to live near them, to associate with them, so full of candor, so kind, so gentle, so careful to avoid offence, so divinely amiable in all things!

Is perfect love to be attained by human beings? Can we love God, here in this world, with all the heart, and soul, and strength, and mind? It is our privilege and duty to have the Spirit of Christ. Shall we exhibit the spirit of the devil? Beloved, let our hearts be set on perfect love; let us give God no rest until we feel our hearts full of love, until all our thoughts and all our lives are full of love to God and love to others. O, when will the church come up to this ground? Only let the church be full of love, and she will be fair as the moon, clear as the sun, and terrible to all wickedness, in high places and low places, as an army with banners.**

---

* see Jonathan Edwards, *Freedom of the Will*, edited by Paul Ramsey, New Haven and London: Yale University Press, 1957. Original edition published in 1754.

** Charles G. Finney, *Lectures to Professing Christians,* (1878) 419-436, *Principles of Victory*, 172-182. For Review: Answer the Study Questions on page 229, Cowles page 242.

The Gospels on Joy

The kingdom of heaven is like treasure hidden in a field. When a man found it, he hid it again, and then in his joy went and sold all he had and bought that field. —Matthew 13:44

Her neighbors and relatives heard that the Lord had shown Elizabeth great mercy, and they shared her joy. —Luke 1:58

But the angel said to the shepherds, "Do not be afraid. I bring you good news that will cause great joy for all the people." —Luke 2:10

Blessed are you when people hate you, when they exclude you and insult you and reject your name as evil, because of the Son of Man. Rejoice in that day and leap for joy, because great is your reward in heaven. For that is how their ancestors treated the prophets. —Luke 6:22-23

Whoever listens to you listens to me; whoever rejects you rejects me; but whoever rejects me rejects him who sent me. The seventy-two returned with joy and said, "Lord, even the demons submit to us in your name." —Luke 10:16-17

At that time Jesus, full of joy through the Holy Spirit, said, "I praise you, Father, Lord of heaven and earth, because you have hidden these things from the wise and learned, and revealed them to little children. Yes, Father, for this is what you were pleased to do." —Luke 10:21

And while they still did not believe it because of joy and amazement, Jesus asked them, "Do you have anything here to eat?" —Luke 24:41

Then they worshiped him and returned to Jerusalem with great joy — Luke 24:52

9

Love Works No Ill
1841

Love worketh no ill to his neighbour: therefore love is the fulfilling of the law.—Romans 13:10—KJV

Love does no harm to its neighbor. Therefore love is the fulfillment of the law.—Romans 13:10—NIV

In discussing this subject, I shall show the love that does not constitute Christian faith and then the kind of love that does constitute Christian faith. Then, I will consider who we should regard as our neighbor and why love works no ill to our neighbor.

The love that does not constitute Christian faith.

The love that flows from true Christian faith is not natural affection or only the type of love of that we have for family and relatives. This needs no comment. The absence of natural affection, as mentioned in the Bible, is evidence of a high degree of depravity; but its exercise is not holiness.

True Christian love is not the love that exists between a man and a woman. This type of love is only a modification of natural affection.

Christian love is not complacency. Complacency is an emotion of delight in its object. It is an involuntary state of mind and exists naturally and often necessarily when an object calculated to excite emotions of complacency is present to the mind. Being an involuntary state of mind, it often has no moral character at all, and when any degree of moral character is to be ascribed to complacency, it is because the emotions are indirectly under the influence of the will. Emotions are consequent upon thoughts, and arise spontaneously in the mind when the attention is directed to the deep consideration of any subject. And as the will controls the attention, it indirectly controls the emotions. And emotions of complacency or displacency have moral character only as they are indirectly produced by the action of the will. Complacency may respect a great many different objects:

Complacency may respect personal beauty. We are so constituted that the presence of beautiful objects naturally excites emotions of complacency or delight in its object. The presence of a beautiful human being naturally and certainly excites emotions of delight, where no feeling of prejudice, envy, or other selfish consideration begets an opposite state of emotion.

Complacency may respect other physical accomplishments; such as, an elegant form, dignified deportment, elegant manners, good breeding, and multitudes of similar things. In such things we naturally take delight, and emotions of complacency naturally and certainly exist in the mind under the consideration of such objects, unless some selfish or envious reason prevents.

Complacency may respect intellectual endowments, a towering intellect, a lofty imagination, great learning, great eloquence, and innumerable similar things may naturally excite emotions of complacency in their objects.

Complacency may respect benefits received or expected. We naturally feel emotions of complacency in those who befriend us or grant us great favors; therefore, people may exercise very strong emotions of love to God on account of favors received or expected from Him without one particle of true Christian faith, but just as naturally as similar emotions of complacency might be exercised towards any other benefactor without reference to any other feature of his character than that which is made by the bestowment of the particular favors which excite gratitude and complacency.

Complacency may respect and be founded in a similarity of views and intentions. Everyone knows it to be true that he naturally feels complacency in those whose views, aims, and objects of pursuit correspond with his own, unless it be in cases where a similarity of aims produce a clashing of interests, as is sometimes the case with competitors in business. We see men and women of the same political creed having complacency in each other. We often see the same among professing Christians who are members of the same sect; they exercise a strong affection for or complacency in each other solely on account of the fact of a similarity of views and prejudices, but in this there is not a particle of true piety.

Complacency may be a mere reciprocation, a mere loving of those who love us and because they love us, but there is no piety in this. The Savior says, "If ye love those that love you, what thank have ye? Do not even sinners love those that love them?" (Luke 6:32).

Complacency may respect character, whether good or bad. We often see individuals exercising a high degree of complacency in each other, because they are associated in vice. On the other hand, we often see persons exercising a high degree of complacency in each other on account of their virtues. People are so constituted that they never can conscientiously approve of a wicked character; but on the contrary, they must always approve of right character. And all moral beings in the absence of selfish reasons for a contrary feeling will naturally experience emotions of delight in right character, when it is the subject of contemplation. But emotions of love or delight in right character do not constitute piety. Nor are they any certain evidence of piety. There is not a moral agent in the universe who knows what the character of God is who does not approve it. Nor one person who may not and perhaps does not, when viewing the character of God in the abstract, experience strong emotions of delight in the moral beauty of His character upon the same principles that he would feel emotions of delight in personal beauty.

Complacency may respect the natural attributes of a being. Thus, the wickedest of men may experience the strongest emotions of admiration and delight in view of the natural attributes of God as manifested in the works of creation without a particle of that love to God that constitutes true religion.

True Christian love is not a fondness for a particular person. The love that constitutes the essence of true Christianity does not respect moral character at all. Nor is it complacency in particular individuals, or a feeling of love of any kind for particular individuals to the neglect of others. God's holiness consists in universal benevolence to all beings, irrespective of their moral character; and for this reason, it led Him to give His only begotten Son to die for His enemies (see Romans 5:10).

True Christian love is not an emotion or mere feeling of any kind. It is not a mere experience or something in which we seem to ourselves to be passive, as we do in the exercise of emotions. A false philosophy has confounded emotions with true Christian faith under the name of religious affections. And it is astonishing and alarming to witness the extent to which this mistake and delusion is entertained by humanity. Hence, they speak of experiencing religion, and they speak of religion as something in which they are passive, something springing up in their own minds involuntarily. They speak of experiencing such and such states of mind, and regard Christianity as something to be experienced, rather than as something to be done. Indeed, *the mistake seems to be almost universal, that the Christian religion belongs to the emotions or feelings rather than to the acts of the will.* Hence, complacency in God and in Christians, because they are holy, is generally regarded, not only as evidence of piety, but as constituting the very essence of piety itself. And multitudes of those who profess to be Christians suppose themselves to be highly spiritual, simply because they are in the exercise of lively emotions of gratitude for favors received, of complacency in God on account of benefits conferred, and of complacency in Christians because they are Christians. Now let me say that these emotions may be the result of a right state of the will or of the exercise of that love which constitutes true Christianity, or they may not.

They do not in any case constitute *the essence* of true Christianity, and may often exist without it. And what ungodly man, who has ever been in the habit of intense thinking upon religious subjects, cannot testify to the truth of this from his own experience. The fact is, *Christianity is something to be done, and not merely to be experienced; something in which a person is voluntarily active, and not passive. Indeed, the foundation of all true Christianity consists in voluntary action, and not in emotion.* By voluntary action I mean, of course, the acts of the voluntary power or the will.

The kind of love that constitutes true Christian faith.

The love that constitutes true Christian faith always belongs to the will; that is, it consists in acts of the will. It is actually a state of the will, in opposition to a single or a series of volitions. There is an important distinction to be made between choice and volition. Choice is the mind's election or selection of an end. Volition consists in those efforts or actions of the will which are put forth to accomplish the end chosen. A man may choose to be a merchant. In obedience to this choice, his will puts forth all those volitions that put his body and mind in motion and that are necessary to accomplish the object chosen. Choice, then, is a state of mind in opposition to those volitions that are exercised for obtaining the end chosen.

The love that constitutes true Christian faith is a fixed, permanent choice or state of the will. Understand that it is *a state, an abiding choice* or preference; and from the very laws of the mind this abiding choice has a controlling influence. If you choose to go to New York City, this choice will naturally and certainly beget those volitions, states of mind, and actions of the body that will accomplish this end, if it is within your power.

The love that constitutes true Christianity is the choice of a supreme end or object of pursuit, or a selection of the great and ultimate end of existence. It is a supreme, permanent, controlling preference or choice of the mind.

True Christian love is benevolence or good-willing; the exact opposite of selfishness. Selfishness is the supreme preference or choice of self-gratification as the grand end of life. Selfishness is choosing or willing our own gratification supremely. This is the foundation of all sin, and the carrying out of selfishness consists in those volitions, states of mind, emotions, and bodily actions that make up the history of the wicked. The love mentioned in the text and constitutes true Christianity is that state of mind demanded by the law of God. Hence, it is said in the text that "love is the fulfilling of the law." It is the mind's supreme election or choice of the universal good of being as the supreme end of existence. And it respects the good of all beings capable of doing or enjoying good. This supremely respects the being of God, as He is capable of doing and enjoying infinitely more good than all other beings. Christian love, therefore, prefers God's good, happiness, and glory to all other things in the universe. Remember, it is benevolence in God and not complacency in God that constitutes the foundation of all true Christianity. Complacency in God is virtue, when it is produced by a virtuous state of the will, but not otherwise. Complacency in the character of God is often mentioned in the Bible as constituting virtue, but always remember that emotions of complacency in God and other holy beings, when they are virtuous at all, instead of constituting the foundation and essence of virtue, are virtue only in its lowest form. I repeat it, *the foundation of all virtue is benevolence to God and to the universe*. Christian love is good willing and doing, in opposition to mere good feeling. I wish to get this idea distinctly before your minds, because there are so many mistakes upon this subject.

The love which constitutes true Christianity is disinterested love. And here again let me beg you not to misunderstand me. For oftentimes, when we speak of disinterested love, it is obvious that we are understood to mean disinterested good emotions, rather than disinterested good willing. When it is said that disinterested love consists in loving God for Who and what He really is, it often seems to be meant that we are to exercise complacency in God on account of His character, and this complacency is represented as disinterested love; but, this is a grand mistake. To love God for Who and what He is, and with that love which constitutes true Christian faith, is to love Him with the love of benevolence, to will His good, His glory, and His happiness. Now, complacency in God's character will naturally and certainly exist where there is true benevolence toward Him, and as I have already said, it may exist where there is no benevolence at all, when His character is viewed as it may be viewed, as a mere abstraction. But forever remember that the true Christian religion consists in benevolence to God and to others, and to all beings capable of loving or receiving good. This benevolence does not respect personal character, but regards the good of every moral and every sentient being whether sinful or holy in proportion to its relative value as that is apprehended by the mind. It longs for the salvation of the wicked as much as for the salvation of the righteous. This is manifestly the temper and spirit of God. This is the spirit of Christ, and this is the essence and substance of true godliness wherever it exists. It would not wantonly injure a fly nor tread upon a worm. It regards happiness as a real good. It longs for the diffusion of universal holiness among all moral agents, and of universal enjoyment among all sentient beings. God delights himself in the happiness of the little chirping birds, and bounding lambs, and leaping fishes, and all the multitudes of animal existences with which the universe is teeming. So every benevolent mind has chosen the promotion of universal good as the supreme end of life. Consequently, its volitions, thoughts, and actions are in deep harmony and sympathy with God and directed to the same end to which He directs His efforts.

Who is our neighbor?

We are to regard all moral beings as our neighbors in whatever country or in whatever world they may exist. We are to regard their interests and happiness according to their relative value. This cannot reasonably and probably will not be doubted. All sentient beings are to be regarded as our neighbors; all those connected with us in the great chain of being. And the good of mere animals is to be regarded and treated by us according to its relative value. *The beasts of the field, the fowls of the air, the fishes of the sea, everything that has life and breath; all are to be regarded as our neighbors.*

Most especially, our neighbors are those moral beings most immediately within our reach, who are the most naturally and certainly affected by our influence—those whose geographical proximity to us brings them within our immediate neighborhood in a most emphatic sense. Our families and those whose habitations are most contiguous to ours, who live in the same town, county, state, or nation, are to be regarded as especially our neighbors, but not to the neglect or annihilation of our relation to the human family and to the universe. Still, we are under special obligations to those more within our reach, whether they are human beings or mere animals. Every sentient being within our reach is to be regarded as emphatically our neighbor.

Why love works no ill to our neighbor.

Love works no ill to our neighbor because it belongs to the will and therefore naturally controls the actions of both body and mind. If love directs the thoughts, it will not think evil of a neighbor. Love consists in choice and directs the volitions; therefore, love will not allow volitions that shall work ill to its neighbor. As love controls the attention, and therefore the emotions, it will neither beget nor allow emotions or desires that work ill to its neighbor. As love controls the volitions and the outward actions, it cannot work ill to its neighbor.

Because love has no tendency to work ill to our neighbor, it respects a neighbor's rights, and aims at securing instead of trampling upon them. Love respects a neighbor's piety, and endeavors by all possible means to make him holy as a means of making him happy. Love regards his holiness and happiness as a great good, and is not reckless of the influence it exerts, either to promote or destroy a neighbor's piety. Love regards the interests and well-being of a neighbor in all respects. Love especially respects the rights, piety, and happiness of those with whom we are most nearly in contact, and who for this reason are more immediately under our influence.

Benevolence does not omit any known duty if our neighbor's interest might suffer: therefore, love does not by omission work ill to its neighbor. Love will avoid tempting our neighbor. Love will not lead our neighbor into imitating a bad example or in other ways falling into sin.

Since love consists in good-willing, or in choosing the universal good of being as the supreme end of life, it will of course beget those volitions and actions that will promote the good of all around us, and especially of those who are near and most immediately affected by our conduct. In the thirteenth chapter of First Corinthians, the Apostle Paul describes this love as the foundation and sum of all virtue; and after asserting in the strongest language that no faith or work is of any value without love, he mentions several of its prominent characteristics with the manifest design of distinguishing that which constitutes true Christianity from everything else. Our translation calls it *charity*. The original word is the same as that which is rendered love in this text. The same word is uniformly used in the original for that state of mind that constitutes the true Christian religion, or the love required by the law of God. This love, Paul says, is "patient and long suffering." And who does not know that we are naturally very patient and long suffering toward those whose happiness is very dear to us, and toward whom we feel truly benevolent. Mere complacency is fitful and evanescent, and depends so much upon the particular exhibition made to our mind at the time as to be transitory from its very nature. See the complacency that parents have in their children. When they are sweet and smiling and lovely, the parent is exceedingly delighted with them. But if they become ill-natured and hateful, here another exhibition is made to the mind, which instead of exciting complacency begets impatience and fretfulness. Just so a mere complacency in God will often be exceedingly fitful and of short duration as the ever varying course of His providence exhibits Him to our minds as robed in smiles or clothed with frowns. But benevolence is not subject to these changes, because it has not its foundation in the moral character, in the naturally pleasing or displeasing manifestations that are made to the mind; instead, *benevolence is good-willing. Benevolence is a patient, persevering, supreme disposition to promote the good of its object.*

A second characteristic named by the Apostle is kindness. "Charity suffereth long and is kind." This is of course a characteristic of benevolence or good-will.

A third characteristic is love "envieth not." Envy is an emotion of unhappiness in view of the prosperity of others. Since the love that constitutes true Christianity consists in benevolence, it is impossible that it should coexist with envy. Benevolence cannot be disturbed and made unhappy by the prosperity of its object. Envy is, therefore, the very opposite of true Christianity and is the offspring of hell. An envious person is "of his father the devil," and the lusts of his father he will do.

A fourth characteristic of Christian love is that it "vaunteth not itself;" or, as rendered in the margin, it is not rash. It is mild and amiable, and not rough and headstrong.

A fifth characteristic of benevolence is that it "is not puffed up." It is not swelling, pompous, showy, Pharisaical, ostentatious, and proud; but exactly the reverse of all this.

A sixth characteristic is love "doth not behave itself unseemly." True politeness consists in the practice of benevolence. And when wicked people affect to be truly polite, they affect to be truly benevolent. They are, to be sure, hypocritical in this; but still, it remains a truth that true politeness manifests itself in a disposition to make everybody happy. So, one of the characteristics of true Christianity is true politeness. Love "doth not behave itself unseemly." There is a natural urbanity and courteousness that is always a characteristic of true benevolence. True Christianity does not need the polish of a dancing school, or to ape the manners of nobility, or the most refined classes of society, in order to exhibit genuine politeness. Who doubts that Jesus Christ was truly polite? His benevolence led Him to seek the comfort and happiness of all around Him. He sought both their temporal and their spiritual good. When at a feast, He chose not the chief seat for himself; instead, He gave others the preference. His benevolence exhibited itself in making as little trouble wherever He went as possible; and consequently when in the house of Martha and Mary, He manifested no disposition to have the sisters give up their time to preparing good dishes for His entertainment. Instead, He commended Mary for listening to His instructions, and reproved Martha for giving herself up to worry about His entertainment. Take any person you please, and let him be filled with the love of God, and he will naturally and certainly exhibit a lovely exterior instead of that which is unseemly. If riding in a stage coach, if in a steam boat, a railroad car, a public house, at home, or abroad in public or in the family circle, he will exhibit a disposition to accommodate, to prevent all unhappiness and all sin, and to make everybody comfortable, holy, and happy. He will not be boorish and unmannerly, rough, outrageous, and unseemly; but will exhibit that wisdom that comes down from heaven, which is "first pure, then peaceable, gentle, and easy to be entreated, full of mercy and good fruits, without partiality, and without hypocrisy" (James 3:17).

A seventh characteristic is love "seeketh not her own." Its supreme object is the promotion of the universal good and happiness of all. Of course it will not be selfish. It will manifest itself in the most assiduous endeavors to make all around as comfortable, as happy, and as holy, as possible.

An eighth characteristic is love "is not easily provoked." Of course benevolence will not easily quarrel with its object. It is not quickly impatient and ready to scold, but is extremely calm and forbearing.

A ninth characteristic is love "thinketh no evil." It not only does not meditate on any evil, but it does not surmise or suspect evil where all appearances are right. A selfish mind is always suspecting hypocrisy in others, because it is conscious of hypocrisy in itself. A hypocrite, a liar, a knave, or a dishonest man is apt of course to suspect others, because he naturally judges others by himself. But an honest, upright, benevolent mind, thinks no evil, unless there is some appearance of evil.

A tenth characteristic is love "speaks no evil." This is not especially mentioned by the Apostle in this connection, but it is a doctrine abundantly taught in the Bible. And if it were not, the very nature of true benevolence renders it certain that love speaks no evil. *Speaking evil is speaking either truth or falsehood with a selfish intention which is prejudicial to the character of anyone and when the circumstances of the case do not demand such speaking as a dictate of benevolence.* Remember, benevolence is the choice of the universal good of being. It is therefore impossible that benevolence should be guilty of evil speaking. It is tender of everyone's reputation as of the apple of its own eye, and love would as soon pluck out its own eyes as to inflict a needless wound upon the character of any one.

An eleventh characteristic is love "rejoiceth not in iniquity, but rejoiceth in the truth." Since all iniquity injures the universe, benevolence must deplore it and cannot rejoice in it. Since truth is the instrument of universal good, benevolence must of course rejoice in the truth.

The Apostle Paul goes on to say, love "beareth all things, believeth all things, hopeth all things, endureth all things." I cannot enlarge upon these particulars. He concludes by saying charity or love "never faileth;" that is, love abides. From its very nature, *love is a state of mind*, and is not fitful and evanescent like emotions. The emotions of the mind are naturally like an effervescence thrown into an excitement, and then they naturally and quickly subside. On the contrary, "love never fails." *Christian love is the supreme, deliberate choice of the mind, or abiding, permanent state of the will*; instead of that feverish excitement which people talk of experiencing, and which they falsely say is true Christianity.

REMARKS

From this subject we learn the delusion of an Antinomian religion. Vast multitudes of those who profess to be Christians suppose religion to consist in frames and feelings instead of good-willing. They can relate what they call a good experience. They can talk of their views, raptures, and peace of mind; and they manifestly suppose true Christianity consists in these experiences. Now, I have already said and wish here to repeat that as these frames and feelings consist in emotions, and are only indirectly under the power of the will. They are the very lowest forms of virtue, and doubtless may exist where there is no true Christian faith at all. They may arise solely out of a mistaken view of God's character and relations, and of our own character and relations. The Universalist doubtless exercises the love of complacency toward the God which he worships. The Antinomian feels complacency in God as he understands His character. Thus, every form of enthusiasm, fanaticism, and delusion, may be united with complacency in an imaginary god. Indeed, it is very easy to see that almost any possible or conceivable state of the emotions or mere feelings may be produced by mistaken views of things. Now, as the mere feelings or emotions of the mind depend upon the views and opinions which are entertained by the mind, very little dependence can be placed upon them, even as evidences of true piety. Much less should it be supposed that true piety consists in them. Many persons are carried away with dreams, and entertain the strangest and most absurd opinions on religious subjects; but their emotions will be found to correspond with their views, thoughts and opinions. And these emotions will sometimes be exceedingly deep and overpowering, and it matters not at all whether these opinions are true or false. Persons will feel just as deeply in a dream, in view of the most absurd and ridiculous things that a dreaming mind can imagine, as if those things were actual realities. Now it would be strange indeed if the reality and depth of these emotions should be depended upon as evidence of the reality of their objects. The solemn fact is that there is a great, very common but ruinous, mistake upon this subject in making Christianity consist in emotions, and what are very commonly termed affections, instead of consisting, as it really does, in the state and actions of the will.

It appears to me that President Jonathan Edwards committed a sad mistake upon this subject when he confounded the sensibility with the will and laid a foundation for a vast amount of delusion.

Let me be understood. *Emotions, or frames and feelings, are the certain and necessary results of a right state of the will, or of the benevolence or good-willing that constitutes true Christianity*. If the will is right, it will direct the attention of the mind to the consideration of those subjects that will naturally and necessarily beget *lively and deep emotions of gratitude, complacency, godly sorrow, and all those states of mind of which Christians speak*, and which they are so apt to conceive as constituting true Christianity. But *these constitute the happiness, rather than the virtue of the mind. They are the reward of holiness, rather than holiness itself.* To be sure, *they are virtuous as far as they are indirectly under the influence of the will*. But they are only virtuous on that account; therefore, they are virtuous in no other sense than thoughts and decisions of conscience may be virtuous. Thought is the spontaneous and necessary acting of mind when the will directs the attention to an object of thought. The decisions of conscience are the necessary decisions of reason when the attention of the mind is directed by the will to a consideration of those subjects that come under the jurisdiction of conscience. Both the thoughts and the decisions of conscience are necessary when the attention of the mind is thus employed by the will. These actions of the mind are, therefore, moral actions in the same sense that the outward or bodily actions are moral actions.

Principles of Joy in the Holy Spirit — Finney's Lessons on Romans

The muscles move at the bidding of the will. Whenever any state of mind or motion of the body is under the control of the will, there is a sense in which these actions have moral character. But separate them from the actions of the will and they have no moral character at all. Now, if the will be right, there is a sense in which the thoughts and decisions of conscience and outward actions may be virtuous; and if the will be wrong, there is a sense in which they are all vicious. Bear in mind that the praise or blameworthiness lies in the voluntary actions of the mind or in the decisions of the will; and, properly speaking, in the decisions of the will alone.

From this subject, it is easy to see that where there is true Christian faith, there must of necessity be a corresponding true Christian life. The emotions do not control the actions of body or mind. Consequently, if the Christian religion consisted in emotion, it might exist in the mind in its reality and strength without being evinced in the outward conduct. For we know that people often exercise the deepest feelings and emotions on subjects, while they refuse or neglect to act in conformity with their feelings. But the same cannot be said of the actions of the will. People always act outwardly in conformity with their volitions. Their outward actions are connected with their acts of their will by a natural necessity. Therefore, good-willing or true Christianity always manifests itself in a holy life. Inaction and supineness in the Christian religion are absurd and impossible where true Christian faith exists. Benevolence or good-willing must produce action and good action by a natural necessity. Therefore, it is absurd and ridiculous to say that a person has true Christian faith and yet is not employed in doing good where he is able to act at all. Remember, I beseech you, that the Christian religion is benevolence or good-willing and not mere feeling or emotion; and because it is good-willing, it necessarily produces good acting. The very essence of Christian faith is activity, exertion, or effort of heart and life to promote universal good. A religion of supineness is therefore not the religion of Christ. Antinomian inaction is as opposite to the true Christian religion as light is to darkness, and a person can no more act truly Christian and give himself up to inaction, ecstasy, peace, and joy than he can do anything else that involves a contradiction. Christian faith consists in the state or acts of the heart or will; and is, therefore, in its very nature, essential activity. I mean as I say. the Christian religion is activity itself. It is the mind willing the good of universal being.

Do you see the great delusion of making the Christian religion consist in a complacent love of God and Christians? I have already said that complacency is an emotion, and where the will or heart is right complacency will always be exercised towards God. *Complacency is the effect and not the essence of true Christian faith.* It appears to me that many mistake in supposing that the love of the brethren which is so largely insisted on in the Bible is complacency rather than benevolence. But a little consideration will show that the love of the brethren insisted upon by Christ and His Apostles is benevolence and not complacency. Benevolence is spoken of as the same kind of love with which Christ loved us. Hence, as Christ laid down his life for us, we should be ready to lay down our lives for the brethren. *The love of God and of Christ for the world was benevolence and not complacency. It was a love exercised to enemies, and not to those that were holy; consequently, it must have been benevolence.*

Do you see the great mistake of those who excuse themselves for their lack of love to the brethren? They make the excuse that they do not see the image of Christ in some of their brothers and sisters in the church. The love that we exercise to the image of Christ is complacency. Their excuse shows that they suppose the love required of them is complacency and not benevolence; consequently, they manifest no holiness and they suppose they have no obligation to exercise love toward those who do not bear the image of Christ as they see it. Now this is a ruinous mistake. For the love which we are required to exercise toward our brothers and sisters in the church is good-will or benevolence; therefore, it does not respect their moral character. A true Christian exercises deep and permanent affection for the brethren, whatever may be their spiritual state. There are many who profess to be Christians who seem to give themselves up to the most censorious and denunciatory speaking; they seem to think that this is proper because they are condemning backsliders or hypocrites. Now, I would humbly ask, is this benevolence? Is this love? To benevolence, complacency can be added where there is a foundation for it, or a manifestation of holy character. Complacency will render it still more certain that the person who exercises it will avoid all evil speaking. Where there is no manifestation of holy character, benevolence will naturally avoid speaking evil or "working ill to our neighbor."

You can see from this subject the delusion of those who profess to be Christian while they transact business upon selfish principles. Selfishness and benevolence are exact and eternal opposites. Not too long ago, a professional man said to me, "I have been surprised that the religion of those who have been long religious does not do more to overcome their selfishness." This is just the same thing as to express surprise that those who have long professed to be religious have no religion. The fact is, *the very beginning of Christian faith, or the new birth itself, is the overthrow of selfishness as the reigning principle of the mind.* Christian faith establishes the principle of benevolence in the mind as a permanent state of the will. Hence, the Bible teaches, "For whatsoever is born of God overcometh the world: and this is the victory that overcometh the world, even our faith. Who is he that overcometh the world, but he that believeth that Jesus is the Son of God?" (1 John 5:4-5). And, "Whosoever is born of God doth not commit sin; for his seed remaineth in him: and he cannot sin, because he is born of God" (1 John 3:9). By this I do not understand the Apostle to mean that a soul that is born of God cannot be seduced into occasional sins by the power of temptation; but that he cannot live in sin or live in a state of sin. He cannot transact his daily business upon selfish principles, which are the essence of all sin. It is therefore absurd and impossible that a benevolent or truly Christian mind should transact business upon selfish principles.

Love, or benevolence and its necessary fruits, is the whole of the Christian religion. I say necessary fruits, because the actions of the mind and body are connected with the actions of the will by a natural necessity; so, the fruits of holiness are the necessary products of a right state of the heart or will.

Where there are no fruits there is no true Christian faith. It is in vain for unfruitful souls, Antinomians, and persons who sit down in inaction, to pretend to be pious Christians. They talk in vain of their views, their experience, and their raptures. Unless the fruits of benevolence, or good-willing, are upon them; unless, like Christ, they go about doing good, when they are able to go about at all, it is a delusion and nonsense for them to suppose that they are truly religious.

We see from this subject the delusion of those individuals, churches, and ecclesiastical bodies that seem to be given up in a great measure to censoriousness and vituperation, engaged it would seem in little else than watching for the haltings and the errors of their brethren, and who seem to be abandoned to a spirit of fretfulness rather than of love or good willing. Of course, I do not accuse the whole Church of being in this state, but speak of those who really are in this state.

You see the delusion of those editors of newspapers whose columns savor of gabble rather than of the sweet benevolence of God. Look into their pages and ask, "Is this the love that works no ill to his neighbor?" Why, instead of working no ill to his neighbor, these newspapers would work the ruin of the world if people had any confidence in what they read in such periodicals. No thanks to some of the editors of the present day if their papers do not work unlimited mischief; it will only be because the readers have ceased to confide in them. Of course, I do not design this remark to be of universal application, but there are lamentable cases to attest the truth of this remark, and it will be acknowledged with sorrow by those who truly love the Lord.

We see the delusion of those whose religion consists in desiring the happiness of those who are at a distance, while it neglects the happiness of those in its immediate neighborhood. Multitudes will go to church and pray for the heathen; they will give money to send the Gospel or the Bible to the heathen; but unhappily, their prayers seem always to overlook those right around them who are more immediately and necessarily affected by their conduct. Their own household help, or clerks, or laborers, are perhaps daily rendered unhappy by their malevolence and peevishness. They are left in a great measure unprayed for, unwarned, unblessed by them. They seem to be engaged in anything but promoting the happiness of those within their reach; and yet, they suppose themselves to be truly religious. But herein is a great delusion. It is the religion of the imagination and desires. It is like the piety of someone who contemplates going on a foreign mission, who feels deeply as he says for the heathen, but never bestirs himself to save the souls of anyone at home. He can go through with his education as lazily as a drone. He can let his own classmates and perhaps his own roommate go down to hell unblessed and unwarned. He can let his own neighborhood and his own kindred sink down to death and hell around him, and yet imagine himself to feel truly benevolent and to long for the salvation of the heathen. He never promotes piety or revivals at home, and yet he works himself into the belief that he shall do it when he goes abroad. But again, I say this is the religion of the imagination, and a deep and ruinous delusion. Let such a one go on to heathen ground and be surrounded with the naked and cold realities of heathenism, and he will find at last his sad mistake. If it were not for his pride of character and fear of the loss of reputation, he would soon find his way back to Christian lands and to the repose and indolence of a contemplative life. How many there are who are in the constant neglect of the happiness of all in their immediate neighborhood, whose prayers and efforts seem always to overleap the heads of all within their reach, and light down upon distant and unknown lands. True benevolence embraces all the world, but it always concerns itself for the time being to secure the well-being of those most immediately within its reach. Those that compose the domestic circle are the objects upon which benevolence necessarily and primarily exerts itself; through these it flows abroad to all that are near, most especially; and it ceases not until it reaches those that are afar off. In this sense it is true that "charity begins at home," but not in the sense in which this is generally understood. This saying is generally supposed to mean that charity regards self-interest first and most; however, the very fact that the term *charity* is used (which is synonymous with *benevolence*) shows that the true meaning of this saying is that *benevolence begins by seeking the happiness of those in its immediate neighborhood*, and continues to extend itself until it reaches those that are afar off.

 The kind of religion or rather of irreligion of which I have just been speaking would be of no benefit if the world were full of it. Suppose everyone had this kind of religion, each one desiring and praying for the happiness of those beyond their reach but neglecting and trampling upon the happiness of all within their reach. Who then would be happy? Everyone employed in making those immediately in contact with them unhappy, and only seeking the happiness of those at a distance, who are in their turn rendering themselves and those immediately around them unhappy while they are desiring and praying for the happiness of others at a distance. Such religion as this would leave the world in wretchedness if everyone on earth possessed it.

Do you see how real religion, true Christianity, makes its possessor happy? There is a sweetness and a divine relish in the exercise of benevolence itself; and in addition to this, the emotions of the mind will usually be in accordance with the state of the will or heart. True Christian faith and benevolence necessarily results in the happiness of the believer.

Do you see what a truly Christian family, neighborhood, or universe would be? Everyone employed in making those around them happy to the full extent of their power. A most divine religion this! Take but a single family, where benevolence is the law of every member. See the husband and wife, brothers and sisters, and all the members of the family; see how careful they are not to injure each other's piety or unnecessarily wound each other's feelings. See how kindly they watch over each other for good. See how watchful they are to each other's interests and happiness. See how pleased each one is to deny himself to promote the general good of all. The law of kindness dwells ever on their tongues. Such a family is a little picture of heaven. Wherever such a family is found, it is an oasis, or a little green spot in the midst of a vast wilderness of moral death.

Do you see the utter unreasonableness of infidelity? Infidels affect to disbelieve the necessity of a change of heart. But what do they mean? Do they not know by their own observation that people are by nature supremely selfish? And can they be happy without a radical change of heart? Could a world of selfish beings make up heaven! Impossible! The idea is absurd and ridiculous! It is self-evident that without that change of heart which consists in a radical change of character from selfishness to benevolence, a person cannot be saved.

Do you see from this subject how to detect false hopes? False professors of Christ as Savior are either inactive in Christian faith and practice, or manifest a legal spirit in opposition to the spirit of love. There are two extremes that should always be guarded against in the church. The one is Antinomianism, which satisfies itself with frames and feelings while it makes little or no exertion for the salvation of the world. The other is a legal zeal that bustles about often harshly and furiously and professes to be working for God when there is an obvious dash of bitterness and misanthropy in the countenance and manner and life. This is not the love that works no ill to his neighbor. It is not the benevolence and spirit of Christ; and all such religion is spurious however zealous, however active, and however apparently useful it may be.

Spurious conversions often throw the mind into a state of fermentation and deep feeling which of course soon subsides. But true conversion to the Christian faith consists in a change of choice; and of course, is an abiding state of mind. Where there are revivals the chaff may be easily discovered from the wheat when the effervescence of excited emotion has passed by. You can then see whether the will is under the control of truth. While the emotions are strong they may induce a series of volitions which would lead for the time being to the conclusion that the will or heart is really changed, but as soon as these emotions subside, if the heart is not changed, the selfish preference will again resume its control. Just in proportion as the excitement ceases will it become apparent in the persons life, spirit, and temper (and especially in his business transactions), that his selfish heart or preference is not changed, and that he is still unregenerate. The fact that the emotions very often induce volition, and many times a series of volitions inconsistent with the governing preference of the will or heart, renders it impossible for us, in the midst of the excitement of a revival, to distinguish clearly between true and false conversions to Christianity; but as the excitement subsides, if we are willing to be guided by the Bible, we can clearly distinguish between those who are born again and those who are not. And we are bound so to distinguish, and to deal faithfully, promptly, and energetically with those who are seen still to remain in selfishness.

Now you see the vast importance of distinguishing that which constitutes the true Christian religion, and all those frames and feelings upon which so much stress is laid in many people in the church who are still inactive in the cause of Christ and who suppose themselves holy simply because they know not what holiness is. They do not understand that their frames and feelings are the result of their views and opinions, and whether their opinions are right or wrong, cannot be known by their frames or emotions, but by the acting of their will. They may have love in the form of emotion. They may have peace and joy and even ecstasy in the form of emotions without one particle of the true Christian faith. Furthermore, if they are not really in a state of efficient good-willing, if they are not engaged in doing good and promoting the individual and general happiness to the extent of their power, it is absolutely certain that they are not truly Christians. O that people understood this fact! O that people knew that true Christian faith leads the believer to benevolence, to the love that is willing to lay down one's life for its neighbor! How much that is called Christianity is really only working continual ill to its neighbor! But blessed be God, the true Christian religion works no ill to its neighbor. Give me then true Christian neighbors, and I am content. Give me irreligious neighbors, and I will try to do them good, for that is benevolence. Let the one hear who has an ear to hear. Amen.*

---

* Charles G. Finney, *The Oberlin Evangelist*, March 3, 1841, *Principles of Liberty*, 167-181. For Review: Answer the Study Questions on page 230, Cowles page 242.

The Gospel of John and Acts on Joy

The bride belongs to the bridegroom. The friend who attends the bridegroom waits and listens for him, and is full of joy when he hears the bridegroom's voice. That joy is mine, and it is now complete. —John 3:29

I have told you this so that my joy may be in you and that your joy may be complete. —John 15:11

Very truly I tell you, you will weep and mourn while the world rejoices. You will grieve, but your grief will turn to joy. A woman giving birth to a child has pain because her time has come; but when her baby is born she forgets the anguish because of her joy that a child is born into the world. So with you: Now is your time of grief, but I will see you again and you will rejoice, and no one will take away your joy. —John 16:20-22

Until now you have not asked for anything in my name. Ask and you will receive, and your joy will be complete. —John 16:24

I am coming to you now, but I say these things while I am still in the world, so that they may have the full measure of my joy within them. —John 17:13

The disciples were filled with joy and with the Holy Spirit. —Acts 13:52

Yet he has not left himself without testimony: He has shown kindness by giving you rain from heaven and crops in their seasons; he provides you with plenty of food and fills your hearts with joy. —Acts 14:17

The jailer brought them into his house and set a meal before them; he was filled with joy because he had come to believe in God—he and his whole household. —Acts 16:34

10

Putting on Christ
1843

But put ye on the Lord Jesus Christ, and make not provision for the flesh, to fulfil the lusts thereof.—Romans 13:14—KJV

Rather, clothe yourselves with the Lord Jesus Christ, and do not think about how to gratify the desires of the sinful nature.—Romans 13:14—NIV

In considering this text, we need to know what Paul intended by this command, what is implied in obeying this command, some essential conditions for obeying this command, that everyone should obey this command, that obeying this command is naturally indispensable to salvation, some consequences of obeying this command, and the consequences of disobeying this command.

What Paul intended by this command.

"To put on a person" is to assume his character and peculiarities as an actor does on the stage. Therefore, this command enjoins the imitation of Jesus Christ, as actors imitate those they represent.

What is implied in obeying this command.

Obeying this command implies the putting away of selfishness. Christ was not selfish. Selfishness is the preference of self-gratification to the will of God and the good of the universe, and Christ never did this. The Apostle adds, "and make no provision for the flesh, to fulfill the lusts thereof." Here, Paul contrasts "putting on Christ," and "making provision for the flesh," which is the same as selfishness. Paul was more philosophical than any of the other sacred writers, and he employs the language "works of the flesh," "following after the flesh," and "carnal mind" to designate the nature of sin. But the whole Bible condemns self-seeking as wrong and inconsistent with the true service of God or imitation of Jesus Christ.

Obeying this command implies living for the same end, goal, or ultimate purpose for which Jesus Christ lived. What was His end or ultimate intention? Not the gratification of self, but the well-being of the universe. Whoever puts on Christ must adopt His end or intention.

Obeying this command implies the same singleness of eye. Christ's eye was not double, but exclusively directed to one end; that was, the glory of God. He never wavered from pursuing this end.

Obeying this command implies such a sympathy with Jesus Christ as to beget an imitation of Him. A profound sympathy is necessary to and naturally begets imitation.

Some essential conditions for obeying this command.

One essential condition is a deep and intense study of Christ's character until you perceive the great principle of His action—until you clearly develop an understanding of the real end for which He lived. Persons attempting to imitate others must give the closest attention to them. This is essential to the success of a dramatic actor or any other artist. Who, when looking at a picture by West, and observing all its delicate shadings, has not been struck with the deep attention which the artist must have given to his subject? One shade is stronger and another weaker, exactly exhibiting the position and form of each limb and the various expressions of countenance and attitude appropriate to the circumstances of the person represented. Now, in order to express these things by colorings on the canvass, the artist must have studied his subject most intensely.* So it is with a good actor. He does not merely commit and rehearse his piece as a schoolboy does on the stage. He does not stand and spout it off in recitation style. He seeks to represent his character in dress, habit, spirit, style, manner, and everything; in this consists the perfection of the dramatic art.

The Apostle commands us thus to put on Christ—to imitate Him—to give intense thought to understand the true idea of His character. Then, he commands us to commit our mind fully to the same end as Christ's, to the same end to which He was devoted. To enjoy a piece of poetry, you must put yourself into the same state of mind in which the poet was when he wrote it. Then as you read the poem, your tone and manner will naturally represent him. This is the difficulty with so many in reading or singing hymns. They read or sing as though they did not at all apprehend the sentiment and without the emotion. Either they do not have the spirit of devotion or they do not give attention to the sentiment of the hymn. But to represent Christ, we must catch His spirit. We must make His grand end and aim our end and aim. Then we shall act as He would act under similar circumstances.

Another essential condition is fully believing that through grace you can put on Christ. If you do not believe you can, of course you cannot. No one can intend to do what he believes he cannot do. It is absurd to suppose the contrary. No one intends to fly like a bird. Why? Because everyone knows he cannot. We may wish to fly like a bird, while we do not believe we can, but to intend it is impossible. So unless you believe you can put on Christ, it is utterly impossible that you should intend to do it, and this is the great reason why so many never actually put on Christ.

An essential condition is not only fully believing that you can put on Christ, but actually intending to put on Christ—intending to make Him your whole example. You must intend to do this; it will never happen by accident.

Principles of Joy in the Holy Spirit — Finney's Lessons on Romans

You must be fully prepared to make any sacrifice to put on Christ. You must count the cost and make up your mind to meet the expense necessary to the accomplishment of this end. You must make any sacrifice of friends, property, or credit which stand in the way. The Lord Jesus Christ teaches this and warns people against making themselves ridiculous by beginning to build without being able to finish. The truth is, unless a person has made up their mind to absolutely sacrifice whatever hinders them from fully putting on Christ, they do not have an understanding of the very first principle of the Christian faith.

You must realize the importance of putting on Christ. Suppose a dramatic author should write an admirable drama adapted powerfully to awaken the attention and arouse the passions of the spectators at its exhibition, but the actors should so poorly prepare themselves, and so poorly act it as perfectly to misrepresent him. It is easy to see how they would injure the credit of both the author and drama. While they profess to be followers of Christ, people who do not fully put on the Lord Jesus Christ are doing Him and His cause the greatest injury of which they are capable. They should then realize the infinite importance of fully representing Him.

Another condition of putting on Christ is keeping up a constant communication and relationship with Him. You must commune with Him in prayer without ceasing. Who does not know that an actor needs to drink into and commune with the spirit of the author profoundly if he would truly represent him. He must get the state of mind of the man who wrote the drama; in short, he must "put on" the writer. If he does not, he will misrepresent him. So there must be constant communion with the Spirit of Christ in order to put Him on and act just as He would.

To put on Christ, you must not rest while you have any unrepented, unconfessed sin between you and Christ. You must keep a clear medium between you and Christ. I will explain what I mean. You have seen two friends who have been for a long time agreed, and have taken sweet counsel together, but by and by a little difference creeps in between them—a little mist begins to obscure the medium, and now, when they meet, you will begin to see it in the eye and countenance. There is a little flutter in their manner, and unless it is immediately removed, it will increase until finally they turn their backs upon each other. So with a husband and wife, how careful they should be to keep a clear medium of mental communion. Suppose a husband has grieved his wife. Now, if he is a man of sensibility, he cannot be at ease. He goes to pray; he remembers the wound which he has inflicted, and he can pray no further. He rises from his knees and goes and confesses to his wife the injury he has done her. The cloud is now removed from between them and he is happy. So with the Christian. If he has grieved Christ and injured His tender feelings, he can have no further communion with Him until he has repented and confessed his faults; then, the tender breathing of mutual love are restored.

If you would put on Christ, you must cease from all self-dependence. As long as you depend on yourself, you will see no need of putting on Christ.

If you would put on Christ, you must avail yourself of His exceeding great and precious promises. You must realize why He gave the promises, and that He gave them to you personally. The Apostle Peter says, "Whereby are given unto us, exceeding great and precious promises, that, by these we might be partakers of the divine nature; having escaped the corruption that is in the world through lust" (2 Peter 1:4). The design of the promises is to beget in us a universal likeness to the Lord Jesus Christ. Now, a promise is good for nothing unless it is believed and applied. Ten thousand promises would be of no more use than a bankbook of checks given to a poor man, if the poor man carried it closed and never used it.

Everyone should obey this command.

Putting on Christ does not mean that everyone should to do exactly the same things which Christ did, because no one is in all respects in the same circumstances as Jesus Christ. As circumstances vary, outward duties differ. Christ practiced celibacy, and in His circumstances this was His duty, but celibacy never could be the duty of the whole human race. The whole human race should not imitate Him in practicing celibacy and in many other ways. However, everyone is obligated to do as He did in so far as their circumstances are the same as His. We are obligated to do what we suppose He would do if He were in our circumstances.

Principles of Joy in the Holy Spirit — Finney's Lessons on Romans

For example, if Christ were a father, a merchant, a mechanic, a lawyer, or a citizen, what would He do? In early life, Christ was a carpenter, and He labored with His father at his trade. Let a carpenter ask these questions, "What sort of a carpenter was Jesus Christ? How honest was He? How did He do His work? How did He associate and converse with His fellow workers?" Now, if you are a carpenter, the kind of carpenter you suppose Christ would be, you are to be. Suppose the Lord Jesus Christ were a merchant, upon what principles would He conduct His business? Or, if Christ were a physician, how would He practice medicine? Would He have avoided visiting and helping the poor in order to establish a medical practice among the rich?

You are bound to consider how Christ would act in your circumstances and do as you think He would do. How important it is for a minister of the gospel to inquire what kind of a pastor Christ would be if He were in his circumstances; and so with everyone for the same reason. If Christ were a physician, what would He do? Would He try to reject poor patients in order to obtain rich patients? When a poor man came soliciting His aid, would Christ say, "I shall not get much money for this; therefore, I do not care whether I attend to it or not"? Now, beloved brethren, who are physicians, are you such as you think Christ would be, taking into the account the difference of circumstances? Similarly, you may take any other occupation, even the lowest; for no occupation that is honest is too low to forbid the supposition of Christ being in similar circumstances. It was with a design to illustrate this that He washed His disciples' feet. In the East they wear sandals, which expose their feet to the hot sands, and it was customary for the lowest servant of the house to wait at the door with water to wash the feet of visitors. The Savior did this to inculcate the lesson of lowliness of heart, and to show the spirit with which all should perform the duties of life. Whatever your condition or situation, whatever you suppose Christ would be and do in your place, you ought to be and do. Furthermore, everyone should ask themselves, "Would Christ pursue my calling, if placed in my circumstances, and would He pursue it as I do?"

That it is a universal duty to put on Christ is evident from the following facts—it is just and right—all can do it by His grace—universal reason demands it—it is essential to the good of the universe—both sinners and saints are really commanded to put on Christ.

Obeying this command is naturally indispensable to salvation.

"Indispensable to salvation" does not mean no one can be saved who has not always done this; but rather, so far as our knowledge extends, we are to put on Christ and live devoted to the same end as Christ. Anything less than this is sin. Nothing short of intending to be or do what Christ would be or do with our understanding and in our circumstances can be acceptable to God. Jesus said, "You cannot serve God and mammon" (Matthew 6:24). What does He mean? He does not mean that you cannot serve God at one time and mammon at another time. He does mean that you must be entirely devoted to God or entirely devoted to mammon, and you cannot serve both God and mammon at the same time. Benevolence is a unit and will always manifest itself in everyone alike in so far as their circumstances are similar.

Jesus Christ was no more than virtuous, and you must be no less, or you cannot be saved. I have often been astonished that people talk as if Christ did something more than His duty, and performed works of supererogation, as if such a thing were possible. Duty is what benevolence requires. Now, if Christ should do more than benevolence requires, it could not be benevolence, nor duty, and consequently, not virtue. I would ask, was God in making the Atonement any more benevolent than He ought to be? If so, He was not virtuous in it. The truth is, people are in the dark on this subject. No being in the universe can perform works of supererogation; for everyone is required to do his whole duty. Christ was perfectly benevolent and this was His duty; and so must you be if you put on Christ. You must be like Him, or you never can be with Him.

Some consequences of obeying this command.

I wish to be exceedingly candid and hold nothing back. I have often marked how much the Lord Jesus Christ differed from many who set themselves up as reformers. He would often press His listeners until almost all of them would forsake Him. Once, everyone left Him except His twelve disciples, and He turned to them and said, "Will you also go away?" (John 6:67). He implied that He would rather lose them than keep back the truth. We must not preach a false Christ.

The first consequence of putting on Christ is having much opposition. You can expect no better usage than Christ received: "It is enough for the servant that he be as his master" (Matthew 10:25). If you put on Christ, you may expect great trials. This is the inheritance of all who "will live godly in Christ Jesus" (2 Timothy 3:12). Look at Paul. While he was a Pharisee, he went on smoothly. The gales of popular favor swelled his sails. But when he became the preacher of the cross of Christ, ah! then he knew what it was to go against wind and tide.

Some will accuse you of having a bad spirit. Some have always brought this charge against the true followers of Jesus Christ, and especially against Christ himself. Jesus said so much about the religious teachers, creeds, and traditions of His people, and He rebuked them so plainly, that they finally tried and executed Christ as a blasphemer.

If you put on Christ, you will need great meekness, and at the same time great decision of character. Without both of these qualities, you cannot endure the shock of a world arrayed against you. You will subject yourself to much misapprehension. People will not understand you. Many wonder why Christians are so misunderstood. But it is not at all amazing. Who was ever more misunderstood than Jesus Christ? The simple fact is: a selfish mind does not understand the principle upon which a true Christian acts. If you are misunderstood, of course you will be misrepresented. This you must expect.

If you put on Christ, it will subject you to the loss of many friends. They will think you are extreme, extravagant, and carrying matters too far. With every new step you take, you will see an additional falling off of your friends. They will walk no more with you. But all the consequences are not evil, because you will inherit Christ's peace of mind, and this is worth more than all the world can give. You will sleep just as sweetly, eat with just as much relish, and enjoy the tranquil hours just as really, as if you had all the world's favor. People often wonder if those who have put on Christ are unhappy. I answer, no. They are the only persons who know what true happiness is. His joy will be fulfilled in you. This is His promise, and His true followers sympathize with Him in all the joys He had.

If you put on Christ, you will share His glory in being the representative of the true God. "I have given them the glory that you gave me, that they may be one as we are one—I in them and you in me—so that they may be brought to complete unity. Then the world will know that you sent me and have loved them even as you have loved me" (John 17:22-23). Christ was sent to reveal the true character of God. He took the law of God which lay on tables of stone and He acted it out. He showed us what God was. Without such a demonstration as He made of His true character, people must have always remained in ignorance. What is God? God is a glorious, infinite, and invisible Spirit lying back in the bosom of eternity where no eye can reach. What finite mind could comprehend God? God must reveal himself; and to this end He concentrated His glory in Jesus Christ and sent Him forth among the human race. Everyone who puts on the Lord Jesus Christ will share this glory with Him, of making known to the world the true character of God.

You will be able to say, with Paul, "For to me, to live is Christ" (Philippians 1:21). The Apostle seems to have had this idea in his mind that Christ lived His life over again in him. So it will be with you. Christ renews His life in His true followers.

You will be able to say from your own consciousness, as John says, "Our fellowship is with the Father and with his Son, Jesus Christ" (1 John 1:3). You will be happy in the highest degree of which you are capable in this life. And you will be no less useful than you are happy.

Consequences of disobeying this requirement.

If you claim to be a Christian and disobey this requirement, you will be a hypocrite and people will know it. Perhaps there are some who succeed in keeping on the mask of hypocrisy. But most betray themselves sooner or later and are known in their true character. You will render peace of mind impossible. You will render yourself justly despicable. Everyone loves to see people live up to their profession, and they naturally cry out against hypocrisy. You will ruin your own soul and do the most you can to ruin others. You will bring upon yourself the endless execration of all beings in the universe, both good and bad.

REMARKS

Inconsistent "Christians" sometimes gain the hollow applause of the unthinking and ungodly. But they never gain the solid respect of any class for any considerable time. Instead of this, they really lose respect. For as soon as their true character appears, people cannot but condemn and abhor them. Their inward lack of confidence in those who claim to be Christians is often exhibited in a trying hour. A fact related in my hearing by a minister made a deep impression on my mind. A wealthy man in the South, who had sat under the preaching of a worldly minister, was taken sick and about to die. His friends asked him if they should send for his minister. He said, "No, I do not want him now. We have been together at the horse races." They urged him to send for somebody, and mentioned several people. But he rejected them all. At last, he told them to call in Tom, one of his colored servants; for, said he, "I have often heard him pray alone." Tom came. He laid his little hat at the door, and inquired what his master wanted. Said the dying man, "Tom, do you pray?" "Yes, master, in my weak way." "Can you pray for your dying master?" "I'll try," he answered. "Come here, then, and pray for me." And Tom drew near, and poured out his soul to God for the dying man. Ah! the master knew in his inmost soul that his minister could not pray. Poor Tom was the man to pray for him.**

The lives of many who claim to Christians are a most terrible burlesque on Christianity. Satan, it would seem, has pushed these into the Church as members to disgrace it. Persons who have a strong sense of the ridiculous are often tempted to laugh at the absurd notions of "Christianity" which some manifest. They never seem to think of asking how Christ would act. I have sometimes seen servants in families where they were called to family worship come in cowering and get behind the door altogether away from the family circle. I wonder if they think it will be so in heaven. In some families, it is not the wish but the choice of the servant, and of course they are not to blame. Since I have been here, I have seen persons take up their hats and leave the house when they see the colored people sitting among the whites. I wonder if such people would do so in heaven. Do let me ask, "Is not this the direct opposite of the spirit of Christ?" How would Christ treat the poor slaves and the colored people if He were in this country?

See the importance of always bearing in mind the person whom you have undertaken to represent and the part you are expected to act. For example, everyone can see that a minister in the pulpit and everywhere else should bear this in mind, and so he should; but no more, really, than any other Christian should in his vocation.

It is becoming to us to inquire whether we have so represented Christ as to give those around us the true idea of Christianity. Suppose a minister should never ask himself what idea of Christianity his people get from him. It is easy to see that he would not be able to convey a very definite idea of Christianity to his people. Everyone who claims to be a Christian should examine themselves. And now, beloved, do you live so as to make the impression that Christianity leads to disinterested benevolence? Who would get that idea from you? A man said to me not long ago, if Christian faith leads to benevolence, I know of but one man in our church who seems to be a Christian. How many do you know in this city? Christianity is nothing less than putting on Christ Do you live so? Do I? If not, what will become of our souls?

Those who do not put on Christ are the worst kind of heretics. There is no heresy so bad as a false profession of Christian faith. Inconsistent "Christians" are the greatest curse to the world that there is in it. Those who claim to be Christians who have not put on Christ should confess to those around them and instantly reform. Confess to your wife, your children, your church, your neighbors. Will you do it?

Sinners are altogether without excuse and are as much bound to put on Christ as those who claim to be Christians. Unless every one of us in his calling fully intends to put on Christ, and keep Him on, we are in the way to hell. If you are not what you think Christ would be in your calling, you are not a Christian. How different putting on Christ is from the common views of what is Christian! All that we see among many who claim to be Christians is pride and starch and fashion and death. Oh! Brothers and

Principles of Joy in the Holy Spirit — Finney's Lessons on Romans

sisters, let us put on the Lord Jesus Christ, and "make no provision for the flesh to fulfill the lusts thereof" (Romans 13:14).***

---

* Most probably, Finney referred to a famous American painter many Americans of his day would have known—the painter Benjamin West was born in Pennsylvania on October 10, 1738 to a Quaker family. He painted historical scenes during and after the time of the American War of Independence. He died on March 11, 1820.

** Finney preached this sermon when slavery based on race was the law of the land in the Southern states. Finney opposed slavery and was active in preaching revivals and encouraging the abolition of slavery. Many slaveholders looked upon their slaves as personal property, just as they looked upon their horses or cattle as personal property, instead of looking upon their slaves as persons (created in the image of God, just as God created them). Slaves did not receive their freedom in the United States of America until after Abraham Lincoln issued the *Emancipation Proclamation* on January 1, 1863, and the Civil War was won by the Northern states and remaining Confederate troops surrendered in May 1865. On December 6, 1865, the *Thirteenth Amendment* to the *United States Constitution* (passed by Congress on January 31, 1865) was finally ratified by the states and slavery was abolished. Slavery still "immorally but legally" exists in some countries today, and this slavery is "justified" in this countries by some false religions.

*** Charles G. Finney, *The Oberlin Evangelist*, March 15, 1843, *Principles of Holiness*, 124-134. For Review: Answer the Study Questions on page 231, Cowles page 242.

11

The Kingdom of God in Consciousness
1861

For the kingdom of God is not meat and drink; but righteousness, and peace, and joy in the Holy Ghost. —Romans 14:17—KJV

For the kingdom of God is not a matter of eating and drinking, but of righteousness, peace and joy in the Holy Spirit. —Romans 14:17—NIV

We need to ask, what is the kingdom of God? What is righteousness? What is peace? What is joy in the Holy Spirit?

What is the kingdom of God?

The kingdom of God is not an outward organization. It is not the visible church or any ecclesiastical establishment whatever. It is not any material or worldly good. The kingdom of God is the reign of Christ the King in the souls of Christians.

What is righteousness?

Righteousness is moral uprightness; the love to God, others, and ourselves which the Bible requires. Righteousness does not belong strictly to muscular action, but to the state of the heart. And righteousness is really the spirit of the moral law existing and established in the heart. Christ promised that He would write His law upon the hearts of His people and engrave it in their inward parts, and they should all know the Lord from the least of them unto the greatest of them. The spirit of the law of Christ or that which the law of Christ really requires in its meaning and intent is supreme, perfect, disinterested (unselfish or not self-centered) love to God and an equal love to others that we have for ourselves.

The law of Christ requires that God should be loved for His own sake, and supremely, because He is supremely and infinitely great and good. The law of Christ also requires that we should love others as we love ourselves; and this love to God and others should be expressed in all appropriate ways in all the relations of life. This love, with all its appropriate expressions in the temper and life and spirit, is righteousness. It is a voluntary love; therefore, it must reveal itself in uprightness of life in every relation in which we exist.

Righteousness is the opposite of unrighteousness. Unrighteousness is a withholding from God and others their due. Unrighteousness is a spirit of not caring for God or others; that treats with contempt the rights and feelings and authority of God and the rights of our neighbors. It is a lack of conformity to the moral law, a voluntary withholding of obedience to God's law. Righteousness is the opposite of this. Righteousness is love positively exercised with all its positive fruits.

Righteousness is real active devotion to the whole mind of God, and also devotion to the interests and well being of human beings. Righteousness is a state of mind in which there is a continual offering of self in a confiding love-service to God. The righteous person serves God diligently and with all their powers, with respect to Him and not for pay. It is a cheerful and willing service; not because we must, but from a supreme interest in God and His cause.

The Kingdom of God in Consciousness

Righteousness always implies diligence and industry and study to please God. Righteousness always implies the avoiding of everything that can displease God; and in short, righteousness consists in the heart's being fully committed to do and suffer all the will of God, and that readily and joyfully for God's own sake.

Righteousness also involves sincere devotion to the interests of others; a willingness to deny self when by so doing we can promote the greater good of others, and that from real regard to our neighbors as to a brother or sister. It is in fact the spirit of universal brotherhood practically carried out.

This, then, is the righteousness which constitutes the great element or peculiarity of the kingdom of God in the soul. It is Christ's righteousness imparted to the soul. It is Christ's law or will taking effect in the soul, and begetting His own righteousness in us; and thus, we come to be partakers of the righteousness of God, not merely by imputation, but by actual experience and active love and service. I pray you, let no one overlook the true goal of righteousness. Do not forget that true righteousness is the very love in kind that is in Christ's own heart, a love that led Him to do all He did and does for sinners and saints.

The love of Christ in us must necessarily express itself in our life, because the connection between this love and outward action is a connection of necessity. This love consists in the will's devotion to God and to the good of all people. It is consecration; it is making common cause with God and others and unifying ourselves with God's state of mind.

What is peace?

Peace of mind is not apathy or a state of indifference to God, His claims, or His service. Peace is the opposite of war, strife, or friction under the government of God. It is the opposite of this; it is a state of cordiality, and of conscious cordiality, existing between the soul and God.

Peace does not consist merely in the soul's being reconciled to God, but also includes the fact that God is reconciled to us, and that this is revealed to us in our consciousness. In this state of mind, we are aware that God has accepted us and forgiven us and that our peace is made with him.

Principles of Joy in the Holy Spirit — Finney's Lessons on Romans

Peace in the kingdom of God is a state of universal satisfaction of mind with God's will as expressed in creation and providence, and in His law and gospel. I say satisfaction with His will, for if in anything we are not satisfied with God, we are stubbornly resisting His control like an unruly child. If we profess to submit, we do it ungraciously and not really. There cannot be peace between us and God as long as a particle of dissatisfaction with God's ways and will remains in our hearts.

This peace is a state of mind in which there is a conscious yielding of everything that God claims. The mind is settled to do so; to make this the universal law of our activity; to accept all God's requirements and yield not merely of necessity, but willingly and cordially to all that He requires of us.

This state of mind is like the calm, deep flow of a river. It is a calm, deep flow of feeling in conscious harmony with God's state of mind. It is remarkable that in this state of mind we are conscious, not of the mind's lying still, and being in a quiescent state, but the sensibility seems to be flowing, a deep current of the mind. And it all flows in one direction. Like a river, there is no conflicting of different currents, some flowing in one direction and some in another.

There may be ripplings in the current. There may be obstructions so that the waters in one place may dam up and boil over the obstructions, but there are no counter currents forcing their way upward and conflicting with the general stream, with the little eddyings here and there, and the obstructions, and boilings up, and flowings around the obstructing objects here and there. Upon the whole, the whole movement of the mind, the intellect, the sensibility, the will, all come flowing in one direction, and the flow is harmony; the flow is peace, the flow is a deep, broad river of life and love.

This peace is like the subdued, settled, satisfied state of a weaned child. As the Psalmist says, "Lord, my heart is not haughty, nor mine eyes lofty; neither do I exercise myself in great matters, or in things too high for me. Surely I have behaved and quieted myself as a child that is weaned of its mother; my soul is even as a weaned child" (Psalm 131:1-2)

Everyone knows that an unsubdued child, unsettled in obedience, is continually chafing under parental authority; and there can be no real

The Kingdom of God in Consciousness

peace between the parent and the child unless the child be actually and thoroughly subdued, so that it will accept the will of the parent as its law of life. And when the child is really and thoroughly subdued, so that it is cheerful and satisfied with its state of subjection; when this state becomes its chosen adopted state, and this subjection is preferred to following its own counsels and its own will, then there is peace between the parent and the child. Then the child itself has peace of mind; then the child itself can be happy. The child is not stubbornly resisting the parent, and keeping up a constant friction with parental authority. Just so is it in the government of God. While the King is striving to set up His kingdom in the heart and the sinner is resisting, there is conviction, remorse, dissatisfaction, struggling, evading, stubbornness, chafing, cavilling; and all the elements of disorder, of sin, of turmoil are in the soul. In this state there can be no peace. This heart cannot be saved; it cannot, by any possibility, go to heaven. This mind can never have peace until it is completely and joyfully and universally subject to the will of God. The peace of the gospel consists in this perfectly subdued, settled, confiding, joyful, quiescent state of mind in respect to God, His government, character, requirements, and dealings.

Peace of mind always implies and includes a state of mind the opposite of condemnation and remorse. In other words, we are conscious, as I have already intimated, of our being accepted; not only of our being at peace with God, but also of His being at peace with us. A state of forgiveness, of being restored to favor, of being on good terms with God through His abounding grace in Jesus Christ are always involved in being at peace with God as a state of mind.

The peace of mind that we have in relation to God through faith in Jesus Christ and the work of the Holy Spirit is the opposite of all unbelieving worry and anxiety that can corrode, fret, or distress the mind. When the kingdom of God is set up in our soul, when we truly embrace the Kingdom of God, not only is it true that we accept God's whole will, but we have such confidence in God, have such spirituality in regard to perceiving God in His universal providence and recognizing God in all the movements of His providence, that the unbelieving worry and corroding anxiety that so much disturb the world is shut out from our mind.

11

Romans 14:17

Principles of Joy in the Holy Spirit — Finney's Lessons on Romans

What is joy in the Holy Spirit?

Joy in the Holy Spirit is not a mere joy arising out of the supposition that we are safe. Although this consideration is a matter of joy, still this is not the joy mentioned here. It is joy in the Holy Spirit. From the union of our spirit with God's Spirit, God's joy is really produced in us. Christ said to His disciples, "These things have I spoken unto you that my joy might remain in you, and that your joy might be full" (John 15:11).

Joy or rejoicing in God is always an element of the kingdom of God in the soul. In the kingdom of God, God's joy and righteousness and peace are so imparted to us by the Holy Spirit that we are really conscious, not only of being partakers of His holiness and of His divine nature, but also of drinking of the river of His own pleasures or joys. Where righteousness and peace are, there Christian joy or joy in God will be.

Joy in the Holy Spirit is rejoicing in God himself. It is not rejoicing in ourselves, either that we are good or that we are saved or that we are going to heaven. God is the direct object in which we rejoice. The contemplation of God and communion with God fill the soul with joy unspeakable; and there is in the soul of the Christian a joy, a deep, abiding, perennial joy, even amidst the trials of this life. We have always in God the same reason for rejoicing in Him; He is always the same glorious, loving, infinite object of joy. The mind that is in harmony with His will cannot but enjoy His peace and rejoice in Him. Such a mind cannot be poor; such a mind cannot lack the grounds and all the elements of rejoicing. Indeed, Christian joy always will be where true Christian faith resides. Christianity involves supreme love to God and equal love to others. Christianity consists in a cordial embracing of God's whole character and will and way, so there will always be joy. Furthermore, even in the midst of sorrows there will be a deep Christian joy. In the midst of the trials of life, in the midst of temptations, in the midst of persecutions, and even in the article of death, there is joy, joy in God.

The mind that is devoted to God cannot be deprived of Christian joy. Christian joy necessarily springs up in the very exercise of love and faith and gratitude. It is the natural and certain result of a truly Christian state of mind. Yes, it is an element of this Christian state of mind; it essentially

The Kingdom of God in Consciousness

belongs to a truly devout state of mind.

REMARKS

Righteousness, peace, and joy in the Holy Spirit must be a matter of consciousness. A Christian faith of which we could not be conscious could not be of much importance to us. If we did not know whether we had Christian faith or not, surely it could not be worth having as far as we are concerned. But the fact is, if we can be conscious of anything, we can and must be conscious of the kingdom of God existing within us.

Just think! The kingdom of God is righteousness and peace and joy in the Holy Spirit; and yet, I can remember the time when it was thought a very dark and suspicious circumstance if a person expressed great confidence that he was a Christian. It was gravely suspected by grave theologians and ministers that such a person was not acquainted with his heart; and to express great doubts with respect to one's own conversion was regarded as an evidence of profound humility. And we would frequently hear the very excellent Mr. So and So, and Dr. Such a One, spoken of as having so many doubts as to whether they were Christians. Now we might earnestly and prayerfully ask, "Where did such views of Christianity come from?"

It must also be a matter of observation in the sense that the kingdom of God within a person must reveal itself in his outward life, temper, and spirit; in his business transactions; in his social and domestic relations; in his public relations; and indeed, in every relationship in his life. If the kingdom of God is within him, then he is an upright man. He is a benevolent man. He is a man devoted to the service of God and to the interests of every person. In business, he is equitable; in politics, he is honest and honorable. In every relationship, he is a Christian.

How very different is this account of the religion of Jesus in the fourteenth chapter of Romans from the experience narrated in the seventh chapter of Romans! The seventh chapter of Romans plainly describes a legal experience in which the kingdom of God is not set up in the heart, but where God is striving to get possession of the heart. The eighth chapter of Romans portrays an experience in which the kingdom of God is set up in the heart. Paul described the person in whom the kingdom of God is set up in their heart, "There is therefore now no condemnation to them which are in Christ Jesus, who walk not after the flesh, but after the Spirit.... That the righteousness of the law might be fulfilled in us, who walk not after the flesh, but after the Spirit" (Romans 8:1, 4).

The experience described in the seventh chapter of Romans is an experience the opposite of the eighth chapter. In the seventh chapter of Romans, religion is all bondage, resolution, purpose, and failing; instead of righteousness, peace, and joy in the Holy Spirit. In the seventh chapter, the soul is described as bound fast in the cords of its own sins; floundering in a pit of mire and clay, and having neither righteousness, nor peace, nor joy in the Holy Spirit. And yet, strange to tell, for centuries, this experience in the seventh chapter of Romans has been regarded as authentic Christian experience by a great portion of the church. There is reason to fear that millions of souls have stopped in the seventh chapter of Romans, taking it for granted that they were converted, having mistaken conviction of sin for true conversion and faith; thus, they have gone down to hell.

How different is this account of the kingdom of God in consciousness from the peaceless religion of many who claim to be Christians. They have no peace of mind. They are restless, resisting the control of God, chafing, complaining, murmuring, resisting the law of Christ, and are in a constant state of turmoil and agitation in regard to their relations to God. Indeed, they know that they have no peace of mind. They know that God's whole will is not cordially accepted by them. They know that they are living in the neglect of known duty. They know that they are shunning the cross daily. They know that they are not universally devoted to God. They know that they are not devoted to the interests of others as well as their own. Of course peace is impossible to them! They are aware that they have not this peace of mind and this state of cordiality between themselves and God. And yet, they think themselves Christians! But the kingdom of God is not within them, for Christ does not reign in their hearts and they are in no sense prepared for heaven. Now, if the kingdom of God is not within them, why should they call themselves Christians?

The Kingdom of God in Consciousness

It is very common for people in this sad condition to fall back and say that they have no dependence except upon Christ and they depend on Christ. But surely, this is a mistake. They do not truly depend on Christ, unless Christ has really set up His throne within their hearts. If they have true faith in Christ, they have true peace, they have true righteousness, they have true joy in the Holy Spirit; but lacking these, it is a sheer delusion to say that they depend on Christ.

But they say, "I do not depend on anything within myself. I do not depend on my prayers, on my own righteousness, on my peace of mind, on my joy, or upon any experience I have." "No," I answer, "you should not depend on any of these as *the ground* of your acceptance with God. But as *the condition* of your going to heaven, as being that without which you cannot go to heaven, you must depend on this righteousness and peace and joy in the Holy Spirit. This state of mind is that without which you can never go to heaven." However perfect it may be, it is not that for which, on the ground of justice, you could be admitted to heaven, but it is that without which heaven is a natural impossibility to you.

Do not, therefore, I pray you, say, "O, I am to be saved by grace, therefore I lay no stress upon my own holiness." But I ask you, my dear sir, "What is salvation? Is not an element of salvation personal holiness or righteousness? True, if saved at all, you are saved by grace. But mark! To be saved by grace is to be made holy by grace, to be made righteous by grace. By grace through faith in Jesus Christ, salvation is having the very state of mind which the text describes, 'righteousness, peace and joy in the Holy Spirit.'"

Let no one then pretend to fall back upon Christ who does not allow Christ to reign in his heart. The religion of many is sheer Antinomianism. They really suppose that they are going to be saved by an imputed without an imparted righteousness. They know that they are living in the daily indulgence of sin. They know that they shun the cross, and always have done so. They know that they never have made a clean statement of confession of sin or washed their hands by restitution. In short, they know that they have never become personally upright, honest, holy; and yet, they think they are going to saved by Christ! They say, "We have believed, and therefore we are forgiven and accepted." They think that by one act of faith they come into a state of perpetual justification. But this is the religion of naked Antinomianism. If this be true, then the law must indeed be repealed and abolished; for if the moral law remains in force, the soul must be condemned if it indulges in sin.

How different is the Christianity described in this text from the joyless religion of multitudes who claim to be Christians. Indeed, it is mournfully common to see those who profess Christianity to seldom or never profess any religious joy. It is no wonder they do not, for they themselves will admit that they are living in the constant indulgence of known sin. In this state, true Christian joy is entirely out of the question. If in this state they have any joy, it will be rejoicing in themselves; in their own supposed safety, and not in God. A joyless religion is a very repulsive religion.

To have the kingdom of God in our consciousness is indispensable to our rightly teaching Christianity. I say teaching Christianity. We may warn others of their danger. We may prove to them their guilt. We may hold forth the threatenings and even the promises of the Bible. We may teach them the doctrines of the faith, but this is not teaching them Christianity; it is not presenting Christianity to them. It is teaching them certain things about Christianity, or rather, saying certain things about Christianity. But true Christianity is a state of mind, a voluntary state, a state of love, with which joy and peace are necessarily connected. Now unless we have this joy and peace, it is impossible that we should convey a correct idea of what Christianity is by what we say and do.

If we do not ourselves love, if we have not personal peace and joy, if we attempt to preach Christianity, we shall continually betray ourselves and show that we are preaching but a hearsay gospel, and trying to teach a faith which we do not experientially understand. The fact is, experience always has a language of its own, and this language can never be supplied by any theory. Truly to preach peace and goodwill, peace and goodwill must be a matter of personal experience and consciousness; truly to preach joy, the heart must be flowing with joy.

The experience of the kingdom in consciousness is essential to rightly living it before the world. It cannot be counterfeited. A person may be very sanctimonious in his outward life and in his looks, in his words and tone of voice; but after all this, there will be insincerity in it, there will be something unnatural, it will be a manifest affectation. To be lived, Christianity must be experienced. If it be in the heart, it will be looked, it will be acted, it will be spoken; it will be made manifest in the very tones of the voice, in an obliging manner, in making efforts to honor God and to do good to others. It will be unselfish, honest, generous, cheerful, joyful. But these things cannot be so counterfeited as to set well upon a person.

Where this consciousness of the kingdom of God really exists, it will produce conviction. It cannot conceal itself. It will be noticeable in any relation of life. A husband will notice it in his wife. He will be struck with it. It will produce conviction of sin. A wife will be struck with it in her husband. Parents in children and children in parents, and in every relationship of life, it will produce conviction of sin. Living the Christian faith is a thing so diverse from the spirit of this world, the kingdom of God is so opposite to the kingdoms of this world, and to the kingdom of Satan, that where it is really set up in any heart it must so express itself in the life, temper, and spirit, as to force conviction of sin wherever it has an opportunity really to manifest itself.

If a human soul does not have this consciousness of the kingdom of God, it will of course seek worldly good. Seeking happiness, satisfaction, and enjoyment is natural to people. A person will either seek his own satisfaction selfishly, or he will seek the general good of God and others unselfishly. If the kingdom of God is established in him, he is an unselfish devotee to the glory of God and the good of others. In this he will find his enjoyment; here he will find the truest enjoyment and the highest kind of enjoyment.

In this state of mind, he does not seek his own enjoyment as his supreme goal; but he inevitably finds happiness, satisfaction, and enjoyment. In this state of mind, he does not seek his own peace, nor his own joy, these are not the objects of his search nor the end at which he aims; yet, he inevitably finds them while he does not seek them, and all the more surely because he does not seek them. But if a person does not have this enjoyment, if he does not have happiness in God, he will seek it in the world. It is in vain to shut him up to a truly Christian life, unless the kingdom of God is established in his heart. If converts to the Christian faith stop short of this consciousness, they will surely turn back.

Principles of Joy in the Holy Spirit — Finney's Lessons on Romans

If the soul has this satisfaction in God, it will not go lusting after worldly good, It has found a joy too sublime, too high, too spiritual, too all-pervading, to leave the mind restless and craving after worldly good. It will not lust for worldly pleasure and worldly ways. It will not plead for merely worldly amusements and pastimes and social conversations. No! It has found the society of God. It has entered into communion with God. It resides in the same palace with the King of Kings. It has an altar and a worship and a sanctuary within itself. It is at home when engaged in the worship and service of God. But deprive the soul of this satisfaction in God, and you cannot keep it; it will go abroad inquiring, "Who will show us any good?"

True converts to Christianity will soon learn to watch unto prayer, that they may pray in the Holy Spirit, and thus keep themselves in the love of God. At first, converts are not aware of how easily they can mar their own peace. They are not aware of how easily they can throw themselves out of sympathy with God, of how easily they can bring a cloud over their souls and wound their own spirits. But if they are really converted, they have the kingdom of God in their consciousness, and they will soon learn what wounds, what brings darkness, what mars their union with God, what disturbs their peace, what separates them from that clear and heavenly union without which they cannot live. They will soon learn the necessity of watchfulness, of much prayerfulness, of engaging as little as is consistent with duty in promiscuous conversation. They will learn to guard against idle words, vain conversation, worldly associations, a wasting of their time, a misuse of their money, a misuse of their tongue—in short they will learn to gird themselves up and walk softly with God. They will find this indispensable to their peace, indispensable to their joy, indispensable to their maintaining their righteousness. They will soon learn that they must either part with God or part with sin; that they must gird up their loins, and live wholly a Christ-centered and devoted life, or they can never have Christian joy and righteousness and peace at all.

Spurious conversions may generally be known by people not realizing the necessity of watchfulness and prayer and constant communion with God. It shows that they have not tasted of the grace of God; that they have not had communion with God; that they have not known what it is

The Kingdom of God in Consciousness

to be born of God and to have the kingdom of God set up within them.

By watching the tendency of those who claim to be Christians, we may generally tell whether true Christian faith is really a matter of experience with them. If we find them loose in the use of their tongues, careless, running hither and thither to please themselves, not caring to spend much time in prayer, not disposed to search their Bibles, not tender and easily wounded by any slip or sin into which they may fall—we may know they are not truly converted. The King has not set up His throne in their hearts. Holiness to the Lord is not written on their hearts. They know not what it is to walk and commune with God.

Sinners know that this which I have described must be true Christianity, and must be what they themselves need. In preaching at a certain place I was discoursing upon Christian faith as an experience; upon the love of God and the peace and joy of the salvation of Christ. As I came out of the pulpit, I was met at the foot of the pulpit stairs by a prominent lawyer, a stranger to me, who wished to be introduced to me. He said to me: "Mr. Finney, after tea, I wish you would make a spiritual call with me. I wish to introduce you to a friend of mine." I replied, "I suppose it is for a Christian purpose." He answered yes. I told him I should be happy to accompany him. He called on me after tea, and took me to the house of his friend, and introduced me to an aged lady, who immediately expressed great joy to see me, and began to tell me what the Lord had done for her soul. She poured out a sweet Christian experience in a conversation of half an hour. Her joy was overflowing. She said the very atmosphere she breathed seemed to be love. This lawyer sat where I could look him in the face without appearing to do so. I had learned that he was not a Christian. I saw the muscles of his face quiver; that it was with difficulty that he could suppress his emotions while the old lady was pouring off from her full heart this flood of true Christian experience. After hearing what she had to say, we rose up and took our leave. As we stepped out into the street, he stepped before me and said, "See there! What do you think of that? I know that is the Christian faith! I know that is what I need, and I never was so determined not to rest short of Christian faith as I am now."

Thus I have found it common, when preaching Christian faith as a matter of experience and consciousness, to find it carrying conviction to the minds even of the most skeptical. I have often heard of their saying, "There, I understand that now. I see that is and must be true Christianity; this is what we all need, or certainly we cannot go to heaven."

Without this experience of the kingdom of God in our consciousness, we cannot enjoy what we call Christian duties. If we attempt to perform our Christian duties without this experience, we shall do it only as a task, as a matter of habit, as something that must not be neglected; as something in which we have no true satisfaction. But with this experience, prayer is a real luxury, and we will love to multiply occasions of prayer. So great is the enjoyment of communion with God, so sacred, so calm, so divinely serene and satisfying, that the soul is never in this world so deeply satisfied as when in the deepest communion with God. Christian conversation with truly spiritual persons is a feast of the soul in which the kingdom of God is set up.

Where the kingdom of God is set up in the heart, labor, pains-taking, and even self-denial for the salvation of souls and the glory of God is spontaneous; it is the natural outburst of an inward flame of love, an inward spring of joy and peace. But where the kingdom of God is not reigning in the heart, much prayer is a great burden and people are shy of conversations about Christianity. They have no heart to speak of Christian faith. They can hardly bring themselves to labor for souls and with souls. When the kingdom of God is not truly set up in their heart, it is a real cross to go and labor personally with souls, a real trial, a matter of fearfulness and timidity. Not knowing the kingdom of God in consciousness, they are ashamed and afraid to go and labor earnestly with their neighbors for the salvation of their souls. While they themselves are in bondage to sin and have no real experience of what they teach or of the kingdom of God burning within them, they are ashamed to labor directly and personally with souls.

Without peace and joy we cannot earnestly and honestly recommend Christianity. If our Christianity is a bondage to sin or legalism and void of peace and joy in God, we may warn others of their danger and their guilt; we can commend the Christian faith to them as a matter of personal prudence, as a decision not to be neglected lest they should lose their souls; but we cannot recommend it in such a sense as to draw people

The Kingdom of God in Consciousness

out of the world into a present embracing of the Christian faith and life. The fact is, people want enjoyment for the present; they want something to interest them now; they want something that they can feel now, realize now, interest themselves in and find some satisfaction in now. But if we do not have this peace and joy, all our representations will naturally repel rather than attract their minds. They will admit, "O, Christianity is something we must attend to, but not now. Your Christianity is a necessity, we admit, sometime before we die. We intend to become Christians sometime; but it is a religion to die by and not live by. It is something to be associated with deathbeds and funerals and mournful occasions, not something in which we can find a present interest, enjoyment, and power."

The kingdom of God in our consciousness is the true and only antidote to being worldly-minded. With the kingdom of God set up in his heart, a person is crucified to the world and can well afford that the world should be crucified to him. With the love, peace, and joy of God's kingdom in experience, he will naturally turn away and hide himself in God, rather than mix up unnecessarily with the bustle, the strife, the bitterness, the slang, the egotism, and the insanity of this world.

Many people stop short of experiencing the Kingdom of God in their consciousness. Even if they profess to be Christians, they make up the masses who are pleading for worldly enjoyment, for society's conversations, for the cultivation of a worldly taste. They run after amusements; they journey and do anything to find enjoyment. They must see sights, they must hear music, they must frequent musical entertainments, they must get up worldly pastimes and parties; these things they will seek because they have nothing better in experience.

If we ask why the great mass of those who claim to be Christians are so worldly-minded, the answer is at hand—they do not have the kingdom of God in consciousness. Not being rooted and grounded in love; not having the peace of God ruling in their hearts; not having the joy of God a perpetual fountain welling up within them; how can it be expected that they will not do as they do? But the most surprising thing is that these worldly "Christians" still hold on to the idea that they are truly Christians. If they would be consistent and say, "We have no Christian faith; we have no consciousness of righteousness and peace and joy in the Holy Spirit. We have no joy in God or Christianity. Do you expect us to deprive ourselves of all enjoyment? We have no satisfaction in our spiritual experience; do you us expect to deprive ourselves of seeking satisfaction elsewhere? We do not know God; we must have worldly enjoyments." Now if they would say this and be consistent, they would cease to be stumbling-blocks to others; people would understand them. The world would not hide behind them. They would not then be a standing contradiction of Christianity and a shocking dishonor to Christ, and in that case they would avow their unchristian character. But as it is, strange to tell, they will maintain their claim to be Christians. They think themselves really Christians. But they are not Christians. They seek the world and lust after it, simply because they have no Christian faith in their consciousness.

It is easy to distinguish between those who love God and those who do not. The people in whose heart the kingdom of God is established follow on to know the Lord more and more perfectly. They are under the influence of a divine charm or enchantment. The love of Christ is constraining them. They have tasted and seen that the Lord is gracious. Why should they turn back and lust after the flesh-pots of Egypt? Why should they gad about seeking the love of the world? They have found the home of their hearts in Christ. They have found their resting place, their joyful habitation, their all-satisfying portion. They cannot exchange these spiritual joys for the gross pleasures of the world. They cannot exchange these sacred moments of communion with God for communion with this world. They cannot afford to abandon God's heavenly ways for the insane ways of a wicked world.

Do you ask, "How shall I come to have this experience of the kingdom of God in my soul?" The answer is plain and scriptural: Receive Christ as your Lord and Savior. Open your heart. Christ says, "Behold, I stand at the door and knock; if any man hear my voice, and open the door, I will come in to him, and will sup with him, and he with me" (Revelation 3:20). Give Christ the key to the whole house, of every room and every closet. Let Christ cleanse the whole—cleanse every apartment. Let Him write, "Holiness to the Lord," upon every wall, and every ceiling, and every door, and everything within you. Open your heart. Commit your-

The Kingdom of God in Consciousness

self to Jesus Christ for this very purpose, that He may write His law and establish His throne forever within you. Do it now! Submit to Christ now. Invite Christ into your heart. Lay all upon His altar and ask Him to baptize you with the Holy Spirit.*

---

* Charles G. Finney, *The Oberlin Evangelist,* April 24, 1861, *Principles of Liberty*, 183-194. For Review: Answer the Study Questions on page 232, Cowles page 245.

Principles of Joy in the Holy Spirit — Finney's Lessons on Romans

The Letters of Paul on Joy

Be joyful in hope, patient in affliction, faithful in prayer. —Romans 12:12

For the kingdom of God is not a matter of eating and drinking, but of righteousness, peace and joy in the Holy Spirit, because anyone who serves Christ in this way is pleasing to God and receives human approval. Let us therefore make every effort to do what leads to peace and to mutual edification. —Romans 14:17-19

May the God of hope fill you with all joy and peace as you trust in him, so that you may overflow with hope by the power of the Holy Spirit. —Romans 15:13

I urge you, brothers and sisters, by our Lord Jesus Christ and by the love of the Spirit, to join me in my struggle by praying to God for me. Pray that I may be kept safe from the unbelievers in Judea and that the contribution I take to Jerusalem may be favorably received by the Lord's people there, so that I may come to you with joy, by God's will, and in your company be refreshed. —Romans 15:30-32

Not that we lord it over your faith, but we work with you for your joy, because it is by faith you stand firm. —2 Corinthians 1:24

I wrote as I did, so that when I came I would not be distressed by those who should have made me rejoice. I had confidence in all of you, that you would all share my joy. —2 Corinthians 2:3

I have spoken to you with great frankness; I take great pride in you. I am greatly encouraged; in all our troubles my joy knows no bounds. —2 Corinthians 7:4

In the midst of a very severe trial, their overflowing joy and their extreme poverty welled up in rich generosity. —2 Corinthians 8:2

12

Total Abstinence a Christian Duty
1850

It is good neither to eat flesh, nor to drink wine, nor any thing whereby thy brother stumbleth, or is offended, or is made weak. —Romans 14:21—KJV

It is better not to eat meat or drink wine or to do anything else that will cause your brother to fall. —Romans 14:21—NIV

When Paul wrote, "It is good," he meant, "It is expedient." In this sense, to say that a certain course "is good" is the same as saying it "is best"—it is for the general good—it is expedient and therefore right that we should neither "eat flesh, nor drink wine, nor anything whereby our brethren stumble, are offended, or are made weak."

In the early ages of Christianity, there were several topics much agitated in the Church, some of which had been referred to Paul for decisions. One of the questions from the Church was whether it was lawful to eat meat, inasmuch as it was customary after animals presented for sacrifice to the idols had been before them for a certain time to expose them for sale in the public meat market. Many, therefore, supposed that in purchasing any meat they might thus, *indirectly*, favor idolatry, because they unknowingly purchased some of the meat which had been offered to the idols. Many, for this reason, abstained from the use of meat altogether, lest, as I have said, they should seem to approve of and support idolatry. In the eighth chapter of the First Epistle to the Corinthians, you will find further reference to this subject; the Apostle concludes by saying, "Wherefore, if meat make my brother to offend, I will eat no flesh while the world standeth, lest I make my brother to offend" (1 Corinthians 8:13). In reply to their inquiries, he told them that it was lawful to eat meat under ordinary circumstances; yet, if so doing was an occasion of stumbling to any weak brother, and did more mischief than would counter-balance the good to be derived from it, he would deny himself for that reason. He said, if his eating meat caused his weak brother to offend, he would "eat no flesh while the world standeth." It was not, in itself, unlawful to eat meat; yet, he taught, it was necessary to take care lest the eating of it should stumble the brethren.

Having been requested to preach on the subject of Temperance, I will begin by defining my position and endeavoring to establish my position. Then, I will answer objections and examine the position of those who make the objections.

My position on the subject of Temperance.

The question of Temperance may be viewed in a great many aspects and it may be argued in a vast variety of ways. For example, it may be discussed as a scientific question, and it has been extensively regarded in this light in America. I do not intend to take up this point, but simply examine the Christian bearings of the question. I am well aware that the scientific view is extremely important; however, it is easy enough to proceed to the discussion of it as a Christian question without entering very fully into the scientific issues. My position is not that the use of intoxicating drinks in any quantity and under all circumstances is necessarily sinful. I do not take the ground that any use of intoxicating drinks is wrong independently of the circumstances under which it is used and the reasons which have prompted such use. I do not take the ground that any use of it is wrong irrespective of the circumstances under which and the reasons for which it is used. I can conceive of circumstances under which it may be supposed to be the duty of an individual to drink—even in quantities sufficiently copious to produce intoxication—in order to meet some constitutional emergency. Physicians maintain this ground and patients may think it necessary under such circumstances; therefore, it is taken innocently. The matter is right or wrong according to the reasons and circumstances which demand its use. Strictly speaking, nothing is right in itself except that love which the law of God commands; nothing is wrong in itself except the opposite state of mind. But it is not my purpose to discuss this question, but only to say that when we would inquire into the lawfulness of any particular act, such as the use of alcohol, we must understand the circumstances under which and the reasons for which it is used in order to understand whether it is right or wrong in an individual case.

The question is not whether it may or may not be used as a medicine when recommended by a competent physician. I do not deny that it may be used as a medicine under certain circumstances. Nor do I say that it is wrong to use wine at the table of the Lord. The *Temperance Question* has suffered much from controversy on this point; for if Christ has ordered the use of wine on that occasion, and as matters are left so that it cannot be positively ascertained whether His wine was alcoholic or not, the question need not be discussed; inasmuch as the quantity used at such times is so very small. Paul enjoined Timothy to "Drink no longer water but take a little wine for his stomach's sake, and his often infirmities" (1 Timothy 5:23). It was lawful, therefore, for Timothy to drink a little. The Apostle did not require him to take much; nor is it necessary or usual to take much at the Communion Table, so this part of the question does not strictly belong to the *Temperance Reformation*.

The question is not whether it is or is not necessary in any case, or whether it is or is not an indispensable article of diet in any case. I would take the negative view, but I cannot make this issue at present, as it would carry me too far from my main design. Nor do I mean just now to affirm that it is in no case useful to persons in robust health, as is commonly supposed. Since I cannot now enter into the scientific bearings of the question, I do not mean to determine whether its use is or is not necessary or beneficial to persons in feeble health. I must make the question one of self-denial for the sake of others. I would like to discuss the question of their real necessity or utility under any circumstances, but I must content myself on this occasion with the assumption that under some circumstances the moderate use of these drinks is useful. Therefore, I will take up the matter this way: *"Is it your duty to forego the use of intoxicating drinks as an act of self-denial for the sake of others?"* I love to discuss the question in this light; because, if these intoxicating drinks are useful, it affords Christians an opportunity to manifestitheir love for the Savior by the sacrifice.

My proposition is simply this: *"The manufacture, sale, and use of intoxicating drinks, as a beverage, or as an article of luxury or of diet—or to provide them, as such, for others—is neither benevolent, nor expedient, and is, therefore, wrong."* Or, in other words, *"Total abstinence from the manufacture, sale, and use of intoxicating drinks as a beverage, or as an article of luxury or of diet, and from offering or providing them for others, as such, under the present circumstances of the Church, is expedient, and therefore a duty."*

Establishing my position.

I admit that the abuse of a good thing is not always a sufficient reason for totally abstaining from its use. Food, clothing, the doctrine of justification by faith, many of the best things are abused. Therefore, it is not a universal rule that the abuse of a good thing is a sufficient reason for totally abstaining from its use. But, I shall have occasion to turn my attention to this admission again; because while I admit that it is not a universal rule; yet, I maintain it is a good rule and binding on people under certain circumstances—it is obligatory upon people under certain circumstances to abstain from a thing that may be useful, or that is in fact useful, on the ground of its great abuse. Although I admit the rule is not universal, I shall endeavour to show that the abuse of this article is a good reason that it should be abandoned as an article of luxury or diet.

Total Abstinence a Christian Duty

Benevolence is a universal duty. All people under all circumstances should love God supremely and their neighbor as themselves; this is a rule of universal obligation. There is no possible exception. But what is benevolence? Benevolence is goodwill. Benevolence implies a willing of every good according to its known relative value. There must be no particular stress laid on a certain good because it is your own irrespective of its relative value. When your neighbor's good is of greater value than your own, it must have the preference. If by denying yourself a small good you can procure for him a greater good, it is your duty to do it.

Jesus Christ acted upon this principle in the atonement. The great principle of benevolence upon which everything turns is this—when by sacrificing to oneself a less good, or by taking upon oneself a less evil than would befall others, or by sacrificing a less good than we can obtain for others, the law which requires us to love our neighbor as ourselves plainly points out the path of duty. It is very easy to see that this principle must be the one upon which Christ acted, and upon which the whole plan of salvation turned. By taking upon himself certain evils, He designed to secure to the universe a good which was greater than the evils which He suffered. Therefore, it was in strict accordance with true benevolence that Christ acted in coming forward to make atonement; for the suffering sacrifice He made was an evil of less magnitude than would have been the consequences of an opposite course. Because of His nature and relations, Christ could magnify the law and make it honorable, save multitudes beyond number from eternal suffering, and secure to them an amount of good far exceeding the amount of His sufferings, although His sufferings were inconceivably great. His benevolence led Christ to make personal sacrifice for the sake of a great good. Thus, the apostles also proceeded upon this principle in carrying out the course their Lord and Master had begun.

Everyone admits the following facts. First, intemperance prevails in this land to an alarming extent, far more than people are generally aware of. Since I have been here in England, I have been surprised to learn how ignorant many people are with regard to the statistics of the extent to which intemperance prevails in this country. However, every person knows and admits that intemperance prevails to an alarming extent.

Second, intemperance is one of the greatest evils which infests society, whether it be regarded physically, morally, or socially. Regarding intemperance in its relation to people's health, it cannot be denied that it is one of the greatest physical evils, producing more sickness and death than any other evil. Considered morally, intemperance does more to demoralise society by drawing thousands into all forms of vice, corrupting the Church and causing it to pour forth some forty or fifty thousand yearly from its resources. Considered socially, it poisons all the fountains of social relations. I could enlarge as well as upon its political aspects; if I had time I might swell this statement and adduce such a mass of statistics and facts which have been gathered and published both in England and America that no one could shrink from admitting that as an evil in society and viewed in all its bearings it has no parallel in the history of this nation or in that of any other nation anywhere.

Third, the good which results to the Church and the world from its use (admitting, for the sake of argument, as I said before, that good does result), yet it cannot be denied that any such good is indefinitely less than the evil which results. Who doubts this? Admitting that some good does result, who does not know that the evil resulting from its use is indefinitely greater than the good?

Fourth, the business of the Christian Church is to reform the world. Its sole business in the world is to enlighten and save it—all that it does in the world is to be done in subserviency to this purpose. Its grand object—the goal for which it lives or ought to live and move and have its being—is to glorify God by saving the world from every form of sin. Christ said, "You are the light of the world" (Matthew 5:14) and "You are the salt of the earth" (Matthew 5:13).

Fifth, the Christian Church is bound to reform the world. Christ has required the Church to convert the world—not of course in their own strength, but in His—and He has promised to be with the Church in it; consequently, it is the duty of Christians to put away every form of iniquity from the world and to make disciples of Christ of all the nations of the earth. Christ requires it. He has promised His aid. Therefore, it is the duty of Christians to reform the world. The reform of the world is indispensable to the success of the Church in its great mission. Intemperance

Total Abstinence a Christian Duty

is so great an evil that the Church can by no means be excused from bringing about its removal.

Sixth, if united, Christians are able to effect this reform, and if the Church uses its money, time, and talents rightly—if it does this—it is able to enlighten the world and settle this question forever by putting away this mighty evil. Now, if this reform is indispensable to the success of the Church—to secure the end for which she lives—it would of course follow (if we may judge from the success which has attended efforts made where the Church has been united) that wherever they will steadily and in a right spirit use the right means, and persevere in enlightening the public mind by bringing the whole force of their precept and example to bear upon it, they may thoroughly rout this enemy of the human race and banish it from the world. A multitude of cases which have occurred in America will show that even a few individuals in a Christian community may exert such an influence as to put certain evils away. But who doubts that if the British Churches were united in this matter, an influence could be brought to bear which would rout this enemy and bring about this reformation. Suppose every minister and member of the Christian Church in these realms should frown upon intemperance, and those of all ranks in society who are professed Christians should undertake at once—with all the force of their influence, both by example and precept—to oppose intemperance, how long, think you, would intemperance fill this land with crime, woe, and mourning? No one can doubt that in the course of a few months these vendors' shops would be locked up and the Church purified. Who, of those who took an opposite course, would then dare show their face in the streets when rebuked from every pulpit and from every Christian in every place? Why, the four winds would blow a rebuke in his face! It is easy to put intemperance away, if the Church, whose duty it is to unite for this purpose, would do so. Now, if it can be done by the Church, and it is necessary to be done, and the evil of its remaining is vastly greater than the evil which would result from putting it away, then it is a simple demonstration that it is the duty of every Christian to do what he can by precept and example and every other lawful means to put this evil away.

Principles of Joy in the Holy Spirit — Finney's Lessons on Romans

Let me say again, it will not be doubted I presume by any who have ever examined the question, that the cessation of the manufacture, sale, and use of intoxicating drink as a beverage or an article of luxury or diet is a condition of success in this enterprise. While a minister uses it himself, he cannot have much influence in staying this tide of desolation. This is generally known and acknowledged in England; in America it has been shown up to a perfect demonstration. We have tried every ground a Christian could take on the question, and the conclusion we have come to is this, we must have total abstinence or total failure; this was our final issue. Let any minister continue the use of it and try to reform his congregation. He will find it is a failure. Let any set of people try the moderate use, everybody will hold their views. No drunkard will claim the right to use it in any other degree than moderately—no one will assert that it is right to drink to intoxication—all take the ground of moderation. Moderation! What is it? Intoxication! What is it? Where is the line? Examine this question and you will find that if the Church is to do anything, it must wholly wash her hands. The Church must take this ground—that as a beverage, an article of luxury or diet, it will not indulge in it. The questions will not now be argued, whether it may or may not be used as a medicine; but, in accordance with the terms of my proposition, I shall endeavour to prove that the law of God which requires universal benevolence requires us to aim at promoting our neighbor's good. If our neighbor is stumbled or injured by what we are doing, even though it may be by his own consent; yet if, after all, the injury to him is vastly greater than the good to us, benevolence demands that we should, for his sake, deny ourselves. Especially is this true, where the difference is very great—where the evil to him is enormous—where the evil is indefinitely greater than the good to us—total abstinence on our part is the only condition of saving him from the evil.

The spirit of the Gospel plainly requires total abstinence. I have already said, it is easy to show that the whole plan of salvation turns upon this great principle of Christian benevolence, of one person denying himself of a good for the sake of obtaining a greater good to others—one individual taking to himself certain sufferings and enduring certain evils in order to avoid the infliction of greater though deserved evils on others.

Total Abstinence a Christian Duty

Now, the apostle acted upon the principle of the gospel when he said that if eating meat should cause his brother to stumble, he would eat no more meat while the world stood. He could do without eating meat—although useful, he could eat other things—although a good, it was not a necessity of life. Eating meat was not necessary, because he could do without it; consequently, the great abuse of eating meat offered to idols was a good reason for his abstaining from using it altogether. The same, he said, was true with regard to wine: "It is good neither to eat flesh, nor to drink wine, nor anything whereby thy brother stumbleth, is offended, or is made weak" (Romans 14:21). Now, by "anything," he did not mean to say he must necessarily forego those things which are indispensable to life or salvation; but he could forego those things which could be spared—which were not indispensable—we should abstain from the use of all such things rather than stumble our brethren. By refusing to do this, we walk uncharitably and contrary to the spirit of the Gospel.

The intelligence and conscience of the Christian world demands that the Church should proceed to take up this question. It seems now to be called up by the providence of God and most pressingly urged upon the Church. The public conscience is beginning to awaken on this subject in England; and, to a still greater extent in America, because more has been said there than has been said here. But I have never been anywhere, since this subject has been so thoroughly discussed, where the consciences of all classes of people—infidels as well as Christians—did not demand at once that the Church should take action. The law of benevolence requires that everyone—not only Christians, but all people—should take up this reform and deny themselves for the sake of the good which may result. The Church of God is manifestly under rebuke on this point. I might mention many instances in which the Spirit has been manifestly grieved by this holding back—cases in which ministers of the Gospel have not been successful—where they did not preach with that unction and power which give the Gospel effect—where the Christians have dwindled away in number, while those who remained had decreased in spirituality. I could bring a great many evidences of this in different denominations of Christians wherever this subject is neglected, since it has come up in the providence of God. It is remarkable to see the extent to which this has been manifested in America, where the displeasure of the Almighty has been visible towards those who have withstood this reformation.

It does strike me, therefore, that as a matter of self-denial, and a Christian duty on the ground of expediency and charity, the question is perfectly plain; still, however, there are many objections, some of which I shall now proceed to answer.

Admitting, then, *for the sake of the argument*, that intoxicating drink is a good; it must also be admitted that it is not indispensable, while it is easy to show that the evils resulting from its abuse are vastly greater than the good derivable from its use; therefore, the law of benevolence plainly demands abstinence, because, upon the whole, the use is an evil rather than a good.

Answers to Objections.

Some object, that "Christ used alcoholic, or fermented wines; and that, if benevolence required abstinence, He would have abstained." This needs to be proved before it is assumed as a certain truth. I do not know that He did; and I will not affirm that He did not. The sweet wines were called "wine," as well as the fermented. To establish the fact that Christ used alcoholic wines, it is said that He was accused of being a gluttonous man and a wine-bibber, a friend of publicans and sinners (see Matthew 11:19). It is argued that since He neither expressly nor implicitly denied that He used wine; therefore, from His non-denial, He did use wine. However, it no more follows that He did, than the fact that He did not deny that He was a glutton implied that He admitted it. But even if He had used wine, the circumstances under which He used it not only justified but might have demanded its use in His case. I have already said that the use of wine is not wrong in itself; it is presumable that in the case of Timothy some urgent reason existed for his abstaining from the use of water, and taking a little wine; but observe, in this case, it was enjoined as a medicine and not as an article of luxury or diet. From Paul's statement, it may fairly be inferred that Timothy was not in the habit of taking wine in any quantities; for it was but little which he was enjoined to take; while, if he had taken it in any quantity before, this injunction would have been unnecessary. It has been supposed that the apostles and their coadjutors said nothing upon the subject of temperance or against the use of alcoholic drinks. It is obvious that Timothy did not use it, and that he actually needed the injunction of the apostle to induce him to do so, even as a medicine. Observe what the apostle says: "It is good neither to eat flesh, nor to drink wine, or anything whereby thy brother stumbleth, or is offended, or is made weak." Therefore, is it likely that after such language as this, the apostle himself used it or recommended it to be used as an article of luxury or diet, especially where the circumstances were such that its abuse was a great stumbling-block to the Church? No! It is not likely that Paul would thus contradict himself!

Others object that if temperance, in the sense here meant, is a specific branch of the great reformation to be carried out and perfected by the Christian Church, "Why did not the Apostolic Church do it?" They had very good reasons for not doing it. There were several other important questions as well as the use of wine, such as war and slavery, for instance, which were not raised as distinct subjects. I know that this fact has been used by some persons, and even by ministers, in such a manner as to lead many persons into infidelity. They say the apostles could not have been inspired men, neither could Christ have been what He professed to be, or He and the apostles would have used all their influence to suppress war and put an end to slavery and intemperance. Let us inquire, for a moment, whether it would have been expedient for them to have done otherwise than they did in this matter. The fact is, they had a previous question to settle. It was by no means generally admitted that Jesus was the Messiah; consequently, if He had attempted to have exercised authority on this point, had made such reforms a prominent object, He would thereby have diverted public attention from the first great question of His Messiahship. So it was with the apostles; the advent, divine authority, and the resurrection of Christ was the first question to be settled. It is easy to see that it was totally inexpedient to raise any excitement on other points till this was settled. First, it was necessary to show that their revelation was divine, that Jesus was the Messiah, and that they were His inspired and duly commissioned servants. Suppose, either by precept or example, they had raised the questions before mentioned, they would have left their main position unsustained, and would have left undone the work they had been particularly commissioned to do. Their first great business was to establish the fact that what they set forth was a revelation from God, and not to take any particular branch of reform and raise a question upon that, thereby diverting public attention from their main question. If the question could once be settled that their message was a revelation from God, it would then be in place for the Church to take it up in its details, and apply its great principles to the annihilation of every form and degree of evil. It took Christ and His apostles their lifetime to settle the great question of the true Messiahship of Jesus, the divine authority of the apostles, and to establish beyond controversy the fact that what they delivered to the world was truly the mind and will of God. Now, they no doubt avoided (and wisely) making issue with many points and branches of reform before the one great question was settled that they were commissioned by God to give to us, a revelation of His will. They no doubt studiously avoided making such issues either by precept or example; hence, it is not strange if they did use wine moderately, as it was the common drink of the country. I suppose they could not well have avoided this without having raised an excitement on the question. I judge this from the fact that the very practice has often provoked vehement discussion as I have sat at table. You cannot abstain without having more or less of this excitement. At some tables where I have refused to take wine, I have been obliged, in self-defence, to enter into a discussion of the question. No doubt this would have been the case with Christ and His apostles; and it might have been—I do not say it was—for this reason that they were unwilling to start a public fermentation on the subject at that time and under those circumstances. Who does not see, as I have said, that the issue to be first made and settled was whether or not their revelation was from God. If you look through the Bible, you will find principles which condemn war, slavery, and intemperance as well as every other form of vice. No one, I presume, will accuse the apostles of being warriors, slave-holders, or intemperate men. But mark! Christianity is never to be chargeable with these evils, because its moral and spiritual principles condemn them everywhere. Nothing is more certain than this, war, slavery, and intemperance, and every other form of iniquity,

Total Abstinence a Christian Duty

is condemned by the Gospel of Christ. Let no one, therefore, reject the Bible on the pretence that it sanctions or connives at such evils as these. God has proceeded step by step in His various reforms as people were able to bear them. There is no occasion for fault-finding either with the Bible or with God's dealings on these questions. By now, I should think that what I have said on this subject will be quite enough to satisfy people who were willing to be satisfied with regard to the example of Christ and the apostles. Admitting they did use wine moderately, the reasons for so doing that I have named, are, I think, too obvious to leave any stumbling-block on this score in the way of any honest mind.

Many take the position that they manufacture, vend, use, and offer alcohol as indispensable to health. Now, more than 1,000 medical men, and among them many of the principal physicians of Great Britain, have testified that alcoholic drink is wholly unnecessary and may be done without in perfect safety. In America, the fact is established in hundreds of thousands of cases. The deacon of the church to which I first belonged was an elderly man who accustomed himself to take alcoholic drinks in small quantities before his meals as "his appetite was poor" and as "his physician had recommended him to do so." Now, soon after my conversion the temperance question came up in the United States generally, and particularly in that neighborhood. As the church began to examine the matter, they found the influence of this deacon greatly in their way. Many of the members were ready to go through with temperance for the sake of the public good; but Deacon Cleary, being an elderly man, did not take up reforms so readily. Finally, some of the brethren ventured to expostulate with him. But he said he was "sure he could not do without it." He was "sure he should die, if he wholly abstained;" but, "he would use it moderately as a medicine." At length, however, he said his life was of no great importance; it was of less importance that he should live than that he should stand in the way of the reform. He thought the devil was trying to take his life and he would rather, therefore, give it up than be a stumbling-block. He said, "You may have my name and whatever influence I possess to help the reform." Now, notice this, in a couple of years his strength was renewed and he became quite a different man. On being asked what he thought of giving up alcohol, he said, "Oh! I am renewing my youth! It was the devil who made me think I could not do without it!" This has been the experience in cases all but innumerable in America; and I have not heard this argument for years. It is not contended for as a necessary article of diet, or at least to my knowledge it has not been for years.

I formerly used it moderately and occasionally myself, but I have now abstained for twenty-five years; and surely I have performed as much labor, I think, as any minister, either in America or in Europe; and I can say that I am better in health now than I was on the day I abandoned its use. I can do more now than I could when I was accustomed sometimes in moderation to use it; and my experience is corroborated in instances beyond number.

Some object that the rights of hospitality demand its use. Now, what is intended by this? The rights of hospitality! Has anyone a right to expect me to do that which is inconsistent with benevolence as a mere matter of hospitality? No! Perhaps you think you will be accused of selfishness instead of benevolence by refusing to provide it. The fact is, if your reputation must suffer for doing your duty, let it suffer; for the person who is not prepared to do this is not prepared to go the length of taking Christ and His apostles as His examples. When people bring up such excuses and accuse others of selfishness, they are not even themselves satisfied with their own reasonings, even while they accuse others of selfishness and of disregarding the rights of hospitality in not offering it—I cannot believe that they are satisfied with such reasoning as theirs.

Some object that they cannot employ laborers without providing it, or giving them the means. They will have it in some way, and if they do not give it to them, they will not work for them. Farmers in our country furnish their laborers with board almost universally; and people have urged that the men will not work unless they give them alcohol in some form. But if they were to advise their laborers not to drink it, setting the example themselves; and if they were to give them in wages the amount of what it would cost to furnish them with alcohol—if they were to do this it would be fair enough; and where it has been done, as far as I know, it has given universal satisfaction. Increase their wages by giving them the worth of the alcohol in money, and soon the laborers will be not only satisfied, but glad that such an experiment was tried! There is no difficulty in getting over this. If Christian employers will but persevere in taking strong and right grounds, their employees will soon be influenced by them not to take it. Finding they do not really need it, they will be glad to receive the money instead.

Some object that teetotalism is made a religion of; therefore, there is danger in inculcating it. Now, I never knew an instance of this kind in my life. On the contrary, we have observed that when we can get people to abstain, they almost invariably come to a more just apprehension of God and religious truth. When we induce them to abstain from these drinks, they see more clearly by far the necessity of a change of heart and a Christian life. Indeed, it is strange to suppose that after clearing a person's whole system of this abomination, we should make him all the more apt to deceive himself! Therefore, this danger is very small. But there is a good deal of danger on the other hand. Those who make this objection do not seem to understand that there is a danger of being deceived by the spirit of alcohol—a danger of confounding the influences of alcohol with those of the Spirit of God. Now, every physiologist is aware that there are certain persons on whose minds stimuli in certain forms produce certain impressions; and in many cases these impressions incline them to think and talk about religion. For instance, when I was quite a lad, I was teaching a school one winter and boarding in a house. The head of the family was an intemperate man, and often came home from the public-house in a state of intoxication, so much so, indeed, as to walk in such a manner that everyone could see he was intoxicated. Now, when he came home in this state, he invariably prayed with his family; while on other occasions, he never said a word on the subject of religion. Such was the tendency of his mind. This is an extreme case, I admit; but I have known multitudes of cases involving the same principle. I have seen men exceedingly fluent in prayer and flippant in religious conversation after taking a little alcohol. I knew a minister who never preached fluently unless he was well steeped in alcohol, and when I rebuked him for it, he told me that he would rather give five dollars for a gill of brandy when he had to preach than preach without it.* After taking alcohol, he could speak, preach, or pray; rob him of that, and he seemed to have no more of the spirit of preaching than a stick or a stone. For years he went on in this way; and when the *Temperance Reformation* compelled him to abandon alcohol, he resorted to opium as a substitute. There is a tendency in many minds to this. But, in justice, I ought to say, that I am not aware that it has been customary in general for ministers of the gospel in America to take alcohol in any form just before going into the pulpit; and never in my life to my recollection did I so much as hear of its being kept in the vestry in any form for the use of ministers or church officers. I cannot but express my astonishment and grief at this custom as I find it exists in some cases in this country. I have sometimes found a man praying with very much apparent fervency; but when I have come near him, I have found his breath smelt of alcohol! Take the alcohol away and see how he would pray then! If you mean to give him fervency, you must give him alcohol. If you would see that there is nothing in him but spiritual death, deprive him of it.

In America, before the *Temperance Reformation*, multitudes of such cases occurred. Many years ago, I was laboring in a town in the State of New York during a revival of religion. I boarded with a deacon who always had a glass full of old cider on his table. His eyes glistened after partaking of it, which he did in large quantities. I spoke to his pastor as to his general character. He said he was "always in the Spirit—always ready." I told him I was afraid he either was, or would be, a drunkard. The minister was quite shocked. Said I, his speech and general appearance are those of a man who keeps himself highly excited with alcohol. The minister never thought of this.

It was customary of the temperance men to send lecturers round where there had been revivals; that they might make their appeal while the public conscience was awake and men's minds were yielding to truth and easily won over to the reform. They visited the place referred to, but this reputed good man resisted the *Temperance Reformation*; and, to the astonishment of everyone, it was found that he was a secret drunkard—that he had often been seen drunk by his family at different times extending over many years. He was, of course, excommunicated from the church as a drunkard. By now, he may be in a drunkard's grave! I have seen such results as this one among those who opposed the *Temperance Reformation* so many times that I have come greatly to fear that ministers or professed

Total Abstinence a Christian Duty

Christians who continue to oppose it will become drunkards.

Another objection is, "Many who became abstainers have turned back to drink again." I have very frequently read this, and have been shocked, I cannot tell how much, to hear it sometimes even from those who claim to be Christians. Admitting its truth, what does it amount to? Even if nearly all go back to drinking—what then? Is it amazing that they do, while the Church stands aloof and opposes the *Temperance Reformation*? Suppose people should attempt any other branch of reform, and the Church with its weightiest influence should oppose them—who would wonder if they became faint-hearted? If the ministers and nearly all the Church should frown, or at least should fail to smile, is it any wonder that the masses should go back thinking they are wrong? Who does not see that it is almost miraculous that such masses should continue to stand by their reformation under such circumstances? Suppose great revivals of religion should spread throughout the land, and great efforts should be made; but, suppose again that the ministers and Churches should rise up and denounce it as the work of the devil and give the whole of their influence against it, discouraging the efforts, and setting their faces firmly against it—if the converts, under these circumstances, backslide, and then the Church say, "There, you see your revival is good for nothing—half of you backslide!" Would it be thought any wonder that they had backslidden? It is easy to see, then, who is the occasion of this going back; and yet these are the very persons to make this a stumbling-block and objection to the reformation.

Some object, "It would be better to seek the conversion of people to God, and aim at making them Christians, and then temperance will take care of itself." But let me say, there are thousands and thousands of people who never can be made Christians until they abandon alcohol. How can such be made Christians, when half the time they are under the influence of alcohol? Again, suppose they were converted. Could they be expected not to fall away—ever and anon to backslide, unless they abstained? If such are to be saved, the proper means must be used, and the stumbling-blocks removed out of their way. I believe the saints will persevere; but I also believe it will be because the stumbling-blocks will be overcome and removed out of the way. It was supposed, when first our missionaries went abroad, that the question of caste would "take care of itself." It was said the natives were "sensitive on the point, therefore do not attack it. Make them Christians, and caste will take care of itself." But one of our missionaries (whose name I was glad to see in the British Banner yesterday attached to an address on the subject), once told me this, "We have done wrong. We have allowed men to believe that they could be Christians, and yet retain their ideas of caste, supposing that Christianity would remove this feeling. But we find we have thus allowed an element to exist in the Church, which, if it remain, will ruin it." He said that when he went back to India he would have to "excommunicate a multitude whose spirit of caste had overcome their Christianity, instead of the opposite course as they had hoped."

But I must pass rapidly over this ground. Some object that good men have used it. So they have. But good men have also engaged in the slave-trade. John Newton, for instance, did so for some time after his conversion. Whitefield was a slave-holder. But they were not fully informed on the point. When such things are done in ignorance, the men may be Christians, notwithstanding. But it does not therefore follow that in these days of light Christians may hold slaves, or vend, or use, or offer alcohol when the truth has been presented to them and an entirely different aspect of the question comes up.

Again, some object, "I can do nothing alone, and my individual example can do but little; therefore, although I care nothing about alcoholic drinks, it is of no use for me, as an individual, to make an effort." Now, the misery is that there are so many who say this when, if everyone would lay aside this plea and take action, there would be a great army in this enterprise and no one would think or talk of being alone! Come up each one of you for himself! Give the influence of your name and your example! When will this work ever be done while each one stands away and says, "If I come, I must come alone!" But if you are obliged to come alone, come alone! At any rate, rid your skirts of this abomination.

The last objection I shall notice is that almost as often as I have brought this subject up in conversation, and other ways, since I have been in this country, I have heard the objection thrown out that the cause of teetotalism has been rendered odious by the imprudence, mismanagement, and false position of its advocates. I have heard the same objection made repeatedly in America to both the anti-slavery and temperance reforms. It has been common in America for those who withhold their influence from these reformations to say, "We are in favor of temperance," or "We are opposed to slavery." "But, we cannot identify ourselves with the abolitionists," or "We cannot identify ourselves with the teetotalers. Because we cannot approve of many of their measures and arguments." I have been in the habit of making this reply: "Brethren, show us a more excellent way. Come forward and take the lead. We will give you the lead, and shall be glad to follow, if you will come forward and give us the benefit of your wisdom and prudence in precept and in example. Why do you stand back? Why do you leave it for others to go forward, and then complain of their want of wisdom? They would have been glad to have availed themselves of your wisdom and experience, if you would have allowed them to have done so. If you will be leaders in this enterprise, we will be glad to have you; and if you will not, why not? Why do you stand back and refuse to put your hand to the work, because there is not so much wisdom exercised in pushing these reforms as you think you might exercise yourselves?" The fact is, it is horrible for those of the highest influence in society to remain silent till those perhaps of less influence, and less wisdom, are compelled to do something, and go forward according to the best of their judgment, and then for these wise men to excuse the withholding their influence altogether, because, they say, the cause is not advocated in the wisest manner!

Examine the position of those who make the objections.

I might assail their position from many points, and examine it in a great many ways; but I prefer, on the present occasion, to present it in the form of what logicians call the *argumentum ad hominem*. Sometimes we have an argument pressed upon an individual in this way; he admits certain truths, and, admitting these truths, we can present an argument, upon his own grounds, that will have a bearing directly upon him in view of his own premises. This is what logicians call *argumentum ad hominem*, and this shall be the form in which I will present this part of the argument.**

Principles of Joy in the Holy Spirit — Finney's Lessons on Romans

In England, you have settled the unlawfulness of slave-holding. Between yourselves and me, there is no difference of opinion on this subject. You believe that making, vending, and holding people as slaves is sinful and a great abomination in the sight of God, and that it ought to be immediately abandoned. I agree. Now, in view of this admission of yours, I remark, that the liquor-trade is as injurious to society as the slave-trade. I can only go rapidly over this part of the subject. For example, who would not rather that his son or daughter, husband or wife, should be torn away and sent into slavery, for there he or she might have the use of reason, and at least be moral and Christian, rather than become the victim of drunkenness? I need not say that I do not in any degree sympathise with slavery. My tongue has not been silent against it, nor has my pen been useless in fighting slavery. I have used both tongue and pen to rebuke this great iniquity.

One of the features of slavery which has, perhaps, been most complained of is its sundering of family ties, tearing children from their parents, and sending its various members to different parts of the country—thus severing them forever. Now, look at alcohol. Does not alcohol do worse than separate them one from another? Yes, indeed! I would rather have my wife torn away and made a slave, and my family broken up, than that we should become a family of drunkards! Who does not know that there are more ways than one to lacerate the heart, tear the family to pieces, and effect domestic ruin? Slavery is bad, but the sale of alcoholic drinks, which ruins thousands of families, is worse than selling them into slavery. The one is bad enough, but the other is still worse. Would you not rather that your own family were sold into slavery than that they should become a family of drunkards? Slaves are made so by force—drunkards are made by their own consent. In being made a slave, a person commits no sin; a person becoming a drunkard ruins both soul and body. Both of them appear wrong under the light which the Gospel pours upon them, when they are presented and developed in their proper aspect.

Inasmuch as the slavery question is settled in this country, and connection therewith accounted a great wickedness, I address the question to you in this shape, because you English people admit that slavery is not to be tolerated and that, however convenient or necessary some may assert it to be, they may not have slaves to be their servants, even if it were impossible to get servants without slaves, as the slaveholders maintain—you will hear no such arguments. I honor you for the ground you take on this question; but I should like to see you take equally consistent ground on the liquor question.

In both cases, the demand sustains the trade. If nobody bought slaves, nobody would raise them: and if nobody used alcohol, it would not be manufactured and sold. More than this; if nobody abused alcohol, though it were a useful article of diet, yet there would not enough be demanded to render it a profitable article of manufacture or sale; it is the enormous abuse of it which makes it so profitable. The sale and manufacture is undertaken upon the assumption of its abuse. I doubt whether there is a single manufacturer or vendor in Great Britain who will deny that it is this abuse which renders it so profitable an article of traffic and that it is made and sold on this assumption. In the cases of both slavery and alcohol manufacture, the enormous quantity advertised for sale increases the demand. When once the advertising began, its exhibition everywhere increased the amount of temptation and the demand increased.

It is remarkable to what an extent both of these evils are sustained and defended by the same arguments. The upholders of these evils appeal to the Bible in the same way. Some say the Bible sanctions and sustains slavery; others are content that the Bible recognizes the existence of slavery and does not condemn it. The same course is taken on the liquor question. They say the evil existed when the inspired men lived and people were allowed to use it. The Bible is quoted as conniving at it. But I have not time fully to trace the parallel, or you would be struck with the extent to which these questions are sustained by the same arguments. Intoxicating drink, then, is a greater social, political, domestic, individual, and moral evil than slavery. It introduces more immorality. It does more injury to the cause of Jesus Christ; it does more to ruin the bodies and souls of people than slavery. No well informed person can consistently deny this.

Both evils are persevered in for the same reason. Their usefulness and necessity are pleaded for in the same manner. The spirit of selfishness acts the same part in both cases. In America, we find the same difficulty in both cases in the way of getting rid of these evils. Both are so firmly fixed in the habits of the people—so many interests are at stake, so much property is invested, both in ardent spirits and in slaves—there are so many difficulties in the way of getting rid of both—it is astonishing to see to what an extent these difficulties are the same. We find the same reluctance to examine the question on the part of those who are connected with either of these trades. Many pulpits were formerly shut to both these questions. Preachers have refused to give notice from the pulpits of meetings on these subjects. There is the same sensibility of rebuke both from the pulpit and through the press. Some said they were not proper questions for the pulpit, especially on the Sabbath.

With reference to intoxicating drink in this country, it is the same as slavery is in ours. In the North of our country, ministers preach in season and out of season against both those evils on the Sabbath as well as on other days; but at first they were sneered at. A great amount of sensitiveness existed in all classes against bringing up discussions on these subjects. It was said it would produce divisions in the churches. So it did. Nevertheless, it must be done. The same sympathy for those who are committed to both of these evils has been manifested under the name of charity. We have been often called upon to be charitable with regard to those engaged in the manufacture, sale, and use of these drinks, as well as towards the slave-dealer and the slaveholder. The same arguments in this respect, too, are used in both cases. There has been the same sacrifice of ministerial character—some ministers have eventually been banished from their pulpits for not sympathizing with these reforms. In America, this has been the case to a lamentable extent. Ministers are now beginning to take high grounds and preach on both questions.

I wish I had all the ministers of Great Britain here before me this evening! I would ask them, "If you continue to stand aloof, in what light will the public come to regard you?" For I have learned that one body of them have actually refused to receive a memorial on the subject (a memorial is a resolution brought before a denominational body, usually composed of ministers and elders, that requires a vote on a subject that will have an effect on the whole denomination)! Now, who does not know that these ministers and elders must suffer in the estimation of those who inquire?

Total Abstinence a Christian Duty

When it comes to be considered that 60,000 of your fellow countrymen annually go down to a drunkard's grave and every year some 40,000 or 50,000 are excommunicated from your churches for this sin—when the people become fully alive to these and multitudes of similar facts which might be stated, they will consider it a shame for the ministers to withhold their influence on this question. Yes! The ministers are deceived if they think the people are satisfied with their present position on this question.

I am glad to find that so many ministers have already given the weight of their example to this reform, and among them the excellent minister of this place (Rev. James Sherman). I congratulate you, brethren, on this point. Since I have been in this country, I have been thrown into the company of ministers and have been shocked! For years, till I came here, I have not seen a minister drink a drop except at the communion table. I have seen enough in America to demonstrate that there no minister can be sustained by public confidence who withholds the influence of his precept and example from the *Temperance Reformation*. And if you will continue to use it, and refuse to rebuke it both by precept and example, you must expect to lose the public confidence; and, as certain as God rules the world, you ought to lose it!

I speak this all in charity. I know very well that the time has been in my own country when the question was not thoroughly understood. Alcohol was used because it was considered necessary; many, however, though still supposing it to be useful, denied themselves on account of its abuse and the great evils which arose from its use.

There is the same tendency to infidelity resulting from the conduct of the churches in reference to both of these questions. In the United States, it has been common for persons to say there can be no truth in Christianity, because the Church, and especially the ministers, do not come out and take decided ground on these questions. The same is going on in this country with respect to the *Temperance Reformation*; multitudes are losing their confidence in ministers and churches, in the Bible, and even in Christianity itself.

I have thus pursued a rapid parallel between the slave traffic and the traffic in alcoholic drinks. I have only suggested points for your consideration. Perhaps I should do well to say that a tract has been written and published in the United States, by one of our best men, pursuing this parallel. I have never myself read this tract, but it made a deep impression, as it well might; for who cannot see that in every part of society intemperance is an evil as injurious as slavery? And when light is cast upon it, the crime of both is great, if not quite equally so?

It costs the Church more to use alcoholic drinks than she can afford. The providence of God plainly calls upon the Church to act now. There is a minister in this country whom I have heard openly oppose the total abstinence question, and declare that he has no sympathy with it. Now, I have been informed that this very man's wife is a drunkard; his eldest son, too, is such a beast of a drunkard that he requires someone constantly to take care of him. The rest of his family will probably go in the same direction. Still, he "has no sympathy with the *Temperance Reformation*!" I myself have seen him drink glass after glass, and that more than once. What infatuation is this! Yet what else could he expect? Let me state that thousands of cases involving the same principle might be adduced where persons have opposed teetotalism until the result has been the ruin of their families, or, at least, of some members of their families.

I once urged a man to become a teetotaler, because I feared he would be a drunkard. He said he would consent "if his wife would go with him." I reasoned for an hour with her; but all in vain. I said, "You will rue this, mark me." She replied, "I'll risk it." Now, in less than five years, her husband has become a drunkard! Perhaps he is now in a drunkard's grave.

While conversing with a brother minister the other day, I was astonished to hear him say that he was struck with the use I made of Leviticus 10:9, which expressly states that priests were not, on pain of death, to take wine or strong drink when going to the services of the sanctuary. He asked, "Is there such a passage as this?" "Yes, there is," I said. He could not believe it, so I got up from the table, took the Bible, and showed him these verses: "And the LORD spake unto Aaron, saying, Do not drink wine nor strong drink, thou, nor thy sons with thee, when ye go into the tabernacle of the congregation, lest ye die: it shall be a statute for ever throughout your generations: And that ye may put difference between holy and unholy, and between unclean and clean; And that ye may teach the children of Israel all the statutes which the LORD hath spoken unto them by the hand of Moses.

Some say, "I take a little, but don't care about it." You take just enough to prevent your rebuking it in those who take much; for they will turn around and ask if you entirely abstain, and your influence in the matter comes to nothing, or rather it confirms them in their evil habit. If you care so little as you say, what a pity it is you range yourself on the opposite side for such a trifle!

I have been informed by one who was a city missionary, and have been repeatedly assured by those who profess to know, that the managers of the City Mission discourage the advocacy of the total abstinence principle by their missionaries. Now, I cannot vouch for the truth of this; but if it is true, such conduct is worthy of unmeasured rebuke, and may well account for their comparatively small success. What! City missionaries, one of whose principal duties it ought to be to secure total abstinence among the poor, discouraged from such efforts! If this is so, it is both shocking and abominable. It may be untrue; I hope it is.

Do the churches in England expect a general revival while they resist this reform and refuse to come up and lay themselves upon the altar? If they do, I am sure they are mistaken. It is perfectly plain that the ministers of this kingdom have not given themselves in earnest to rebuke this sin, and carry forward the temperance reform. I have occasion to know that some ministers and others, who are themselves abstainers, nevertheless provide alcoholic drinks for their guests—who do not hesitate to put alcoholic drinks upon their tables for the use of others. Some of them seldom preach against drinking, and when they do, they are in the habit of giving notice beforehand that they are going to preach against drinking and that those who do not like to be rebuked may absent themselves. Thus they try to satisfy their consciences, either with bearing the silent testimony of their example against it, or, at most, by preaching perhaps only once a year a sermon on the subject. Now, is it not plain that this is rather an apology for a temperance effort rather than anything like laying themselves upon the altar with a determination to push this reformation? What does it mean? Why do they not on all occasions rebuke this as one of the reigning sins and evils of the day and of the land? Why do they not

Principles of Joy in the Holy Spirit — Finney's Lessons on Romans

speak against it, pray against it, write against it, rebuke it everywhere and on all occasions like men who have resolutely undertaken to put away one of the greatest abominations of the world?

The fact is, the great mass of ministers using wine and other intoxicating drinks directly countenance this evil as it exists in society. Comparatively few are abstainers, and those, either because they fear they shall offend their brethren in the ministry, or their churches or congregations, or all these together, do very little, I fear, to promote this great reform, and put away this wide-spread and overwhelming evil. And is this the way for ministers of God to treat one of the greatest, most widespread, and most desolating of evils that ever cursed any country? Why, really it is lamentable to see to what an extent the leaders of the sacramental hosts of God's elect compromise with this evil! If they hold their peace much longer the stones will cry out against them, and society will universally rebuke them. For if this is not so, then those laws of mind that have so strongly developed themselves in every other country will fail to do so in this country. But there is no mistake. The public conscience is beginning to arouse itself, and there is a murmuring deep and increasing that will eventually speak forth in accents that must be understood. The time is come for the Church and her ministers to speak out and rebuke this evil everywhere and on all occasions. Will not the brethren come up to the work?

When I was first settled in New York City in 1832, I found that one of the elders of the church was a spirit-dealer. The *Temperance Reformation* was but, as it were, beginning to excite public attention. I reasoned with him in private, but without effect; I then exposed his business in my public preaching, and when he objected to my doing so, I told him that as often as I went into that pulpit he might expect that I should rebuke both him and his business till he either forsook the congregation or abandoned the abominable traffic. I did so, and did not let him rest till he left his seat, and went to another congregation; and his place was filled by a better man.

But I see I have trespassed too long on your time. The subject is so extensive as to need a course of lectures. I have condensed as much as possible and endeavoured to present the subject as fully as I could in one

Total Abstinence a Christian Duty

lecture; however, I must now leave the subject with a word of appeal to the ladies of England. The female sex are deeply interested in this question. You are wives, mothers, sisters; do you not see the multitudes of husbands, fathers, brothers going to destruction through the use of these drinks? Will you not give the benefit of the whole weight of your precept and example against this crying evil? Shall women withhold their influence from a cause that appeals so strongly to the sympathies and the hearts of all classes of people? If the female sex were to unite their efforts, and wholly discountenance the use of alcoholic drinks, and refuse to associate with those who do use them, in one year they might effect a change which would be the admiration of the world. Will they not come up to the work?***

---

* A "gill" is a unit of measure especially in regard to alcoholic beverages. In Great Britain, 1 imperial gill is 5 imperial fluid ounces. Customarily in the United States of America, 1 US gill is 4 US fluid ounces. 1 imperial gill is equivalent to 1.2 US gills.

** Carefully note Finney's definition of *argumentum ad hominem* (which means, *arguing against the person*), for in his use, Finney carefully avoids using personal attacks upon those he argues against, while he does call the sinner to repentance. Finney is *arguing against the person* in the sense of showing the inconsistencies or contradictions in their beliefs and reasonings. Today, we might say that Finney uses the *reductio ad absurdum* argument, which reduces the opponent's arguments to absurdity. Today, logicians consider the *argumentum ad hominem* to be fallacious, but not in the sense that Finney applies his arguments. For Finney, it is inconsistent, if not absurd, to be opposed to slavery and not also opposed to the use of alcoholic drinks for recreation or diet.

*** Charles G. Finney, "The Penny Pulpit," preached on Thursday evening, June 27, 1850, at the Surrey Chapel, Southwark, London, England. Founded by the Rev. Roland Hill, the chapel existed from 1783-1881, and was the site of the first Sunday school in London. When Finney preached at Surrey Chapel, the Rev. James Sherman, a Congregational minister, was the pastor. For Review: Answer the Study Questions on page 233, Cowles page 245.

Principles of Joy in the Holy Spirit — Finney's Lessons on Romans

The Letters of Paul on Joy

But the fruit of the Spirit is love, joy, peace, forbearance, kindness, goodness, faithfulness, gentleness and self-control. Against such things there is no law. —Galatians 5:22-23

I thank my God every time I remember you. In all my prayers for all of you, I always pray with joy because of your partnership in the gospel from the first day until now. —Philippians 1:3-5

Convinced of this, I know that I will remain, and I will continue with all of you for your progress and joy in the faith. —Philippians 1:25

Therefore if you have any encouragement from being united with Christ, if any comfort from his love, if any common sharing in the Spirit, if any tenderness and compassion, then make my joy complete by being like-minded, having the same love, being one in spirit and of one mind. —Philippians 2:1-2

Therefore, my brothers and sisters, you whom I love and long for, my joy and crown, stand firm in the Lord in this way, dear friends! — Philippians 4:1

You became imitators of us and of the Lord, for you welcomed the message in the midst of severe suffering with the joy given by the Holy Spirit. —1 Thessalonians 1:6

Indeed, you are our glory and joy. —1 Thessalonians 2:20

How can we thank God enough for you in return for all the joy we have in the presence of our God because of you? —1 Thessalonians 3:9

Your love has given me great joy and encouragement, because you, brother, have refreshed the hearts of the Lord's people. —Philemon 1:7

13

Doubtful Actions are Sinful
1837

And he that doubteth is damned if he eat, because he eateth not of faith: for whatsoever is not of faith is sin. —Romans 14:23—KJV

But the man who has doubts is condemned if he eats, because his eating is not from faith; and everything that does not come from faith is sin.—Romans 14:23—NIV

IT was a custom among the idolatrous heathen to offer the bodies of slain beasts in sacrifice, and a part of every beast that was offered belonged to the priest. The priests used to send their portion to market to sell, and it was sold in the meat market as any other meat. The Christian Jews that were scattered everywhere were very particular as to what meats they ate, so as not even to run the least danger of violating the Mosaic law; therefore, they raised doubts and created disputes and difficulties among the churches. This was one of the subjects about which the Corinthian church was divided and agitated, until they finally wrote to the Apostle Paul for directions. A part of the First Epistle to the Corinthians was doubtless written as a reply to such inquiries. It seems there were some who carried their scruples so far that they thought it improper to eat any meat at all; for if they went to market for it, they were continually in danger of buying meat that was offered to idols. Others thought it made no difference; they had a right to eat meat and they would buy it in the market as they found it and give themselves no trouble about the matter. To quell the dispute, they wrote to Paul, and in the eighth chapter of the First Epistle to the Corinthians Paul takes up the subject and discusses it fully:

> Now about food sacrificed to idols: We know that "We all possess knowledge." But knowledge puffs up while love builds up. Those who think they know something do not yet know as they ought to know. But whoever loves God is known by God. So then, about eating food sacrificed to idols: We know that "An idol is nothing at all in the world" and that "There is no God but one." For even if there are so-called gods, whether in heaven or on earth (as indeed there are many "gods" and many "lords"), yet for us there is but one God, the Father, from whom all things came and for whom we live; and there is but one Lord, Jesus Christ, through whom all things came and through whom we live. But not everyone possesses this knowledge. Some people are still so accustomed to idols that when they eat sacrificial food they think of it as having been sacrificed to a god, and since their conscience is weak, it is defiled. But food does not bring us near to God; we are no worse if we do not eat, and no better if we do.
>
> (1 Corinthians 8:1-8)

Their "conscience is defiled;" that is, the one whose "conscience is weak" regards it as meat offered to an idol, and eating the meat as really practising idolatry. Paul continued:

> Be careful, however, that the exercise of your rights does not become a stumbling block to the weak. For if someone with a weak conscience sees you, with all your knowledge, eating in an idol's temple, won't that person be emboldened to eat what is sacrificed to idols? So this weak brother or sister, for whom Christ died, is

Doubtful Actions are Sinful

destroyed by your knowledge. When you sin against them in this way and wound their weak conscience, you sin against Christ. Therefore, if what I eat causes my brother or sister to fall into sin, I will never eat meat again, so that I will not cause them to fall."
(1 Corinthians 8:9-13)

Although they might have a sufficient knowledge on the subject to know that an idol is nothing and cannot make any change in the meat itself; yet, if they should be seen eating meat that was known to have been offered to an idol, those who were weak might be emboldened by it to eat the sacrifices as such, or as an act of worship to the idol, supposing all the while that they were but following the example of their more enlightened brethren. Paul continued, "When you sin against them in this way and wound their weak conscience, you sin against Christ. Therefore, if what I eat causes my brother or sister to fall into sin, I will never eat meat again, so that I will not cause them to fall" (1 Corinthians 8:12-13). This is Paul's benevolent conclusion: he would rather not eat meat than be the occasion of drawing a weak brother or sister away into idolatry. For, in fact, to sin so against a weak brother or sister is to sin against Christ.

In writing to the Romans, Paul takes up the same subject, because the same dispute existed there. After laying down some general maxims and principles, he gives this rule: "Accept the one whose faith is weak, without quarreling over disputable matters. One person's faith allows them to eat anything, but another, whose faith is weak, eats only vegetables" (Romans 14:1-2). There were some among them who chose to live entirely on vegetables, rather than run the risk of buying in the butcher's slaughterhouse meat that might have been offered in sacrifice to idols. Others ate their meat as usual, buying what was offered at the marketplace and asking no questions for the sake of conscience. Those who lived on vegetables charged the others with idolatry. And those who ate meat accused the others of superstition and weakness. This was wrong; for Paul continued, "The one who eats everything must not treat with contempt the one who does not, and the one who does not eat everything must not judge the one who does, for God has accepted them. Who are you to judge someone else's servant? To their own master, servants stand or fall. And they will stand, for the Lord is able to make them stand" (Romans 14:3-4).

There was also a controversy about observing the Jewish festival and holy days. Some supposed that God required this, and therefore they observed them. Others neglected them, because they supposed God did not require the observance. Paul wrote,

> One person considers one day more sacred than another; another considers every day alike. Each of them should be fully convinced in their own mind. Whoever regards one day as special does so to the Lord. Whoever eats meat does so to the Lord, for they give thanks to God; and whoever abstains does so to the Lord and gives thanks to God. For none of us lives for ourselves alone, and none of us dies for ourselves alone. If we live, we live for the Lord; and if we die, we die for the Lord. So, whether we live or die, we belong to the Lord. For this very reason, Christ died and returned to life so that he might be the Lord of both the dead and the living. You, then, why do you judge your brother or sister? Or why do you treat them with contempt? For we will all stand before God's judgment seat. It is written: "As surely as I live," says the Lord, "every knee will bow before me; every tongue will acknowledge God." So then, each of us will give an account of ourselves to God. Therefore let us stop passing judgment on one another. Instead, make up your mind not to put any stumbling block or obstacle in the way of a brother or sister. But if anyone regards something as unclean, then for that person it is unclean (Romans 14:5-14).

Especially notice what Paul wrote: "If your brother or sister is distressed because of what you eat, you are no longer acting in love. Do not by your eating destroy someone for whom Christ died" (Romans 14:15). Paul knows that the distinction of meats into clean meats and unclean meats is not binding under Christ. However, to the one who believes in this distinction between clean and unclean meats, to that person it is a crime to eat indiscriminately; because, if he does what he believes to be contrary to the commands of God, it is wrong for him. "All food is clean, but it is wrong for a person to eat anything that causes someone else to stumble" (Romans 14:20). Everyone should be persuaded in his own mind that what he is doing is right. If a person eats meats called unclean,

Doubtful Actions are Sinful

not being clear in his mind that it is right to do so, he offends God. It is good neither to eat meat, nor to drink wine, nor to do anything whereby your brother stumbles, or is offended, or is made weak.

This is a very useful hint to those winebibbers and beer guzzlers who think the cause of temperance is going to be ruined by giving up wine and beer, when it is obvious to every person of the least observation that these things are the greatest hindrance to the cause all over the country.

Paul concluded the fourteenth chapter of Romans with these commands,

> Therefore do not let what you know is good be spoken of as evil. For the kingdom of God is not a matter of eating and drinking, but of righteousness, peace and joy in the Holy Spirit, because anyone who serves Christ in this way is pleasing to God and receives human approval. Let us therefore make every effort to do what leads to peace and to mutual edification. Do not destroy the work of God for the sake of food. All food is clean, but it is wrong for a person to eat anything that causes someone else to stumble. It is better not to eat meat or drink wine or to do anything else that will cause your brother or sister to fall. So whatever you believe about these things keep between yourself and God. Blessed is the one who does not condemn himself by what he approves. But whoever has doubts is condemned if they eat, because their eating is not from faith; and everything that does not come from faith is sin (Romans 14:16-23).

"Whoever has doubts is condemned" means "judged guilty of breaking the law of God." If a person doubts whether it is lawful to do a thing, and while in that state of doubt he does it, he displeases God. He breaks the law and is condemned whether the thing be in itself right or wrong. I have been thus particular in explaining the text in its connexion with the context because I wished fully to satisfy your minds of the correctness of the principle laid down; that, *"If a person does that of which he doubts the lawfulness, he sins, and is condemned for it in the sight of God. Whether it is lawful itself is not the question. If he doubts its lawfulness, it is wrong in him."*

There is one exception which ought to be noticed here; and that is where a person as honestly and fully doubts the lawfulness of omitting to do something as he does the lawfulness of doing it. Jonathan Edwards meets this exactly in his 39th resolution: *"Resolved, never to do any thing that I so much question the lawfulness of, as that I intend, at the same time, to consider and examine afterwards, whether it be lawful or not: except I as much question the lawfulness of the omission."** A person may have equal doubts whether he is bound to do a thing or not to do it. Then all that can be said is that he must act according to the best light he can get. But where he doubts the lawfulness of the act, but has no cause to doubt the lawfulness of the omission, and yet does it, he sins and is condemned before God, and must repent or be damned. In further examination of the subject, I propose to show why a person is criminal for doing something he doubts is lawful, show the application to some cases, offer a few inferences and remarks.

Why a person is criminal for doing something he doubts is lawful.

One reason an individual is condemned if he does something he doubts is lawful is, if God so far enlightens his mind as to make him doubt the lawfulness of an act, he is bound to stop there and examine the question and settle it to his satisfaction. To illustrate this: suppose your child desires to do a certain thing, or suppose he is invited by his companions to go somewhere, and he doubts whether you would be willing, do you not see that it is his duty to ask you? If one of his schoolmates invites him home, and he doubts whether you would like it, and he goes anyway, is not this obviously wrong?

Or suppose a person cast away on a desolate island, where he finds no human being, and he takes up his abode in a solitary cave, considering himself as all alone and destitute of friends or relief or hope. But every morning he finds a supply of nutritious and wholesome food prepared for him, and set by the mouth of his cave sufficient for his needs that day. What is his duty? Do you say, he does not know that there is a being on the island, and therefore he is not under obligations to anyone? Does not gratitude, on the other hand, require him to search and find out his unseen friend, and thank him for his kindness? He cannot say, "I doubt

Doubtful Actions are Sinful

whether there is any being here; therefore, I will do nothing but eat my allowance and take my ease and care for nothing." His not searching for his benefactor would of itself convict him of as desperate wickedness of heart as if he knew who it was and refused to return thanks for the favors received.

Suppose an atheist opens his eyes on this blessed light of heaven, and breathes this air sending health and vigor through his frame. Here is evidence enough of the being of God to set him on the inquiry after that Great Being who provides all these means of life and happiness. And if he does not inquire for more truth, if he does not care, if he sets his heart against God, he shows that he has the heart as well as the intellect of an atheist. He has, to say the least, evidence that there may be a God. What then is his business? Plainly, it is to set himself honestly, and with a most child-like and reverent spirit, to inquire after God and pay Him reverence. If, when he has so much light as to doubt whether there may not be a God, he still goes around as if there were none, and does not inquire for truth and obey it, he shows that his heart is wrong, and that he says in his heart, "Let there be no God."

Consider a deist, and here is the Bible claiming to be a revelation from God. Many good people have believed it to be so. The evidences are such as to have perfectly satisfied the most acute and upright minds of its truth. The evidences, both external and internal are of great weight. To say there are no evidences is itself enough to bring anyone's soundness of mind into question, or his honesty. There is, to say the least that can be said, sufficient evidence to create a doubt whether it is a fable and an imposture. This is in fact but a small part, but we will take it on this ground. Now is it his duty to reject it? No deist pretends that he can be so fully persuaded in his own mind as to be free from all doubt. All he dares to attempt is to raise cavils and create doubts on the other side. Here, then, it is his duty to stop, and not oppose the Bible, until he can prove without a doubt that it is not from God.

Now consider the unitarian. Granting (what is by no means true) that the evidence in the Bible is not sufficient to remove all doubts that Jesus Christ is God; still, it affords evidence enough to raise a doubt on the other side. The unitarian has no right to reject the doctrine of the divinity

13

Romans 14:23

of Christ as untrue, but he is bound humbly to search the scriptures and satisfy himself. Now, no intelligent and honest person can say that the scriptures afford no evidence of the divinity of Christ. The Bible affords evidence which has convinced and fully satisfied thousands of the acutest minds, and many who before making their study opposed the doctrine. No one can reject the doctrine without a doubt, because there is evidence that the Bible may be true. And if the Bible is true (and there is no reason to doubt that it is true), then he rejects it at his peril.

Consider the universalist. Where is the person who can say that he has not so much as a doubt that there is not a hell, where sinners go after death into endless torment. He is bound to stop and inquire, and search the Bible. It is not enough for him to say he does not believe in a hell. It may be there is, and if he rejects it, and goes on reckless of the truth whether there is or not, that itself makes him a rebel against God. He doubts whether there is not a hell which he ought to avoid, and yet acts as if he was certain and had no doubts. He is condemned. I once knew a physician who was a universalist; he has gone to eternity to try the reality of his speculations. He once told me that he had strong doubts of the truth of Universalism, and had mentioned his doubts to his Universalist minister, who confessed that he, too, doubted its truth, and he did not believe there was a universalist in the world who did not.

If a person does something when he doubts if it is lawful, it shows that he is selfish and has other objects besides doing the will of God. It shows that he wants to do it to gratify himself. He doubts whether God will approve of it, and yet he does it. Is he not a rebel? If he honestly wished to serve God, when he doubted he would stop and inquire and examine until he was satisfied. But to go forward while he is in doubt shows that he is selfish and wicked and is willing to do it whether God is pleased or not, and that he wants to do it whether it is right or wrong. He does it because he wants to do it, and not because it is right.

To do something when you doubt if it is lawful is to impeach God's goodness. You assume it is uncertain whether God has given a sufficient revelation of His will, so that you might know your duty if you would. You virtually say that the path of duty is left so doubtful that you must decide at a venture. Such action indicates slothfulness and stupidity of

Doubtful Actions are Sinful

mind. It shows that you would rather act wrong than use the necessary diligence to learn and know the path of duty. It shows that you are either negligent or dishonest in your inquiries. It manifests a reckless spirit. It shows a lack of conscience, an indifference to right, a setting aside of the authority of God, a disposition not to do God's will, and not to care whether He is pleased or displeased, a desperate recklessness and headlong temper, that is the height of wickedness.

The principle then, which is so clearly laid down in the text and context, and also in the chapter which I read from the First Epistle to the Corinthians, is fully sustained by examination: *It is sin for a person to do a thing when he doubts the lawfulness of it, for this he is condemned before God, and he must repent or be damned.*

The application to some cases.

First, I will mention some cases where a person may be equally in doubt with respect to the lawfulness of a thing whether he is bound to do it or not do it. For example, take the subject of using wine at the Communion Table. Since the *Temperance Reformation* has brought up the question about the use of wine, and various wines have been analyzed and the quantity of alcohol they contain has been disclosed, and the difficulty shown of getting wines in this country that are not highly alcoholic, it has been seriously doubted by some whether it is right to use such wines as we can get here in celebrating the Lord's Supper. Some are strong in the belief that wine is an essential part of the ordinance, and that we ought to use the best wine we can get, and there leave the matter. Others say that we ought not to use alcoholic or intoxicating wine at all, and that as wine is not in their view essential to the ordinance, it is better to use some other drink. Both these classes of people are undoubtedly equally conscientious, and desirous to do what they have most reason to believe is agreeable to the will of God. Others are also in doubt on the matter. I can easily conceive that some conscientious persons may be very seriously in doubt which way to act. They are doubtful whether it is right to use alcoholic wine, and are doubtful whether it is right to use any other drink in the sacrament. Here is a case that comes under President Edwards' rule,

"Where it is doubtful in my mind, whether I ought to do it or not to do it;" so, people must decide according to the best light they can get, honestly and with a single desire to know and do what is most pleasing to God.

I do not intend to discuss the question of using wine at communion, nor is this the proper place for a full examination of the subject. I introduced it now merely for the purpose of illustration. But since it is before us, I will make two or three remarks.

I have never apprehended so much evil as some do from the use of common wine at the communion table. I have not felt alarmed at the danger or evil of taking a sip of wine, a teaspoonful or so, once a month, or once in two months, or three months. I do not believe that the disease of intemperance (and intemperance, you know, is in reality a disease of the body) will be either created or continued by so slight a cause. Nor do I believe it is going to injure the Temperance cause so much as some have supposed. Therefore, where a person uses wine as we have been accustomed to do, and is fully persuaded in his own mind, he does not sin.

On the other hand, I do not think that the use of wine is any way essential to the ordinance of communion. Very much has been said and written and printed on the subject, which has darkened counsel by words without knowledge. To my mind, there are stronger reasons than I have any where seen exhibited for supposing that wine is not essential to this ordinance. Great pains have been taken to prove that our Savior used wine that was unfermented when He instituted the Lord's Supper, and which therefore contained no alcohol. Indeed, this has been the point chiefly in debate. But in fact it seems just as irrelevant as it would to discuss the question whether He used wheat or oaten bread, or whether it was leavened or unleavened. Why do we not hear this question vehemently discussed? Because all regard it as unessential.

In order to settle this question about the wine, we should ask what is the meaning of the ordinance of the Lord's Supper: "What did our Savior design to do?" *It was to take the two staple articles for the support of life, food and drink, and use them to represent the necessity and virtue of the atonement.* It is plain that Christ had that view of the Lord's Supper, for it corresponds with what He says, "My flesh is meat indeed, and my blood is drink indeed" (John 6:55). So He poured out water in the temple, and said, "If any man thirst, let him come unto me and drink" (John 7:37). Jesus called himself the "Bread of Life" (John 6:35; 6:48). Thus, it was customary to show the value of Christ's sufferings by food and drink. Why did He take bread instead of some other article of food? Those who know the history and usages of that country will see that Jesus chose that article of food which was in most common use among the people. When I was in Malta, it seemed as if a great number of the people lived on bread alone. They would go in crowds to the marketplace and each buy a piece of coarse bread and stand and eat it. Thus, the most common and the most universally wholesome article of diet is chosen by Christ to represent His flesh. Then, why did Jesus take wine to drink? For the same reason; wine is the common drink of the people, especially at their meals, in all those countries. It is sold there for about a cent a bottle, wine being cheaper than small beer is here. In Sicily, I was informed that wine was sold for five cents a gallon, and I do not know but it was about as cheap as water. And you will observe that the Lord's Supper was first observed at the close of the feast of the Passover, at which the Jews always used wine. Therefore, the meaning of the Savior in this ordinance is: *"As food and drink are essential to the life of the body, so His body and blood, or His atonement, are essential to the life of the soul."* For myself, I am fully convinced that wine is not essential to the communion service, and I should not hesitate to give water to any individual who conscientiously preferred it. Let it be the common food and drink of the country, the support of life to the body, and it answers the purpose of the institution. If I were a missionary among the Eskimo Indians, where they live on dried seal's flesh and snow-water, I would administer the Lord's Supper in those substances. It would convey to their minds the idea that they cannot live without Jesus Christ.

I say, then, that if an individual is fully persuaded in his own mind, he does not sin in giving up the use of wine. Let this church be fully persuaded in their own minds, and I shall have no scruple to do either way if they will substitute any other wholesome drink that is in common use instead of wine. However, I have no objection myself against going on in the old way of using wine.

Principles of Joy in the Holy Spirit — Finney's Lessons on Romans

Now, do not lose sight of the great principle that is under discussion. It is this: *where a man doubts honestly whether it is lawful to do a thing, and doubts equally, on the other hand, whether it is lawful to omit doing it, he must pray over the matter, and search the scriptures, and get the best light he can on the subject, and then act.* And when he does this, he is by no means to be judged or censured by others for the course he takes. "Who are you to judge someone else's servant?" (Romans 14:4). No one is authorized to make his own conscience the rule of his neighbor's conduct.

A similar case is where a minister is so situated that it is necessary for him to go a distance on the Sabbath to preach, as when he preaches to two congregations and similarly. Here he may honestly doubt what is his duty. If he goes, he appears to strangers to disregard the Sabbath. If he does not go, the people will have no preaching. The direction is, let him search the scriptures and get the best light he can and make it a subject of prayer, weigh the subject thoroughly and act according to his best judgment. So in the case of a Sabbath-school teacher. He may live at a distance from the school, and be obliged to travel to it on the Sabbath, or they will have no school. And he may honestly doubt which is his duty, to remain in his own church on the Sabbath, or to travel there, five, eight, or ten miles to a destitute neighborhood to keep up the Sabbath school. Here he must decide for himself according to the best light he can get. Let no one set himself up to judge over a humble and conscientious disciple of the Lord Jesus Christ.

You see that in all these cases it is understood and is plain that the purpose is to honor God, and the sole ground of doubt is which course will really honor God. In reference to all laws of this kind, Paul says, "Whoever regards one day as special does so to the Lord. Whoever eats meat does so to the Lord, for they give thanks to God; and whoever abstains does so to the Lord and gives thanks to God" (Romans 14:6). The design is to do right, and the doubt is as to the means of doing it in the best manner.

Now I will mention some cases where the design or purpose is wrong, where the object is to gratify self and the individual has doubts whether he may do it lawfully. I shall refer to cases concerning which there is a difference of opinion—to acts of which the least that can be said is that a person must have doubts of their being lawful.

Doubtful Actions are Sinful

For instance, consider the making or vending of alcoholic drinks. After all that has been said on this subject, and all the light that has been thrown upon the question, is there a person living in this land who can say he sees no reason to doubt the lawfulness of this business? To say the least that can be said, there can be no honest mind but must be brought to doubt its lawfulness. Indeed, we suppose there is no honest mind but must know it is unlawful and criminal. But take the most charitable supposition possible for the distiller or the vender, and suppose he is not fully convinced of its unlawfulness. We say he must at least doubt its lawfulness. What is he to do then? Is he to shut his eyes to the light and go on regardless of truth so long as he can keep from seeing it? No. He may cavil and raise objections as much as he pleases, but he knows that he has doubts about the lawfulness of his business. And if he doubts and still persists in doing it without taking the trouble to examine and see what is right, he is just as sure to be damned as if he went on in the face of knowledge. You hear these distillers and sellers say, "Why, I am not fully persuaded in my own mind, that the Bible forbids making or vending ardent spirits." Well, suppose you are not fully convinced, suppose all your possible and conceivable objections and cavils are not removed, what then? You know you have doubts about its lawfulness. And it is not necessary to take such ground to convict you of doing wrong. If you doubt its lawfulness, and yet persist in doing it, you are in the way to hell.

Consider a situation where an individual is engaged in an employment that requires him to break the Sabbath. For instance, attending a post office that is open on the Sabbath, or attending to a turnpike gate, or working in a steamboat, or any other employment that is not work of necessity. There are always some things that must be done on the Sabbath, they are works of absolute necessity or of mercy. But suppose a case in which the labor is not necessary, as in the transportation of the U.S. mail on the Sabbath or something similar. The least that can be said, the lowest ground that can be taken by charity itself without turning fool, is that the lawfulness of such employment is doubtful. And if they persist in doing it, they sin and are on the way to hell. God has sent out the penalty of His law against them, and if they do not repent they must be damned.

Principles of Joy in the Holy Spirit — Finney's Lessons on Romans

Think about owning stocks in steamboat and railroad companies, in stages and canal boats, and other businesses that break the Sabbath. Can any such owner truly say he does not doubt the lawfulness of such an investment of capital? Can charity stoop lower than to say a person must strongly doubt whether such labor is a work of necessity or mercy? It is not necessary in the case to demonstrate that it is unlawful, though that can be done fully, but only to show so much light as to create a doubt of its lawfulness. Then, if he persists in doing it with that doubt unsatisfied, he is condemned and lost.

The same remarks will apply to all sorts of lotteries and gambling. Take the case of those indulgences of appetite which are subject of controversy and which to say the least are of doubtful right: the drinking of wine and beer and other fermented intoxicating liquors. In the present aspect of the temperance cause, is it not questionable at least whether making use of these drinks is not transgressing the rule laid down by the apostle, "It is better not to eat meat or drink wine or to do anything else that will cause your brother or sister to fall" (Romans 14:21). No one can make me believe he has no doubts of the lawfulness of doing it. There is no certain proof of its lawfulness, and there is strong proof of its unlawfulness, and everyone who does it while he doubts the lawfulness is condemned and if he persists is damned. If there is any sophistry in all this, I should like to know it, for I do not wish to deceive others nor to be deceived myself. But I am entirely deceived if this is not a simple, direct, and necessary inference from the sentiment of the text.

Can anyone pretend that he has no doubt that it is agreeable to the will of God for him to use tobacco? No one can pretend that he doubts the lawfulness of his omission of these things. Does anyone living think that he is bound in duty to make use of wine or strong beer or tobacco as a luxury? No. The doubt is all on one side. What shall we say then of the person who doubts the lawfulness of it and still fills his face with the poisonous weed? He is condemned.

I might also refer to tea and coffee. It is known generally that these substances are not nutritious at all, and that nearly eight millions of dollars are spent annually for them in this country. Now, will anyone pretend that he does not doubt the lawfulness of spending all this money for that

Doubtful Actions are Sinful

which is of no use, and which are well known to all who have examined the subject to be positively injurious, intolerable to weak stomachs, and as much as the strongest can dispose of? And all this, while the various benevolent societies of the age are loudly calling for help to send the gospel abroad and save a world from hell! To think of the church alone spending millions upon their tea tables, is there no doubt here?

Apply this principle to various amusements. Take the theater for instance. Vast multitudes of those who profess Christian faith attend the theater. And they contend that the Bible no where forbids it. Now mark—what person who professes to be a Christian ever went to a theater and did not doubt whether he was doing what was lawful. I by no means admit that it is a point which is only doubtful. I suppose it is a very plain case, and can be shown to be, that it is unlawful. But I am now only meeting those of you, if there are any here, who go to the theater and are trying to cover up yourselves in the refuge that the Bible nowhere expressly forbids it.

What about parties of pleasure; where people go and eat and drink to excess? Is there no reason to doubt whether that is such a use of time and money as God requires? Look at the starving poor and consider the effect of this gaiety and extravagance and see if you will ever go to another such party, or make one, without doubting its lawfulness. Where can you find a man or a woman who will go so far as to say they have no doubt? Probably there is not one honest mind who will say this. And if you doubt, and still do it, you are condemned.

You see that this principle touches a whole class of things about which there is a controversy, and where people attempt to parry off by saying it is not worse than to do such and such. Thus they try to get away from the condemning sentence of God's law. But in fact, if there is a doubt, it is their duty to abstain.

Take the case of balls, of novel reading, and other methods of wasting time. Is this God's way to spend your lives? Can you say you have no doubt of it? Think about making calls on the Sabbath. People will make a call and then make an apology about it, saying, "I did not know as it was quite right, but I thought I would venture it." He is a Sabbath breaker in heart, at all events, because he doubts.

Consider compliance with worldly customs on New Years Day. The ladies are all at home, and the gentlemen are running all about town to call on them. The ladies make great preparations and treat them with cake, wine, and punch enough to poison them almost to death; while they all bow down to the goddess of fashion. Is there a lady here that does not doubt the lawfulness of all this? I say it can be demonstrated to be wicked, but I only ask the ladies of this city. Is it not doubtful whether this is all lawful? I should call in question the sanity of the man or woman that had no doubt of the lawfulness of such a custom in the midst of such prevailing intemperance as exists in this city. Who among you will practise it again? Practise it if you dare at the peril of your soul. If you do that which is merely doubtful, God frowns and condemns and His voice must be regarded. I know people try to excuse the matter and say it is well to have a day appropriated to such calls, when every lady is at home and every gentleman freed from business and all that. And all that is very well. But when it is seen to be so abused, and to produce so much evil, I ask every Christian here if you can help doubting its lawfulness? And if it be doubtful, it comes under the rule: "If meat make my brother to offend;" if keeping New Years Day leads to so much gluttony, drunkenness, and wickedness, does it not bring the lawfulness of it into doubt? Yes, that is the least that can be said, and they who doubt and yet do it sin against God.

Consider compliance with the extravagant fashions of the day. Christian lady! Have you never doubted, do you not now doubt, whether it is lawful for you to copy these fashions brought from foreign countries, and from places which it were a shame even to name in this assembly? Have you no doubt about it? And if you doubt and do it, you are condemned and must repent of your sin, or you will be lost forever!

What about marriages between Christians and unrepentant sinners? This excuse always comes up: "It is not certain that these marriages are not lawful." Does not the Bible and the nature of the case make it at least doubtful whether these marriages are right? Indeed, it can be demonstrated to be unlawful. But suppose it could not be reduced to demonstration. What Christian ever did it and did not doubt whether it was lawful? And the person who doubts is condemned. Consider the

Doubtful Actions are Sinful

Christian man or woman who is forming such a connection—doubting all the way whether it is right—trying to pray down conscience under the pretext of praying for light, praying all round your duty, and yet pressing on to marry. Be careful! You know you doubt the lawfulness of what you propose; remember that the one who doubts is damned.

Here is a principle that will stand by you when you attempt to rebuke sin and the power of society is employed to face you down and put you on the defensive, demanding that you bring absolute proof of the sinfulness of a cherished practice. Remember, the burden of proof does not lie with you to show beyond a doubt the absolute unlawfulness of the thing. If you can show sufficient reason to question its lawfulness, and to create a valid doubt whether it is according to the will of God, you shift the burden of proof to the other side. And unless they can remove the doubt, and show that there is no room for doubt, they have no right to continue; if they do, they sin against God.

REMARKS

The knowledge of duty is not indispensable to moral obligation, but the possession of *the means* of knowledge is sufficient to make a person responsible. If a person has the means of knowing whether it is right or wrong, he is bound to use the means, and is bound to inquire and ascertain, at his peril. If those are condemned and adjudged worthy of damnation who do what they doubt is lawful, what shall we say of the multitudes who are doing continually that which they know and confess to be wrong? Woe to the person who practises what he condemns, and happy is the person who does not condemn what he allows.

To avoid their duty, hypocrites often try to hide behind their doubts. The hypocrite is unwilling to be enlightened. He does not want to know the truth, because he does not wish to obey the Lord. Therefore, he hides behind his doubts and turns away his eye from the light and will not look or examine to see what his duty is. In this way, he tries to shield himself from responsibility. But God will drag the hypocrite out from behind his refuge of lies by the principle laid down in the text, that their very doubts condemn them.

Principles of Joy in the Holy Spirit — Finney's Lessons on Romans

Many will not be enlightened on the subject of temperance. They persist in drinking or selling rum, because they are not fully convinced it is wrong. They will not read a tract or a paper or attend a temperance meeting for fear they shall be convinced they are wrong. Many are resolved to indulge in the use of wine and strong beer, and they will not listen to any thing calculated to convince them of the wrong. It shows that they are determined to indulge in sin, and they hope to hide behind their doubts. What better evidence could they give that they are hypocrites?

Who in all these United States can say that he has no doubt of the lawfulness of slavery? Yet the great body of the people will not listen to anything on the subject, and they go into a passion if you name it, and it is even seriously proposed, both at the north and at the south, to pass laws forbidding inquiry and discussion on the subject. Now, suppose these laws should be passed for the purpose of enabling the nation to shelter itself behind its doubts whether slavery is a sin—that ought to be abolished immediately—will that help the matter? Not at all. If they continue to hold people as property in slavery, while they doubt its lawfulness, they are condemned before God, and we may be sure their sin will find them out and God will let them know how He regards it.

It is amazing to see the foolishness of people on this subject—as if by refusing to get clear of their doubts they could get clear of their sin. Think of the people of the south; Christians and even ministers refusing to read a paper on the subject of slavery, and perhaps sending it back with abusive or threatening words. Threatening? For what? For reasoning with them about their duty. It can be demonstrated absolutely that slavery is unlawful, and ought to be repented of and given up like any other sin. But suppose they only doubt the lawfulness of slavery and do not mean to be enlightened, they are condemned of God. Let them know that they cannot put this thing down; they cannot clear themselves of it. As long as they doubt its lawfulness, they cannot hold anyone in slavery without sin, and that they do doubt its lawfulness is demonstrated by this opposition to discussion.

We may suppose a case, and perhaps there may be some such in the southern country, where a person doubts the lawfulness of holding slaves and equally doubts the lawfulness of emancipating them in their present

Doubtful Actions are Sinful

state of ignorance and dependence. In that case, he comes under Jonathan Edward's rule, and it is his duty not to fly in a passion with those who would call his attention to it, not to send back newspapers and refuse to read, but to inquire on all hands for light, and examine the question honestly in the light of the word of God, until his doubts are cleared up. The least he can do is to set himself with all his power to educate them and train them to take care of themselves as fast and as thoroughly as possible, and to put them in a state where they can be set at liberty and succeed in caring for themselves.

It is obvious that there is very little conscience in the church. See what multitudes are persisting in doing what they strongly doubt is lawful. There is even less love to God than there is conscience. No one can pretend that love for God is the cause of following the fashions, practising indulgences, and other things that people doubt is lawful. They do not persist in these things because they love God. No, they persist because they wish to do them, to gratify themselves, and they would rather run the risk of doing wrong than have their doubts cleared up. It is because they have so little love for God and so little care for the honor of God.

Do not say in your prayers, "O Lord, if I have sinned in this thing, O Lord, forgive me the sin." If you have done what you doubt is lawful, you have sinned, whether the thing itself be right or wrong. And you must repent, and ask forgiveness for that thing.

Are you convinced that doing what you doubt is lawful, is sin? If you are, will you from this time relinquish everything that you doubt is lawful? Every amusement, every indulgence, every practice, every pursuit? Will you? Or will you stand condemned before the solemn judgment seat of Jesus Christ? If you will not relinquish these things, you prove you are unrepentant and do not intend to obey God. If you do not repent, you bring down upon your head God's condemnation and wrath forever.**

---

*Jonathan Edwards, *The Works of Jonathan Edwards*, Volume One, Edinburgh: The Banner of Truth Trust, 1834, 1974, pg. xxi.

** Charles G. Finney, *Lectures to Professing Christians* (1837, 1878), 36-58, *Principles of Victory*, 183-196. For Review: Answer the Study Questions on page 234, Cowles page 245.

The Letters of Paul on Joy

But the fruit of the Spirit is love, joy, peace, forbearance, kindness, goodness, faithfulness, gentleness and self-control. Against such things there is no law. —Galatians 5:22-23

I thank my God every time I remember you. In all my prayers for all of you, I always pray with joy because of your partnership in the gospel from the first day until now. —Philippians 1:3-5

Convinced of this, I know that I will remain, and I will continue with all of you for your progress and joy in the faith. —Philippians 1:25

Therefore if you have any encouragement from being united with Christ, if any comfort from his love, if any common sharing in the Spirit, if any tenderness and compassion, then make my joy complete by being like-minded, having the same love, being one in spirit and of one mind. —Philippians 2:1-2

Therefore, my brothers and sisters, you whom I love and long for, my joy and crown, stand firm in the Lord in this way, dear friends! —Philippians 4:1

You became imitators of us and of the Lord, for you welcomed the message in the midst of severe suffering with the joy given by the Holy Spirit. —1 Thessalonians 1:6

Indeed, you are our glory and joy. —1 Thessalonians 2:20

How can we thank God enough for you in return for all the joy we have in the presence of our God because of you? —1 Thessalonians 3:9

Your love has given me great joy and encouragement, because you, brother, have refreshed the hearts of the Lord's people. —Philemon 1:7

Study Questions for Individuals and Groups

The study questions in *Principles of Joy in the Holy Spirit* will serve as a review and help you focus your thoughts on some of the main teachings in each of Charles Finney's sermons or lessons on Paul's *Letter to the Romans*. You can use these questions for personal enrichment and for small group study. Experience indicates that probably no more than five questions can be discussed fully in one hour, so you may want to omit some questions, hold a longer discussion, or cover each lesson in two meetings (encouraging people to read the lesson again before your next meeting). The study questions that are obviously phrased for a group discussion can be thought about and answered individually. All of your answers could be written in a personal journal. For additional help in the interpretation of Finney's lessons on Romans, refer to the commentary on the various verses by Henry Cowles which follows these questions, beginning on page 235.

Principles of Joy in the Holy Spirit — Finney's Lessons on Romans

1. Men, Ignorant of God's Righteousness, Would Establish Their Own

1. Today, in what ways do people seem to completely disregard the need for personal righteousness, or the need to try to establish their own righteousness?

2. Today, what types of people try to establish their own righteousness and what might be some of their basic beliefs?

3. What seems to be the root cause or influence for disobeying God, what does God's law require of every intelligent being in the universe, and in what ways can God's law by obeyed?

4. Of what value were the ceremonial laws supposed to be to the Jews and how did they understand or misunderstand them?

5. What was God's high aim with the precept and the penalty of His law and in what ways can people understand or misunderstand His law?

6. What are some ways that those who say they believe in God try to establish their own righteousness?

7. Why do some people try to reform their behavior, what might influence them to want to do so, and what is the result? What do they really need to do and what is the result?

8. What types of behavior, both inside and outside of the church, could you use to illustrate a spirit of legalism? Why is a spirit of legalism so dangerous to those seeking salvation and to those who think they are saved?

9. Why did Jesus need to honor the law of God and how did He honor the law of God in order to save sinners?

10. Why does God consider it important for people to be *personally righteous,* how can this be achieved, and how does a person live righteously?

2. The Way to be Holy

1. Give one or more good reasons why God did not abolish the law for those who believe in Jesus Christ for salvation.

2. If physical laws were founded on the arbitrary will of God, why would it be a problem for everyone; especially for scientists, inventors, and engineers? Describe or define the term "moral law." If the moral law were founded on the arbitrary will of God, why would it be a problem for everyone, especially for believers?

3. On what is the moral law founded and why is this important for God and all intelligent beings?

4. What is the "moral obligation" of every intelligent being? Why would God find it impossible to remove the moral obligation from intelligent beings?

5. What is "legal justification" and what is "gospel justification"? How is Jesus always legally justified? Why is it impossible for sinners to be legally justified? How can sinners be given and receive gospel justification?

6. How does Finney describe the doctrine of "imputed righteousness" and what are some of his reasons for not accepting this doctrine?

7. What did Paul intend by teaching that Christ was "the end of the law for righteousness"? How does his teaching overcome legalism?

8. What is necessary for people to heartily obey God, and how does God win the heart obedience of people?

9. Why is faith in God's holy moral character important, and how did and does God demonstrate His moral character to intelligent beings?

10. How does God expect a person who is holy *in Christ* to act and live?

3. On Believing with the Heart

1. What are some primary differences between intellectual faith and heart-faith? Which is more important? Why?

2. Of what value is the intellectual faith of demons? How common do you think intellectual faith *alone* is among those who profess to be Christians? Why might this be so and how is this demonstrated by them?

3. What should result from true heart-faith? Why will heart-faith continue to be important for believers in heaven?

4. How or in what ways does heart-faith relate to knowing truths about God and how God works? How does heart-faith help with Bible study?

5. Why are there mysteries about God? Why is heart-faith important when thinking about these mysteries or acts of God that we do not understand? What seems to you to be the greatest mystery about God? How does heart-faith help you face that mystery and keep trusting God?

6. Give some reasons why God can always be trusted in spite of what we sometimes see all around us or experience ourselves.

7. What inspires heart-faith in a person and how does a person acquire heart-faith?

8. How does God win our love? What are some things God has done to win our love? Why does God want to win our love?

9. How does love for God relate to a person's obedience and righteousness?

10. Give some examples from the Bible as to why the Bible commends the faith of Abraham. How can you demonstrate a strong faith in God?

4. Conformity to the World

1. What are some practices where you live that indicate conformity to the world; practices that Christians should avoid? Which of the practices that you noted do many Christians seem to follow today? Why do you suppose they do these things?

2. What does Finney say is "the principle of this world"? Do you agree with or disagree? Give reasons for your answer.

3. How does doing business on the principle of this world differ from doing business dishonestly? In what ways might a person be honest while doing business on the principle of this world?

4. What commitments should you make when you join a church? What commitments do some make today when they join a church that seem to be based on the principle of this world?

5. What are some of the things than can happen when those who call themselves Christians act on the same principles upon which the world acts?

6. What does Finney mean by "following the fashions"? Why does he say this is harmful? Do you agree or disagree? Explain your answer.

7. In your opinion, what is Finney's strongest argument against following the fashions.

8. What is Finney's assessment of politics, candidates, and political parties? Based on your experience and knowledge, do you agree or disagree with Finney? Why or why not?

9. What does Finney advise Christians, who have the right to vote, to do when political parties are corrupt? What do you think of Finney's advice on how to vote and whether to follow a political party?

10. What are some of the advantages of refusing to conform to the world in business, fashion, and politics? What changes do you need to make in your life? Will you make them now?

5. *How to Prevent Our Employments from Injuring Our Souls*

1. Compare the King James Version of Romans 12:11 (printed on page 63) with other translations of the Bible. What lesson or lessons do you learn from the King James translation that you do not learn from the other translations? What do Bible students gain from comparing and contrasting different translations on a scripture text?

2. Look up the words "idleness" and "slothfulness." How does idleness differ from resting, recreation, and relaxing after working? Why are work and rest both necessary to our mental, physical, and spiritual health?

3. Explain why idleness and slothfulness are wholly inconsistent with true love for God and others?

4. In what ways is sponging similar to stealing? How might someone try to sponge off of God? What might you say to someone known for sponging?

5. What are some characteristics of lawful employment?

6. What are some characteristics of unlawful employment?

7. How might employment that is otherwise lawful become unlawful?

8. What might you say to someone in your church who is fervently pursuing an employment that they are obviously unqualified to conduct?

9. In what ways can we pursue our employments for the love of God and the glory of God, and for the love of others?

10. In what ways should every Christian's employment be similar to the employment of a good and faithful minister of the Gospel?

6. Being in Debt

1. Give some reasons why the Bible and Finney teach that love with its natural fruits is a perpetual obligation? What are some natural fruits of love? Compare your list of fruits of love with the fruit of the Spirit (see Galatians 5:19-26; Ephesians 5:6-11).

2. What is the proper meaning of owing someone? What are some of the terms that should be complied with before a laborer is paid for his work? Why should Christians be familiar with these terms and comply with them?

3. At what point or points does owing someone become a debt and a sin?

4. What is prospective debt and when should you pay a prospective debt?

5. Why is being in debt a sin, but owing someone not a sin? Why does God declare being in debt a sin?

6. Explain debt in such a way that it should be obvious to anyone that debt is a sin and should be condemned by God and others.

7. Why can being in debt be the same as lying and stealing?

8. Why do some churches refuse to discipline their members when they violate the laws of God in the Bible? What will God do in situations where a church or a minister refuses to discipline members? How do some church members avoid attempts by a church or minister to discipline them? What may God do when they apparently avoid discipline?

9. What does Finney teach about giving when you are in debt? How does giving differ from your obligations to the Church?

10. What does Finney teach that a creditor has no right to do to a debtor? What is his reason? What does a debtor have no right to do to a creditor?

7. Nature of True Virtue

1. How does Finney define and describe *natural affection*? Why is *natural affection* not the type of love required in Romans 13:8-10?

2. What is *complacency* according to Finney's definition? Why does Finney say there is no virtue in *complacency*? Do you agree or disagree? Why or why not?

3. According to the Bible and Finney, who are the people God requires us to love? With what types of love can we not love the sinner? Why?

4. How do some people confuse fondness for God with true love for God? How can fondness for God without true love for God influence people to mistreat God in word and deed?

5. How is desiring to love God different from loving God? What difference does it make if someone desires to love God, but does not truly love God? How can this distinction be confusing for some people?

6. In what ways can some people mistake acting out of pity with acting out of true love? Why is acting out of pity instead of acting out of true love not a virtue?

7. What is *benevolence*? What is a basic or fundamental difference between acting out of benevolence and acting out of some other type of love that Finney described?

8. What is *ultimate intention*? How does someone know their ultimate intention? How does someone's ultimate intention influence their choices and volitions? What is your ultimate intention?

9. Why must equality and impartiality be attributes of true love, of benevolence? Why might these be difficult to practice?

10. Explain the relationship between God's love and the Atonement. Why is this type of love true virtue?

8. *Love is the Whole of Religion*

1. Distinguish between love as complacency and love as benevolence. Describe the type of beings toward whom we can extend love as complacency. Describe the type of beings toward whom we can extend love as benevolence.

2. Distinguish between love as affection and love as emotion. Which love is virtuous? Why is it virtuous instead of the other.

3. How can a person rid themselves of improper or undesirable emotions?

4. What does God require of us?

5. How can someone be like God?

6. What does Finney teach about the relationship of love to faith and of faith to love?

7. What does Finney teach about repentance? What does he say true repentance implies?

8. How can someone increase in love throughout eternity?

9. Name two things that are essential for us to have perfect love. What are some important effects of perfect love in the life of the true Christian?

10. How can perfect love to God save people from serving God because of legal motives or legalism?

9. Love Works No Ill

1. What does Finney mean when he says people of vice can have complacency in each other and people of virtue can have complacency in each other, but people of virtue cannot have complacency in people of vice?

2. Explain why God's holiness led Him to give His Son to die for His enemies.

3. Explain why Christian love is not an emotion or mere feeling, but why emotions of gratitude to God and complacency in God can follow a right state of the will.

4. What does Finney mean by "a state of the will" in contrast to a simple or a series of volitions?

5. List and explain three aspects or qualities of true Christian love.

6. Define selfishness. Why is selfishness the foundation of all sin?

7. Explain the difference in meanings: disinterested, interested, and uninterested. Why does disinterested love constitute true Christianity?

8. Who is our neighbor? Who does Finney exclude as our neighbor? Who is most especially our neighbor?

9. Why do true Christians work no ill to their neighbors? What will true Christians do to their neighbors and what will they avoid doing to them?

10. How does Finney define and describe "speaking evil"? When is it appropriate for someone to tell the truth about the evil someone has done or is doing?

10. Putting on Christ

1. What does Finney and Paul mean by "putting on Christ"? What analogy or example does Finney use to better explain or illustrate what "putting on Christ" means?

2. For what end, purpose, or intention did Christ live? For what end should those who put on Christ live? For what end do you live?

3. What relationship does believing have to "putting on Christ"? What is the difference between believing some facts about Christ and intending to put on Christ? What difference does this make for someone now and forever?

4. What are some things Finney says the believer must be willing to sacrifice to put in Christ? Do you agree or disagree? What are some things you would add to Finney's list today? How important is the willingness to sacrifice in living the Christian life? Explain your answer.

5. When are people obligated to do as Christ did? When are people not obligated to do as Christ did? What example does Finney give to illustrate this? Why might his illustration be important to the Church? How can we know when we are to do as Christ did?

6. What can we do to help us know what Christ would do in our circumstances? What are some examples that Finney gives to illustrate how people can know what Christ would do?

7. Why did Jesus Christ wash His disciples feet? What can believers do today that is similar?

8. Can you go to heaven if you are devoted to money or mammon and not devoted to Jesus Christ? How can you know if you are devoted to mammon and not to Jesus Christ? What kinds of ideas and behavior indicate your devotion? How do love and devotion relate to each other?

9. What was the duty of Jesus Christ? What is your duty?

10. What are some things you can expect in this life if you put on Christ? Do you think the benefits outweigh the sacrifices? Why?

11. *The Kingdom of God in Consciousness*

1. What does the Kingdom of God mean in Romans 14:17? What does it mean to have the Kingdom of God in your consciousness?

2. What is righteousness? What does the law of Christ require?

3. What is righteousness as a state of mind? How can we have the righteousness that God requires?

4. What is peace and peace as a state of mind? Who are involved in the peace that Paul writes about in Romans 14:17?

5. When we are at peace with God, what are some of the facts that we become aware of in our experience? Why must we have peace with God to be truly effective in preaching, teaching, or sharing the gospel of Christ?

6. How does Finney say the parent and child relationship should be? How does Finney compare and contrast this relationship with the type of relationship we should have with God?

7. What is joy in the Holy Spirit? How does someone receive and maintain joy in the Holy Spirit as a state of mind?

8. How is the Kingdom of God in a Christian revealed to the one who has the Kingdom of God within them and to other observers?

9. How does Finney compare and contrast Romans 7 and Romans 14?

10. What can make for or lead to a peaceless and joyless religion?

12. Total Abstinence a Christian Duty

1. What does Finney say is right in itself and wrong in itself? How are we to decide individual cases of right and wrong?

2. What does Finney mean by the principle of "self-denial for the sake of others"? Give some examples where Christians might deny themselves the enjoyment of something good in order to benefit others?

3. What is benevolence? When is it benevolent or your duty to deny yourself something when it concerns your neighbors? How does Finney relate his teaching on benevolence and self-denial to the atonement?

4. According to Finney, what is the business of the Christian Church? Do you agree or disagree? What appears to be the business of churches today, or the business of some churches today?

5. How does Finney relate his teaching on benevolence to the Christian's duty of total abstinence? How does he illustrate his argument using Paul's discussion of eating meat?

6. How much wine did Timothy drink before Paul wrote to him? Why did Paul tell Timothy to drink wine? How much did he tell Timothy to drink? Does this justify drinking wine as a luxury or matter of diet? Why?

7. What does Finney say was the first business of, or the great question to be answered by, Jesus and the Apostles? How does Finney relate this to their not teaching against war, slavery, and intoxicating drinks?

8. How might some people confuse the influence of alcohol or drugs with the influence of the Spirit of God? How can this be dangerous?

9. How can being under the influence of alcohol or drugs hinder someone from becoming a Christian? How can the church help these people?

Principles of Joy in the Holy Spirit — Finney's Lessons on Romans

10. How does Finney compare and contrast the damage done to a person and a family from slavery and from drunkenness? Which is worse? Why?

13. Doubtful Actions are Sinful

1. How does our benevolence as Christians influence us to avoid doing what might lead others into sin?

2. How does our choosing to act out of love for God and others help us avoid legalism in matters, even supposedly minor matters, of differing opinions about what a Christian should or should not do?

3. Explain the meaning of Jonathan Edwards' 39th Resolution. Apply it to a problem facing people or the church today.

4. If we doubt whether an action is lawful or not, what should we do?

5. How might you relate Finney's example of a person on a desolate island to an atheist or agnostic?

6. What does it imply about someone when they do what they doubt is lawful? What might you say to someone you see doing this?

7. If you do something you doubt is lawful, why are you condemned before God and should repent?

8. What advice would you give a church regarding the use of wine at a service of communion?

9. Why did Christ institute the Lord's Supper? What does His use of bread and wine mean? What communion elements might be used today to teach His lesson to new believers in a church?

10. Explain and apply today: "No one is authorized to make his own conscience the rule of his neighbor's conduct."

Henry Cowles
Editor of the "Oberlin Evangelist"
1803-1881

*Professor of Church History, Hebrew,
and Old Testament Literature*

Principles of Joy in the Holy Spirit — Finney's Lessons on Romans

Biographical Sketch of Professor Henry Cowles

The Reverend Henry Cowles was born in Norfolk, Connecticut in 1803. He graduated from Yale and was ordained in 1828. He became professor of languages at Oberlin College in September 1835. His heart was in the work, and all he asked was a place to lay out his strength. In 1838, he took the chair of Church History in the seminary, and of Hebrew and Old Testament Literature in 1840. In 1848, in consequence of straitened means on the part of the college, and the necessity of reducing expenses, he resigned his work in the seminary, and took the editorship of the *Oberlin Evangelist*.

When the *Evangelist* ceased publication in 1862, Professor Cowles was about sixty years of age. The habit of communicating his thought to others by writing was strong upon him, and by what seemed a divine leading he entered upon the work of writing commentaries upon the Scriptures. He commenced with parts of the Old Testament, and went on, year after year, adding volume to volume, devoting to it all his energies and all his resources, through a period of seventeen years. In 1881, he issued the last volume, and the result remains with us—a commentary on the entire scriptures, full of practical wisdom and the ripe fruits of scholarship. He died in September of that same year. The interests of the college through all these years filled his heart and hands.

It would be much more satisfactory to give the family life of these men, to look into their homes and observe there the results of Christian character and fidelity. By the side of each one of these men there stood a woman of like spirit and faith, whose life in the community was no less valuable; and children were gathered around them whose work and life it would be pleasant to follow, but this opens too wide a field.

Condensed and edited from, *Oberlin: the Colony and the College, 1833-1883*, by James J. Fairchild, President of Oberlin College, Oberlin, Ohio: E.J. Goodrich, 1883, pages 284-287.

Henry Cowles
Commentary on Romans

Romans 10:3-10

Romans 10:3-4—*For they being ignorant of God's righteousness, and going about to establish their own righteousness, have not submitted themselves unto the righteousness of God. For Christ is the end of the law for righteousness to every one that believeth.*

"God's righteousness" is used here in the same sense as generally throughout this epistle and particularly in its very opening (*For therein is the righteousness of God revealed from faith to faith: as it is written, The just shall live by faith* (Romans 1:17). God's mode of making people intrinsically righteous at heart and justifying them before the law is through faith in Christ. The Jews being ignorant of this mode, and seeking laboriously to establish a mode of their own, have not yielded their submission to God's method. Enamored of their own system, they have been blind

Principles of Joy in the Holy Spirit — Finney's Lessons on Romans

to the moral beauty and unbelieving as to the truth of God's far better way. For they have quite failed to see that Christ accomplishes the very end sought by the law with reference to every true believer. Of course the primary end of all law is virtue, goodness—to be secured by inducing perfect obedience. In Christ, this perfect obedience is secured far more surely and far more fully under the operation of more effective principles, bringing in a richer, purer moral power so much in the line of moral transformation of character. Then, moreover, for the purpose of justification for sinners before the law, Christ provides through His atonement for the fullest and freest pardon of sin—a result for which mere law makes no provision and in its very nature never can. Hence, every requisite for salvation is provided perfectly in Christ.

Romans 10:5-10—*For Moses describeth the righteousness which is of the law, That the man which doeth those things shall live by them. But the righteousness which is of faith speaketh on this wise, Say not in thine heart, Who shall ascend into heaven? (that is, to bring Christ down from above:) Or, Who shall descend into the deep? (that is, to bring up Christ again from the dead.) But what saith it? The word is nigh thee, even in thy mouth, and in thy heart: that is, the word of faith, which we preach; That if thou shalt confess with thy mouth the Lord Jesus, and shalt believe in thine heart that God hath raised him from the dead, thou shalt be saved. For with the heart man believeth unto righteousness; and with the mouth confession is made unto salvation.*

The close translation of verse 5 is, "For Moses wrote that the man who fulfils the righteousness which is of law shall live in it" *i.e.* by means of it. Perfect obedience ensures life—his highest well-being.

Over against this, Paul presents in a very striking way the righteousness which is reached through faith. He comprises all in two main things: (a) Belief with the heart; (b) Confession with the lips—the things believed in being: the Lord Jesus whom God hath raised from the dead; and confession with the mouth being apparently made prominent here as a testimony to the sincerity and heartiness of this belief. It should be remembered that in those times confession with the lips had a significance little known and not easily over-estimated now. Often it carried with it the loss of all for Christ. Very noticeable is the stress laid upon *"believing with the heart,"* in the sense of most sincere belief, coupled with the thorough obedience of the soul to the legitimate demands of the truth believed.

The thoughtful reader will ask, "What does Paul mean in verses 6-8? What bearing has all this upon the righteousness of faith?"

Briefly put, I take the answer to be this: Paul wishes to show that gospel faith is exceedingly simple, and to all honestly enquiring minds, very easily intelligible. The subject is not too lofty to be understood, so that someone must ascend to heaven to bring down Christ to some nearer point of observation: it is not so profound that Christ must be brought up from the great abyss in order to come within the range of human knowledge; but it is very nigh thee, close at hand, readily seen; readily comprehended. This method of setting forth things difficult of apprehension by conceiving them to be in the great heights of heaven above or in the deep caverns of the earth below is a Jewish conception. Paul found it in Moses: "For this commandment which I command thee this day, it is not hidden from thee, neither is it far off. It is not in heaven, that thou shouldest say, Who shall go up for us to heaven, and bring it unto us, that we may hear it, and do it? Neither is it beyond the sea, that thou shouldest say, Who shall go over the sea for us, and bring it unto us, that we may hear it, and do it? But the word is very nigh unto thee, in thy mouth, and in thy heart, that thou mayest do it" (Deuteronomy 30: 11-14). In one point, Paul seems to have taken the liberty to change the figure, *i.e.* from going over the great sea to going down into the great deep, apparently to make it suggest more naturally the bringing up of Christ again from the dead. The change is only of the letter; not of the spirit of the text.

Now, as to the point of this illustration, nothing can be more clear. It is this: *believing in Christ is a perfectly simple thing*; has in it nothing mysterious, nothing abstruse and incomprehensible; is a matter which a very child may understand. It is very nigh thee, in thy mouth and in thy heart—this doctrine of faith which we preach. *It is but to confess the Lord Jesus as the promised Messiah, the proffered Redeemer, and with thy heart believe on Him for the salvation He comes to bring*—that is all. You receive Christ for Who and What He is; you accept Him as to all He brings to you; you give Him your heart and your life. You trust Him as your Savior. This is believing unto righteousness; the result of such faith is salvation from sin in the heart and also salvation from the curse of the broken law. Jesus sanctifies; Jesus justifies. In the final result, Jesus glorifies. There is nothing beyond these that human souls can need.

---

*Cowles, Henry, *The Longer Epistles of Paul*, New York: D. Appleton & Company, 1880, pages 126-129. [Henceforth, Cowles, page #.]

Romans 12:1-2

I beseech you therefore, brethren, by the mercies of God, that ye present your bodies a living sacrifice, holy, acceptable unto God, which is your reasonable service. And be not conformed to this world: but be ye transformed by the renewing of your mind, that ye may prove what is that good, and acceptable, and perfect, will of God.

The second part of this great epistle commences here—the first part, devoted to gospel truth—the great doctrines which are unto salvation, closing with the previous chapter. Here therefore Paul opens the practical part, bearing upon the various duties of the Christian life. Sensibly and most pertinently, all Christian life begins with supreme consecration to the service of God. Verses 1-2 involve the solemn purpose and the earnest endeavor to conform both the spirit and the life—not to the world, but to the perfect will of God.

Paul assumed that the reader of this chapter has already read the chapters preceding this, and therefore has before his mind all those exceeding great mercies which are embosomed in the glorious gospel scheme. The righteousness of God by faith in Christ; peace with God; a state exempt from all condemnation before the law; a living union with Christ; the indwelling Spirit; victory over sin; all things working together for good and glory unspeakable in the future world. What could be greater and what more can be added to swell the volume of these mercies of God to the uttermost limit possible for mortals to receive! By all these mercies, therefore, says Paul, "I beseech you that ye present your bodies a living sacrifice unto God, in holiness such as is acceptable to Him—all which is your reasonable service, reasonably due from you to God in return for so great mercies. The figure comes from the Jewish sacrifices—supposably from the "whole burnt offering," the significance of which was the consecration of all to God. In the case of animals offered to God in sacrifice, their life was taken and their flesh, being consecrated to God, was consumed on the altar, or used appropriately in modes prescribed. But in the case of Christians presenting their bodies, the sacrifice was to be a "living" one. Of course the "body" is spoken of ("present your *bodies*") because the figure before the mind—animals offered in sacrifice—suggested the consecration of the *body*. But, of his intelligent creatures God asks, not the body only or mainly, but the spirit primarily—the very soul—as Paul proceeds immediately to show. The consecration of even our bodily members and organs is to be made, not by laying human flesh upon an altar of stone, but by the willing, loving devotion—the consecration by an act of mind of all we have and all we are to the service of God.

"Conformed" and "transformed" conceive of people as having in themselves a power to shape their own free activities and their own voluntary character. It supposes them competent on the one hand to resist and rule out of their souls the spirit of the world; and on the other, to transform their own heart and life into harmony with the perfect will of God. However, *let it not be thought that this power of self-renovation and self-culture will be applied to purpose and with all success without the help of the Spirit and the truth of God*. Rather the gospel truth is: *Nothing without God's Spirit as our renewing help; everything with and by means of Christ dwelling in us by His Spirit*, "I can do all things through Christ which strengtheneth me" (Philippians 4:13). Let it then be well borne in mind that this offering of ourselves a living sacrifice holy unto God carries with it the not being conformed to this world, on the one hand; and on the other, the being transformed by the constant renewing of the mind so as to make full proof of what the will of God is; that which is good, well pleasing [unto him], and therefore wanting in nothing. The word "prove" ["that ye may *prove*"] is very expressive. It means—that you may make full proof of in your own experience—that you not only make the trial, but really accomplish the thing you try to do—prove it in your own experience. Paul has the same word here, "*Proving* what is acceptable unto the Lord" (Ephesians 5:10).—Cowles, page 142-144.

Romans 12:9-13

Let love be without dissimulation. Abhor that which is evil; cleave to that which is good. Be kindly affectioned one to another with brotherly love; in honour preferring one another; Not slothful in business; fervent in spirit; serving the Lord; Rejoicing in hope; patient in tribulation; continuing instant in prayer; Distributing to the necessity of saints; given to hospitality.

Love appropriately leads the train of Christian virtues—love in the sense of good will, real benevolence. Let not this love be hypocritical. Let it be real with no mere pretences; the love of the heart and not the vain show of it.

Abhor the evil; cleave to the good. Turn with utmost aversion from whatever is evil; let all your proclivities be toward and unto the good.—In brotherly love be affectionate toward each other; outdo each other, if possible, in mutual respect for others. Let this be your ambition—to surpass all in the deference and respect you manifest toward others.—In matters requiring diligence never slothful; in spirit, evermore fervent; rendering service to the Lord and doing all things as unto him.—Under all circumstances rejoicing in hope; patient in tribulation; constant in prayer, *"praying always with all prayer and supplication"*—imparting freely to meet the necessities of the saints; making their interests common with your own. Also, honor diligently the claims of hospitality.—Cowles, pages 147-148.

Romans 13:8-14

Owe no man any thing, but to love one another: for he that loveth another hath fulfilled the law. For this, Thou shalt not commit adultery, Thou shalt not kill, Thou shalt not steal, Thou shalt not bear false witness, Thou shalt not covet; and if there be any other commandment, it is briefly comprehended in this saying, namely, Thou shalt love thy neighbour as thyself.

Love worketh no ill to his neighbour: therefore love is the fulfilling of the law. And that, knowing the time, that now it is high time to awake out of sleep: for now is our salvation nearer than when we believed. The night is far spent, the day is at hand: let us therefore cast off the works of darkness, and let us put on the armour of light. Let us walk honestly, as in the day; not in rioting and drunkenness, not in chambering and wantonness, not in strife and envying. But put ye on the Lord Jesus Christ, and make not provision for the flesh, to fulfil the lusts thereof.

In point of grammatical form the first word of verse 8, "owe," might be either indicative or imperative; *i.e.* either—you do owe nothing to any-one but love, for love fulfils all law; or owe you no one any thing; pay every honest debt.—The "former might seem to find some support, from the logic of the passage—"*for* love fulfils all law."—But strongly against this indicative construction are these facts: (a) That the whole current of thought here is imperative—a series of precepts—"Pay ye tribute;" "Render to all their dues" *etc.*—(b) That the sense of the indicative has an air of limitation: we can never owe anything but love—which is quite out of harmony with the drift of the passage, and would lie dangerously open to abuse.—It is better, therefore (with the King James Version) to retain the imperative; Owe nothing to any man; pay every honest debt; or better still, make no debt—certainly not any debt of doubtful sort as to payment.—Suddenly at this point, the claims of the law of love flash upon Paul's mind, and he subjoins as an after thought: Owe nothing save the debts of love; these you can never exhaust—never can payoff so entirely that no more shall remain to be paid. The moral claims of that grand law, all put sensibly into that one precept *love one another*—must endure as long as life; as long as society exists; as long as there are fellow-beings whom your love can bless.

In verse 9, Paul would show by specifying the precepts of the decalogue that these forbidden acts violate the law of love and consequently that love does truly fulfil the whole spirit of the law.

The one comprehensive precept—"Thou shalt love thy neighbor as thyself--carries in itself all the prohibitions of the second table of the, decalogue--against disrespect to parents; adultery; theft, falsehood, covetousness; so that all the law might be truthfully put into that affirmative form—*equal and impartial love to all*. Inasmuch as from its nature love must seek evermore "the well-being and never the ill of one's neighbor" *i.e.* of everyone who comes within reach of your acts and influence; therefore, love cannot work any ill to a neighbor, and must be the fulfilling of all the law.

In the sense of Paul, love is not merely a tender emotion, but is the good-willing of the heart, honestly, sincerely purposed, and earnestly carried into action for the good and never for the ill of the neighbor who is so near that your loving heart and well-doing hand can reach him. Paul always thinks of this love as *"working"*—not merely weeping emotional tears—but actively laboring to *bless*.

The reader should carefully notice that this love is due to "thy neighbor"—no other condition or qualification being put into this law. He is not assumed to be your *benefactor*—either in the past or hopefully in the future; *i.e.* this law of loving is not supposed to limit the people to be loved and benefitted to those who have shown favors or good will to you. Moreover, this "neighbor" is not described as being personally agreeable—a man to your taste; or to be on the same social plane with yourself—of the same caste in society. The only mark by which you are to know him is that he is your neighbor; *i.e.* so near to you that your love can reach him with good will and benefactions. This is all that you need to know of him to identify him as the object of your love. And in the application of this rule, there is not the least occasion to measure *distance* in feet or in miles: if the person is within your reach, then love him and do him good. Plainly, Paul *might* have said, "Love everybody in earth or heaven; love all sentient beings whose happiness is a good to be sought." But, to put the law in a more practical shape and to lead the thought toward the good-*doing* which the law demands, Paul chose to say—*your neighbor*.

To the exercise of this great, broad duty of love, Paul here names some special inducements arising from peculiar circumstances. The *times* were making urgent demands for wakeful energy. Life is not only short but with many might be drawing near its end. As to all of them that wonderful redemption which would come at death was nearer than when they first believed. Let them live therefore under a sense of the nearness of that other world, and of the very short time that remained for the labors of earth. Men who are coming so near to the light of heaven should repel the works of darkness and turn away with loathing from every thing that breathes the spirit of darkness—from all those deeds of shame that slink away from even the dull vision of human eyes.—A nobler life, congenial to a far purer light, should command their aspirations. Let them put on the spirit and imitate the life of the Lord Jesus, and no longer plan for a fleshly life but rather for the life of Christ and of heaven.—Cowles, pages 153-156.

Romans 14:15-23

But if thy brother be grieved with thy meat, now walkest thou not charitably. Destroy not him with thy meat, for whom Christ died. Let not then your good be evil spoken of: For the kingdom of God is not meat and drink; but righteousness, and peace, and joy in the Holy Ghost. For he that in these things serveth Christ is acceptable to God, and approved of men. Let us therefore follow after the things which make for peace, and things wherewith one may edify another. For meat destroy not the work of God. All things indeed are pure; but it is evil for that man who eateth with offence. It is good neither to eat flesh, nor to drink wine, nor any thing whereby thy brother stumbleth, or is offended, or is made weak. Hast thou faith? have it to thyself before God. Happy is he that condemneth not himself in that thing which he alloweth. And he that doubteth is damned if he eat, because he eateth not of faith: for whatsoever is not of faith is sin.

If thy brother is grieved with thy habits of eating, thy walk before him and as to him is not according to love. Let not thy eating destroy a soul for whom Christ died. This assumes that your course may break down his conscience; may lead him to feel that he need have no conscience, and so he may lose his soul. Beware, therefore, lest your course may weaken the power of conscience in the case of your brother, inasmuch as he may assume that your conscientious convictions are like his, and consequently that you are reckless of conscience. Take care lest what is really good in you be evil spoken of, in the present case, lest it be taken as proof that you have no conscientiousness toward God.

Try to make your brethren understand that in your view the kingdom of God consists not in what men eat or drink, nor in what they abstain from eating or drinking; but *"in righteousness, peace, and joy in the Holy Ghost."* Labor to disabuse them of their extreme notions of ritualism and to instill into their place of power just views of the spiritual nature of Christ's kingdom. To serve Christ in these things is pleasing to God, and will ultimately approve itself to sensible people.

Still putting the same noble principles in new aspects, Paul urges them to follow what conduces to peace, harmony of feeling, real love, and mutual edification. Do not destroy for the sake of so small a thing as meat God's work of grace in your brother's heart. Think of the sacrifice Christ has made for the saving of human souls. And ask yourself, "Can you not forego all meat, denying yourself if need be this small indulgence in order to promote the interest for which Christ died; or at least to avoid thwarting His endeavors and sacrifices for the saving of souls?"

All things of this sort are in themselves pure enough; the evil lies in their being an offence to thy weak brother. Better never to eat any flesh or drink any wine than to offend thy brother's conscience and so cause him to stumble and fall.

In verse 22, the older manuscripts make a slight change in the construction of the first clause, yet not affecting the sense; thus, "The faith which thou hast, have to thyself before God." Enjoy the quiet of mind and the peaceful exemption from the small bondage which these unfortunate scruples impose; yet at the same time, abstain from indulging yourself openly in anything which would or might seriously harm your Christian brother. Blessed is the man who has no scruples of a weak, ill taught conscience condemning him in what he approves. But on the other hand, he who doubts, whose conscience does not approve, is condemned if he eats because it is not according to his convictions of right, is not according to his then present conceptions and belief as to his Christian duty. Whatever violates or even lacks the support of these convictions is sin. *People must live according to their convictions of personal duty.* God does not demand of us that these ideas of duty be objectively perfect; but he does require, that having formed them honestly and with the best light and the best wisdom at our command, we should obey them implicitly. Obedience to our best convictions thus formed is in our case obedience to God. To disregard them is to disown God's authority.—Cowles, pages 160-162.

Select Bibliography

Lectures to Professing Christians by Charles G. Finney, Oberlin, Ohio: E. J. Goodrich, 1878. The London: Milner and Company, 1837 edition contains an additional sermon, "Why Sinners Hate God."

Principles of Prayer by Charles G. Finney, compiled and edited by Louis Gifford Parkhurst, Jr., Minneapolis: Bethany House Publishers, 1980.

Principles of Victory by Charles G. Finney, compiled and edited by Louis Gifford Parkhurst, Jr., Minneapolis: Bethany House Publishers, 1981.

Principles of Liberty by Charles G. Finney, compiled and edited by Louis Gifford Parkhurst, Jr., Minneapolis: Bethany House Publishers, 1983.

Principles of Holiness by Charles G. Finney, compiled and edited by Louis Gifford Parkhurst, Jr., Minneapolis: Bethany House Publishers, 1984.

Principles of Righteousness: Finney's Lessons on Romans, Volume I by Charles G. Finney, compiled and edited by Louis Gifford Parkhurst, Jr., Edmond, Oklahoma: Agion Press, 2006.

Principles of Peace: Finney's Lessons on Romans, Volume II by Charles G. Finney, compiled and edited by Louis Gifford Parkhurst, Jr., Edmond, Oklahoma: Agion Press, 2010.

Principles of Joy in the Holy Spirit: Finney's Lessons on Romans, Volume III by Charles G. Finney, compiled and edited by Louis Gifford Parkhurst, Jr., Edmond, Oklahoma: Agion Press, 2012.

Sermons of Gospel Themes by Charles G. Finney, New York: Fleming H. Revell Company, 1876.

Sermons on Important Subjects by Charles G. Finney, New York: John S. Taylor, 1836.

Sermons on the Way of Salvation by Charles G. Finney, Oberlin, Ohio: Edwin J. Goodrich, 1891. These sermons were collected and edited after Finney's death by Finney's biographer, G. F. Wright.

Kindle & Nook Bibliography

Francis and Edith Schaeffer: Expanded and Updated Edition by L.G. Parkhurst, Edmond: Agion Press, 2011.

How God Teaches Us to Pray: Lessons from the Lives of Francis and Edith Schaeffer: Expanded and Updated Edition by L.G. Parkhurst, Edmond: Agion Press, 2011.

Prayer Steps to Serenity: Daily Quiet Time Edition: Expanded and Updated Edition by L.G. Parkhurst, Edmond: Agion Press, 2011.

www.ingramcontent.com/pod-product-compliance
Lightning Source LLC
Chambersburg PA
CBHW031240290426
44109CB00012B/374